BARBARA PYM

BARBARA PYM

A Critical Biography

Anne M. Wyatt-Brown

University of Missouri Press • Columbia and London

Copyright © 1992 by

The Curators of the University of Missouri

University of Missouri Press, Columbia, Missouri 65201

Printed and bound in the United States of America

All rights reserved

5   4   3   2   1   96   95   94   93   92

Library of Congress Cataloging-in-Publication Data

Wyatt-Brown, Anna M., 1939–

    Barbara Pym : a critical biography / Anne M. Wyatt-Brown.

      p. cm.

    Includes bibliographical references and index.

    ISBN 0–8262–0820–7 (alk. paper)

    1. Pym, Barbara 2. Novelists, English—20th century—Biography.

    I. Title.

    PR6066.Y58Z96   1992

    823'.941—dc20

    [B]   92–5092

                                           CIP

Designer: Kristie Lee

Typesetter: Connell-Zeko Type & Graphics

Printer and Binder: Thomson-Shore, Inc.

Typeface: Palatino and Brighton Light

To Bert and Natalie

Contents

Preface

Barbara Pym's novels have always aroused an impassioned reaction. Readers either like or dislike them intensely; few are indifferent. Despite the detachment of her narrative voice, Pym wrote as a partisan in the battle of life. She was determined to be heard. Although few readers attempt to explain why they react so strongly to Pym's novels, examining one's visceral response makes a useful point of departure.

I will begin with my own reaction. Like many people, I learned about Pym's novels from reading a 1977 article in the *Times Literary Supplement*, in which well-known critics evaluated the literary reputations of novelists of the previous seventy-five years.[1] I saw the article in the spring of 1978 when I was working on an article about E. M. Forster at Princeton University, where my husband and I were visiting fellows. Frederick Crews, who was lecturing there, suggested that the *Times Literary Supplement* survey would help me complete my project. While hunting for comments about Forster, I was diverted by Lord David Cecil's name. His recommendation of Barbara Pym's novels convinced me to seek them out that June when a research trip took me to King's College, Cambridge, to read the E. M. Forster papers. Pym's novels did not appear in the United States until autumn 1978.[2]

That summer English bookstores carried cheap reprints of *Excellent Women* and *A Glass of Blessings*. In contrast *Quartet in Autumn* was more expensive, and for that mundane reason, I began with *Excellent Women*. The humor immediately attracted me, as well as the flavor of postwar London. The trivial details of Mildred Lathbury's daily life seemed fascinating. As a child I had wondered what it would be like to live through the austerities of the English postwar period instead of leading a relatively comfortable life in America. Moreover, Mildred's Pimlico parish seemed familiar despite its being English. My parents had been active in the parish of an Episcopal church in downtown Baltimore. During the late 1940s and 1950s, so many unattached women—spinsters and widows—had attended services that I had formed the opinion that men—especially fathers— were an endangered species. In our house, church gossip was a staple of parental conversation. My mother complained yearly that the unworldly rector would not let the ladies of the parish charge enough for their handiwork at the annual Christmas bazaar.

For all these reasons, *Excellent Women* amused and delighted me. Here was a novel written from the perspective of those spinsters whose lives had worried me. As I read on, however, I began to hope for a happy ending. It seemed obvious that despite Rocky Napier's easy charm, Mildred was becoming attached to the austere but morally upright Everard Bone, and I could think of no impediment to their marriage. Therefore, upon reaching the novel's abrupt end, I felt shocked by the arbitrariness with which Pym snatched happiness from Mildred's grasp. I kept peering at the last pages of my copy to see if some part had been accidentally omitted. I felt betrayed and puzzled. I returned to my Forster project, temporarily putting Pym's novels aside.

For all that, however, I continued to be drawn to Pym's fiction. I ordered *Some Tame Gazelle*, when it was later reprinted, and read it with great pleasure. Once again, however, the novel challenged any easy romanticism. This time I noted Belinda Bede's passionate denunciation of her sister's possible marriage, her paean of praise to the sisterly life. Belinda's, and I felt sure Pym's, feeling was palpable. Meantime my work in the Forster papers in Cambridge had convinced me that, as in the case of Forster, there might well be a connection between Pym's attitude toward marriage and her creativity.[3] In 1983 I began to draft an article on Pym's views of marriage but was hindered by the lack of information about her life.

As I later discovered, Barbara Brothers had already published a chapter on Pym, in which she suggested that the novelist deliberately punctured her heroines' romantic attitudes. Brothers argued that Pym heralded "the dignity of the quotidian" in her novels. Pym forces us to pay attention to the plight of those individuals whom other writers reject as being too insignificant for fiction.[4] If one followed Brothers's argument to its logical conclusion, however, one might reasonably assume that Barbara Pym was a very independent woman, a feminist before her time. I was not quite so sure. Pym's characters shared too many of the familiar characteristics of the excellent women in our parish. Feminism was the furthest thing from their minds. Moreover, fresh from my exploration of the factors that had inhibited Forster's creativity, I was eager to explore the reasons for Pym's sixteen years of silence.

Then in 1984, Hazel Holt and Hilary Pym Walton published some of Pym's autobiographical writings in *A Very Private Eye*. The mystery of Pym's silence was answered. As Barbara Everett put it, "*Not getting published was almost more intrinsic to her career than its opposite.*" *A Very Private Eye* also provides evidence that despite the surface tranquility of Pym's life, conflict played an important role in her developing art. The picture of Pym that emerges is of a woman who overvalued men and who repeatedly attached herself to unsuitable choices. Moreover, the romantic, girlish tone of Pym's private writings is at variance with the strong, self-contained, ironic narrative voice she later painstakingly constructed in her best novels. Unfortunately, the two coeditors made no attempt to analyze that difference, leaving it to reviewers to describe the discrepancy between her art and her life. Peter Ackroyd said that Pym's "ordinariness . . . is combined with extreme oddness. . . ." She leaves a dominant impression, he concluded, "of a single-minded, almost obsessive, woman."[5] Many of Pym's loyal admirers were disturbed by the woman depicted in the book. Sometime in 1985, a friend of my parents queried me about Pym's life. Bluntly she asked how a woman who was capable of writing such wonderful novels could be so dependent on men. She found Pym's desperation undignified.

Such a judgment, however, ignores the role that dejection played in Pym's life. Although few would have guessed from reading her novels that she often had gloomy moments, the evidence in her papers is overwhelming. Pym's comedy represents a victory over internal and external constraints. Being a writer helped her to resist succumbing to despair. Anthony Storr, the British psychoanalyst, has suggested that depression—even the mild and intermittent kind that caused Pym to have headaches and some moments of writer's block—can be a creative spur. He points out that some very imaginative and inspiring individuals have suffered from despondency—figures as disparate as Michelangelo, Winston Churchill, Sylvia Plath, and Anne Sexton. Indeed without their creativity, Storr argues, they might have surrendered to melancholia. My thesis is that Pym's art allowed her to triumph over social constraints, both those imposed upon her and those she unwittingly inflicted upon herself. As Silvano Arieti has remarked, "Creativity is one of the major means by which the human being liberates himself from the fetters not only of his conditioned responses, but also of his usual choices."[6] Pym's dissatisfaction with her life actually encouraged the development of her creativity.

Like Forster, Pym began writing in youth to determine who she was. In middle age, at the point when Forster turned from novels to criticism, Pym continued to produce novels, partly to reassure herself that her observations were significant. After all, many people in her daily life ignored her presence or took her for granted. Novel writing was not just the part-time occupation she claimed it was. It was a lifeline. When, in girlhood, she found some aspects of her daily life unsatisfactory, she turned to novels, poetry, films, and music to construct a self more to her liking. Not only did she write stories, poems, letters, and journals, but she read voraciously, listened attentively to music of all sorts, and frequented the movies. Although she altered her fictive self over time, having a role mattered to her. Jay Martin's suggestion that many writers "find their identities in literature—literature of all kinds" helps us keep this observation about Pym in proportion.[7]

At the moment, Pym scholars must choose between two schools of writing about the lives of refined, generally upper-middle-class women writers. On the one hand, the older tradition has been brilliantly exemplified by Victoria Glendinning in her insightful but deliberately unpsychological biography of Elizabeth Bowen. Unfortunately, Glendinning's approach limits our appreciation for Bowen's later writing. If Bowen's emotional conflicts are dismissed, her writer's block in her final years is inexplicable. Also the discontinuities of her final novels, *The Little Girls* and *Eva Trout*, seem merely signs of decline rather than a prescient representation of contemporary life. Indeed, Bowen's later fiction represents a heroic attempt to confront the ghosts of her childhood. On the other hand, the new tradition has been well represented by Jean Strouse's *Alice James*, Linda Wagner-Martin's *Sylvia Plath*, and Diane Middlebrook's *Anne Sexton*. All three studies make convincing and responsible use of what Richard Ellmann calls "biographical speculations" to connect the "writer's experience and his or her art."[8] I prefer the psychoanalytic approach. All too often excessive "respect" for the subject leads to genteel, sanitized studies, which ignore the very issues that shaped the subject's art. Pym's reputation will surely withstand my scrutiny. Many other Pym critics have done a fine job describing her comic sensibility. It is time to examine the unexpected subsoil from which Pym's comedy emerged.

Like Forster, Pym's life was sadder and more limited than I had expected it to be, but like him she wrestled with intractable problems and emerged triumphant in life through her art. Both sides of the story need to be told. For example, Forster in *Howards End* notes that Beethoven acknowledges the power of evil. In the Fifth Symphony, he intersperses triumphant passages with others in which "goblins" seem to threaten our very existence. Says Forster, "That is why one can trust Beethoven when he says other things."[9] I wish to demonstrate that Barbara Pym earned her comic vision. Her humor was based on an acceptance of suffering and did not come easily to her. Like most of us, she often did silly things—indeed *A Very Private Eye* accentuates that side of her youth unduly. It lacks the commentary that would place her behavior in a proper context. An honest and searching inquiry will increase our respect.

In recounting Pym's life, I do not reject social explanations. One must realize the effect of environment and gender on her development. At the same time, family dynamics are important. We know relatively little about her parents. Yet Pym's writings (both published and unpublished) reveal that from them she learned to eschew self-scrutiny. Pym's refusal to probe, I contend, reflects a fundamentally pessimistic view of the world. At the same time, psychology and social analysis must be leavened by common sense and literary appreciation. While we recognize that Pym, like most of us, was shaped by social forces, we marvel at the way she managed to transform those constraints.

In raising the question of Pym's psychology, I recognize the limitations of the enterprise. No amount of detective work on my part will provide completely satisfying answers to our questions. Psychoanalytic theory cannot capture Pym's essence, nor account completely for the sources of her saving humor, but it will deepen our understanding of her predicament. Moreover, no critic should claim to psychoanalyze a writer. Analysis, after all, demands a living, reacting, and sometimes resisting subject. On the other hand, psychoanalytic techniques can aid our inquiry. Roy Schafer has suggested that the "analytic project . . . may be called *fictive*. Fictive, not in the sense of artificial, inauthentic, or illusory, but in the sense of a relationship constructed by two people under highly specialized dialogic circumstances." The analyst, he suggests, becomes a coexplorer with the patient. Many literary critics have applied these

principles to narrative. For example, when assessing autobiographical material they, like the analyst, use countertransference as a
guide to their interpretations.[10] In that spirit I am exploring Pym's
psychic life and raising pertinent questions.

In the course of writing this book, I found that only a limited
number of psychoanalysts have concentrated on relatively normal
people whose talents have helped them transform personal anxieties into art. The analysts whose work I cite include D. W. Winnicott,
Karen Horney, Alice Miller, Erik Erikson, Jay Martin, and Anthony
Storr, all of whom have an interest in the nature of human creativity.
On the whole, however, psychoanalysts do not write about people
like Pym. People of her temperament—mildly depressed but otherwise normal—seldom seek the psychiatric couch and therefore do
not enter the relevant literature. Pym had no serious mental problems and never consulted a psychiatrist. Not even in moments of
transient depression did she question the family respect for reti-
cence with which she had been reared. Nonetheless, part of her
suffering, both in her professional and personal life, resulted from
psychological conflicts that she never tried to understand, let alone
master.

Another important aspect of Pym's life is her artistic development
throughout the life cycle, particularly the problems of career she
faced at mid-life. Although Elliott Jaques first advanced a theory of
mid-life change in 1965, only recently have scholars begun to examine the work of individual novelists and poets for signs of a late
style. We need to ask if Jaques's generalizations will help to explain
changes that appear in Pym's later writing. David Gutmann has
challenged Jaques's insistence that creative elders are dominated by
"the fear of death." Pym's case provides some evidence for Gutmann's position and suggests the need to refine Jaques's findings.
Pym had her crisis much later than the men Jaques describes, but
facing death, as he suggested, did alter her art. Although she never
underwent psychoanalysis, her strong religious beliefs and rejuve-
nated creativity spared her from the worst fears of dying, thus
confirming Gutmann's contention.[11] My exploration of her life and
work will add to the continuing debate about the effect of aging on
the later lives and creative work of artists.

Finally, this study will draw on the work of writing theorists,
who have studied the struggles of beginning writers but rarely
have the opportunity to develop an extended case history.[12] Thanks
to the Pym papers at the Bodleian we have examples of Pym's unpublished manuscripts, literary notebooks, and discarded frag-

ments, from girlhood to her final days. As a result, we can see what forces made it difficult for her to launch her career successfully, then later interrupted her success at mid-life. In sum, we have a rare opportunity to understand a writer's feelings at every stage of her career.

Acknowledgments

I owe a debt of gratitude to the following people, without whom this book would not have been written: Roger Salomon, who suggested that I should write on Barbara Pym; Jean Harker, the organizer of the Pym conference, July 5, 1986, for making material available to me; the principal of St. Hilda's, Oxford, who graciously granted me an interview in May 1986; Colin Harris, of the Bodleian Library, for cooperation and speedy assistance; Hilary Pym Walton and Hazel Holt, who granted interviews and answered queries.

Help of a different sort came from assorted friends. Janice Rossen, John Seelye, Judith Oster, and Anita Rutman patiently read my manuscript and offered pertinent suggestions, which I gratefully incorporated. Carolyn Smith and Felicity Trueblood bore with me while I struggled onward. Judith and David Fischer gave me a place to live in Oxford during May 1986, while I finished my research. Their daughter Suzanna brought a copy of Hazel Holt's biography to me from London in January 1991, so that I could complete my revisions on time. Sonia Scott-Fleming, an Oxford novelist, made the novelist's life come alive for me. Giles Gunn and Lawrence Friedman over the years have read my work and offered good advice and assistance when I needed it most.

Sponsored Research and the English Department, University of Florida, gave me the funds that made the 1985 research trip possible. The staff at the University of Missouri Press, under the leadership of Beverly Jarrett, has done a thoroughly professional job shepherding the book through its many stages. The press's anonymous readers and editors have offered much good advice and support, both of which have improved the manuscript considerably.

xvii

This book is dedicated to my husband, Bert, and our daughter, Natalie. Bert read endless versions, gave moral support, cooked dinner, and shared his ideas about depression and creativity. His painstaking editing improved my efforts considerably. Natalie allowed me to go to Oxford in 1985 and 1986 to do the research, even though she really would have preferred me to stay home. Subsequently she has encouraged me at every turn and given me good advice.

Permissions have been granted by the following: the *Gerontologist* gave permission to reuse parts of "Late Style in the Novels of Barbara Pym and Penelope Mortimer," the *Gerontologist* 28 (Dec. 1988): 835–39.

Permission to quote from the Pym papers in two previous articles was granted by the Bodleian Library, Oxford; Hazel Holt, the literary executor of the Pym estate; and Hilary Pym Walton, Pym's sister.

Abbreviations

PYM MSS   Manuscript numbers of the Barbara Pym papers,
          the Bodleian Library

Novels

AQ	*An Academic Question*
CS	*Civil to Strangers*
CH	*Crampton Hodnet*
EW	*Excellent Women*
FGL	*A Few Green Leaves*
GF	*Gervase and Flora*
GB	*A Glass of Blessings*
HFN	*Home Front Novel*
JP	*Jane and Prudence*
LTA	*Less than Angels*
LR	*The Lumber Room*
MD	*The Magic Diamond*
NFR	*No Fond Return of Love*
QA	*Quartet in Autumn*
SVS	*So Very Secret*
STG	*Some Tame Gazelle*
STR	*Something to Remember*
SDD	*The Sweet Dove Died*
UA	*An Unsuitable Attachment*
VPE	*A Very Private Eye*
YMFD	*Young Men in Fancy Dress*

BARBARA PYM

Introduction
Creativity and the Life Cycle

Barbara Pym wrote a series of comic novels about well-bred, upper-middle-class individuals, who are doomed by their inhibitions, ineptitude, or sheer misfortune to a life of singleness and marginality. Pym's fiction has much in common with that of a small band of contemporary novelists—Elizabeth Taylor, Penelope Mortimer, Molly Keane, Elizabeth Jolley, and Anita Brookner. They were all born in the first third of the twentieth century, and their fiction reflects slightly old-fashioned attitudes toward gender relations. In fact, Jolley, Brookner, and Keane owe some of their current popularity and the ease with which they find an international market to the rediscovery of Pym in 1977. Pym's subsequent popular success established a clearly defined market for eccentric fiction by women writers.

Despite the originality and incisiveness of her fiction, Pym has been dismissed by many academics and serious literary critics. Her conservative views and extremely accessible style made her an outsider in the literary circles to which she aspired. Scholars lavish praise upon the works of Margaret Drabble, Doris Lessing, and Iris Murdoch with critical studies but practically ignore Barbara Pym. Their denser prose and more complex plots establish them clearly as writers of import, whereas Pym's emphasis on the domestic and the personal, rather than on feminist, psychological, and philosophical issues, has led to a mistaken condescension toward her work. For example, the novelist A. S. Byatt claims that Pym appeals to "fogies

1

of various ages." In her view, "the new philistinism and the old" together have created a spurious academic interest in Pym.[1]

Yet Pym's novels are important. She was brought up in a comfortable middle-class family and absorbed traditional assumptions about the importance of family life and community values. From early in childhood, she felt herself an outsider, and she found it easier to observe others than to participate fully in the social round she scrutinized with such keen eyes. Her alienation was later exacerbated by her unwanted spinsterhood, which taught her what it was like to belong on the fringes of a group, as an expendable observer rather than as an active participant.

In consequence, Pym's novels present a very significant, if minority opinion about social attitudes. They are not overtly feminist. Indeed the novelist herself defined success as having a husband. Nonetheless, being a female was central to her experience. She shared the perspective of marginal women of her generation, who, despite education and cultivation, felt they had no recognizable role left in the modern world. She observed that social changes had undermined their inherited status. Yet Pym presents this alienation with comic good humor. Her novels have a subversive flavor, rather like the wry stories mothers and daughters have traditionally exchanged about male absurdities and female forbearance.

Pym's novels have shown considerable popular appeal. Readers have appreciated her sympathetic wit, comic flair, and gift of expression. But no critic has hitherto attempted to unwind the many strands that created the texture of her life and work. Read from a life-cycle perspective, her novels contribute to the understanding of gender specialists, gerontologists, writing and reading theorists, and psychoanalysts, as well as to any dispassionate person interested in the careers of talented women. To grasp the unique contribution of her work, however, one must view her novels in all their quirky particularity.

One can start with the issue of feminism. Most mainstream feminist critics have ignored Pym's novels; yet, Barbara Stevens Heusel, in a review of Janice Rossen's *The World of Barbara Pym*, expressed the hope that Rossen's book would encourage someone else to produce "a hard-hitting feminist critique." Such a study would "teach us to value spinsterhood, just as Yeats taught us to see the richness inherent in old age."[2] Would that the matter were so simple. Unfortunately, Pym entertained complicated and conflicting ideas about men and romance. Indeed, her views were considered extremely old-fashioned even by editors in the 1930s.

Pym's personal psychology, not her social environment, constrained her. Ivy Compton-Burnett, who inhabited a similar stratum of society, exploited her own peculiarities. Unlike Pym, she revelled in both her "single state" and middle age, according to her biographer, Hilary Spurling.[3] In contrast, Pym was much more conventional and retiring. She did not dramatize her idiosyncracies but suffered when she was unable to resolve her conflicting desires for artistic independence and the dependency of a traditional marriage.

To make matters worse, Pym judged her deportment by traditional standards. For example, throughout her life she did her best to hide all evidence of hurt and anger. Hence her narratives reveal depression, not fury. Humor and wit masked a deeply submerged hostility in her novels. Never did she frankly discuss her emotions. She was no forthright May Sarton, who sought to express even negative feelings with a rare degree of honesty. According to Carolyn Heilbrun, on one occasion Sarton decided that she had inadvertently suppressed her anger in a work. She deliberately "retold the record of her anger," in the next. Pym took pride in her self-control and paid the penalty of depression and low self-esteem. Her only outlet was to create a subversive subtext, one which reflects the way women have traditionally talked about men behind their backs. Some of her more formidable protagonists, like Belinda Bede in *Some Tame Gazelle* and Mildred Lathbury in *Excellent Women*, exact a delicate revenge upon the pompous or unreliable men in their lives by means of their interior monologues.[4] Conservative or not, Pym's views on gender ought not to be ignored. They must be carefully evaluated not only to understand what forces inhibited the novelist in both her life and her writing but also to appreciate her astonishing insights into female behavior and values, even though such conduct and principles do not conform with current attitudes.

The same can be said of applying other kinds of theories to a study of Pym's career. Pym's example can yield important information about the development of writing vocations and the effect of aging upon that process. Her work constitutes a rich resource. Georges Gusdorf, the dean of autobiographical studies, once suggested, "Every novel is an autobiography by intermediary." To understand the interactions between Pym's life and work, one must carefully examine her literary notebooks and novels, looking for the origins of creative ideas among the minutiae of daily life. Repetitive themes also provide clues to her hidden inner life, to what Norman Holland would call "an identity theme."[5] Finally, the totality of Pym's life should be viewed in the context of changing societal attitudes toward women and female fantasies about romance. These attitudes help to explain some of the anomalies of her experience, in particular the twists and turns that made her career unique among novelists of her caliber.

Since Pym's death in 1980, scholars and critics have examined many important topics in Pym's work. Yet no one has systematically related Pym's life to her writing. Of course, her biographer and literary executor, Hazel Holt, has supplied very important data based upon her extended friendship with Pym and her sister, Hilary Walton. Scholars have analyzed Pym's novels and described with some care her attitudes toward marriage, men, spinsters, homosexuals, anthropology, the Anglican Church, and the traditions of romance fiction. So far no one has sought to analyze her psychic structure. Yet Pym left us her scribbles and tentative first attempts, early manuscripts and rough drafts—what Philippe Lejeune calls pre-texts. These fledgling efforts often reveal the buried origins of her creativity more directly than do the novels themselves.[6]

Indeed, careful examination of Pym's literary legacy suggests that much of her writing was autobiographical, something that was not apparent during her lifetime. The severely limited aspirations of her characters can be attributed to the self-imposed restrictions that characterized her own adult behavior. Also her novels contain private fantasies, which she found difficult to explore in any other fashion, combined with the vignettes of absurd behavior that she assiduously recorded in a series of small notebooks. Erving Goffman has suggested that tales like these help us keep our equilibrium: "We press these stories to the wind; they keep the world from unsettling us."[7] Pym's obsessions with such observations suggests her anxiety, as well as her fascination with human eccentricity.

Pym's creativity and her emotional life cannot be completely separated, for the writer herself never fully detached her life from her fiction. In childhood, when life failed to meet the expectations of her powerful imagination, she began spinning vivid fantasies based on her favorite books. She constantly converted mundane reality into appealing fiction. As a result, her novels and her life are inextricably connected. Indeed, much of her material came from the surface of her daily life, or from free-floating and repetitive fantasies. Thus the origin of many of her fictional ideas can be rather confidently traced. Had she been more spontaneous in her creativity, it would be more difficult to track down the sources of her inspiration.

Pym's comedy is neither comfortably traditionalist nor revolutionary. Instead, like E. M. Forster, she straddled both extremes, drawing on a sense of tradition while occasionally subverting comedy's central tenets. In some ways Pym's situation was similar to Forster's. His homosexuality made him far more critical of the conservative social values depicted by comedy than he might otherwise have been. Pym's talent for observation and hierarchical assessment made her, like many other women writers, a natural practitioner of the comedy of manners.[8] Yet, the deprivations of her emotional life estranged her from some aspects of conventional attitudes, forcing her to treat them from her own eccentric perspective. Her best novels challenge comedy's complacent endorsement of the importance of marriage. Her novels, therefore, do not descend directly from Jane Austen, nor are they in the Trollopean tradition of genial acceptance of human frailty. Instead, Pym explored the lives of forgotten people in a most unusual fashion.

Pym did not have an easy time launching her career, but her troubles lay within. There is no evidence of overt editorial discrimination against her in youth for being a woman. In fact Oxford benefited her as much as it did her male contemporaries. Several of her friends had genuine literary talent; both Robert Liddell and Honor Tracy went on to become distinguished novelists. After university the three of them pooled their knowledge about the publishing world. They read work-in-progress with enthusiasm, offered helpful criticism, and, whenever possible, helped one another find interested publishers.[9]

Unlike Robert Liddell, however, Pym was never single-minded in her devotion to art. Nor was she as realistic about the publishing world. She belonged to a transitional generation of women. Born in 1913, just prior to World War I, she grew up with the expectation that she would marry. To her dismay, disastrous encounters with men in young adulthood suggested that she was doomed to disappointment. Consequently she had to seek her pleasures in fiction rather than in marriage. Of course, the single life had its compensations, and many times Pym acknowledged them. But for the most part she felt troubled by her inability to attract a man's love. Although in her novels she often asserted that spinsterhood has its value, privately she sometimes regretted her single state.

Pym never confronted the relative value of marriage and spinsterhood directly. Indirect hints suggest that her attitudes fluctuated, reflecting how much confidence she felt in her ability to be a successful writer. Not until her late thirties and early forties did she begin to find herself as a writer. Then she modified her fantasies to create most unusual heroines, whose independence is impressive. She describes one of them, Mildred Lathbury of *Excellent Women,* as a "spinster without ties—inquisitive, willing to help others / an onlooker [who] sees most of the game etc."[10] Pym's confidence ebbed away in her later forties. In contrast to Mildred, Dulcie Mainwaring in *No Fond Return of Love* goes to extraordinary lengths to pursue a man, who lacks even the superficial charm of Mildred's inaccessible beloved.

In general, as Barbara Brothers has pointed out, Pym's heroines nourish romantic aspirations but must learn to withstand emotional deprivation. Janice Rossen has also observed that in many of the novels Pym seems haunted by the figure of Jane Eyre, though her versions of that plot generally deny the possibility of "a reunion with a Rochester figure."[11] Eradicating most vestiges of romantic hopefulness was more easily done in her novels than in her life. The manuscripts and literary notebooks make clear that Pym never outgrew her youthful obsession with both *Jane Eyre* and the vicarage novels of Charlotte Yonge. Not until maturity did Pym convert the theme of companions, governesses, and the Anglican church into a penetrating study of old age and dependency in *Quartet in Autumn.*

Growing older added yet another dimension to Pym's work. Her literary career had been problematical from the start. After Oxford, she returned to her parents for eight years while she attempted to convert her fantasies and hurt feelings into novels. During that troubled time, she often longed to grow old quickly, because she assumed that the elderly were no longer afflicted by their passions. The experience of aging turned out to be far more trying than she had imagined. Not only were her romantic dreams repeatedly shattered, but her professional life unexpectedly disintegrated. Her seventh novel, *An Unsuitable Attachment,* was rejected in 1963, when she was nearly fifty. Subsequent efforts to find another publisher were unavailing. Then, in her late fifties, serious ill health began. Despite many vicissitudes, she continued to write. In fact, her illnesses gave her badly needed new insights that eventually revitalized her moribund career. *Quartet in Autumn,* the novel she wrote about the difficulties of aging, is her masterpiece. It won her an enormous audience both in England and in the United States.

Historical events also affected Pym's professional life. Pym's career spanned a period of intense social upheaval and change. During that time the response of readers and critics alike was colored by their altering expectations of what a novel should contain. At some points, Pym's novels met those unspoken criteria, but at other moments they seemed deficient. This interaction explains why Pym had a moment of real popularity in 1952 with *Excellent Women* and then was judged expendable in 1963, even though she had maintained a consistent outlook on the world throughout those years.

Although Pym always had a keen eye for current social habits and was the first to spot a changing trend, her novels sometimes appeared to be strangely disconnected from any particular time or place. For example, Robert Graham thought that Pym was "ahead of her time" in the 1950s when she described the bohemian life of Catherine Oliphant in *Less than Angels*, who unashamedly lives with "a younger man whom she appears to support." By the mid-1960s when Pym was trying to publish *An Unsuitable Attachment* and *The Sweet Dove Died*, Graham asserted that her once "daring" themes had become "commonplace." Manuscript evidence explains the apparent contradiction. Most of Pym's literary ideas came from her daily life, or from revisions of her past. Catherine's affair represents a version of Pym's romance with Henry Harvey at Oxford. The homosexual Piers Longridge in *A Glass of Blessings* may well have shocked some readers in the decorous 1950s, but Pym's interest in homosexuality had begun at Oxford nearly twenty years before. Furthermore, at the time when she was writing the novel, she was busily taking notes on the daily life of some homosexual neighbors in Barnes.[12]

One might suppose that Pym's literary reputation is now firmly established, but two factors continue to challenge her stature as a novelist. The first is that reviewers have often disagreed about the worthiness of her writing. From the start, some believed that she was Jane Austen's natural successor and that her work was representative of a great tradition, while others forcefully disputed the claim.[13] The second point centers around the revelations found in *A Very Private Eye*, the edited autobiography brought out posthumously by Pym's literary executor, Hazel Holt, and Pym's sister, Hilary Walton. The discrepancy between the frivolity and sexual desperation evident in the private documents and the restraint of the novels was so marked that Pym's readers have been forced to reappraise her work in the light of sometimes pathetic biographical facts. While that reappraisal is taking place, her reputation will be subject to challenge, like Forster's, whose literary standing has also been unsettled by biographical revelations. But as in the case of Forster, the more we know about Pym's life, the more remarkable her achievements seem. Few individuals have been capable of turning even the supposedly trivial events of their marginal lives into the material of rich, funny, and powerful novels.

In reassessing the importance of Barbara Pym, certain points are beyond dispute. She wrote from her own perspective: always as a woman, later as an aging person, and finally as a sufferer facing death. She always felt like an outsider. She knew all the social rules but never learned how to make them operate for her benefit. When she felt thwarted by her inability to control her destiny, she used fiction to restore some sense of mastery. Throughout her career, being a writer was intensely important to her. She wanted to be read, and she hoped that her readers would respond to what she wrote. Despite years when she was unable to find a willing publisher, she continued to write. She found composing essential for maintaining her equilibrium and identity.

The personal wellspring of Pym's novels makes them unique in modern times. Other writers sometimes write about lonely women (Anita Brookner, Penelope Mortimer) and display a capacity for detachment that is something like Pym's (Molly Keane). Some have captured the same sensitivity to domestic life (Elizabeth Taylor, Penelope Mortimer). Others are equally interested in spinsters and eccentricity (Elizabeth Jolley). But what makes Pym special is the originality of her mind. She knew she saw life from an unusual angle. Like her character Letty, she was well aware "that the position of an unmarried, unattached, ageing woman is of no interest whatever to the writer of modern fiction" (QA, 3). During her most creative phases she had every intention of changing that situation. Moreover, she had enough of the anthropologist in her to be aware that she was recording a way of life and kinds of people that were fast disappearing from the scene. Unlike an anthropologist, however, she noticed the absurdities of human behavior in mundane places. Even a bus trip could provide data. She would listen to the conversations that went on around her, such as one she recorded May 26, 1934 (VPE, 40).[14] Who else would have regarded the sight of a man in a library "eating a sandwich with a knife and fork, a glass of milk near at hand" as a possible tidbit for a novel? (VPE, 266)

Valuable though her novels are, however, equally important are her papers in the Bodleian Library. Like E. M. Forster's papers, Pym's diaries, letters, and manuscripts are accessible to scholars. Forster himself made the decision to open his life to investigation. In old age he encouraged free inquiry under restricted circumstances. He talked openly to his biographer, P. N. Furbank, and deeded his papers to the King's College Library. Of course, in his prime he had deflected public scrutiny of his personal life. Pym was ambivalent about allowing outsiders to read her journals after her death. On March 5, 1978, toward the end of her life, she consulted the poet Philip Larkin about the disposal of her manuscripts (*VPE*, 314). He had been her friend and literary mentor since the 1960s. At some point she removed passages from diaries to protect her privacy, but she never carried through with a deed of gift. Instead, her sister Hilary Walton gave the papers to the Bodleian after her death.[15]

Ambivalent or not, Pym's life and private thoughts, like Forster's, are open to critical evaluation. In consequence, we have more insight into her psychology than is generally the case with writers. Although her public career was conventional, her private one was not. At Oxford, competing for the attention of attractive men stirred up anxieties that were not easily allayed. In reaction, she schooled herself to behave in an emotionally restrained fashion. In a diary entry of April 19–21, 1940, Pym reported that she had learned to avoid emotional outbursts. She no longer cried when she felt melancholy but reminded herself that the pain would subside in time (*VPE*, 103). She became so successful at hiding her unhappiness that only her sister, Hilary Walton, and a few old friends knew about her unrequited loves. She taught herself to sit like "Patience on a monument,/ Smiling at grief."[16] While she proudly maintained a brave front to make life pleasant for herself and for others, in her diary April 7, 1940, she admitted that she longed for more. The solution, she reported, was to write (*VPE*, 103).

Pym's diaries and notebooks make it possible to reconstruct the story of her life, to reexperience her anguish, pain, stoicism, and great good humor. She was an inveterate notetaker. One can trace many of the sources of her inspiration for her novels back through the manuscripts and eventually into her notebooks. Her notebooks provide glimpses of both the artist at work and the maturing woman. She began as a novice learning her trade and became an experienced novelist and expert editor. In fact, Pym's editing techniques sustained her after the rejection of *An Unsuitable Attachment*, when inspiration was at a low ebb. At the same time, we have a clear picture of an individual going through life's transitions. She struggled with the problems of autonomy and romance at Oxford and during her years at home. She spied on her young neighbors to give her life interest in middle age. Otherwise the repetitious routines of her existence might have been fatal to her literary technique. We can measure the effect of rejection on her work and on her life. After all, having twenty-one editors turn down a single book, *The Sweet Dove Died*, would incline most authors to self-doubt. At the same time, Pym was growing older and facing the new crisis of retirement.

Then, surprisingly she became revitalized in old age and at sixty-four was rediscovered by the reading public. Not only did a new publisher, Macmillan, bring out *Quartet in Autumn* to critical acclaim, but the following year they turned the once-rejected novel, *The Sweet Dove Died*, into a best seller, having made only six minor revisions. Shortly thereafter, she had to face imminent death, and the notebooks reveal how the news affected her final novel. From her record of private griefs and moments of joy, it is now possible to develop a clearer picture of Pym's creative process than is often the case with novelists. This then will be a large part of Pym's legacy and is a matter worth celebrating.

1

Constructing the Lumber Room

$\mathcal{L}$ove and death, Pym's dominant themes, appear in *The Magic Diamond*, an operetta she wrote at the age of nine and staged with her sister and cousins. Children's writing can provide an early sign of creativity, as well as give insight into a person's later psychological development. Indeed, the findings of writing specialists suggest that the two issues are closely related. Young writers instinctively use the familiar conventions of fairy tales to construct stories that explore and transform their experiences. The very act of composition helps them to sort out their own feelings and learn to make sense of their world. Of course, not all children are encouraged to develop their natural creativity. Too great an emphasis on abstract school writing can make them feel incompetent, and many learn to distrust their own ability. Barbara Pym was lucky in this regard. Her talents surfaced early in life, and her family delighted in her gifts.[1]

Even a casual glimpse at *The Magic Diamond* suggests that despite its humor it is a curious and candid text. Pym was too young to attempt to mask her fears. Thus she addresses the problem of marriage with a startling directness. Childlike though this early opera is, it embodies some of the strengths and weaknesses of her later work. Like most young writers, Pym used a fairy-tale frame, but she also drew on Gilbert and Sullivan plots. Her parents had performed in several musical operettas, so they were familiar to both the Pym sisters.[2]

Pym's opera violates some important conventions of fairy tales.

The subtext of its plot depicts the perils of growing up. Its chief protagonists are completely paralyzed by the unpleasant alternatives they face. The main characters include King Antonio, Queen Mayflower, their daughter, Princess Rosebud, Prince George, and the evil Wizard. Prince George, the hero, in an obvious bid to assert his manhood, has stolen the Wizard's magic but now finds his life threatened. The Wizard declares that George must choose between having his head chopped off and attempting to retrieve the Magic Diamond from the guardianship of a hundred dragons. George's dilemma is typical of fairy tales and myths, in which the sometimes timid hero is often rescued by the intervention of friendly animals. This prince, however, never begins his quest. Both fates seem much too dangerous to him. He begs Rosebud, who was played by young Barbara, to advise him. Unfortunately, his beloved feels equally bemused. Eventually, the Wizard becomes exasperated at the delay. After listening to George and Rosebud worry about whom she will marry if George is killed, the Wizard threatens to marry the princess himself. He claims that the king has decreed that Rosebud shall be the Wizard's wife after George is dead. At this point the king intervenes, contradicts the evil Wizard, and has him put in prison.[3]

According to Bruno Bettelheim's analysis, fairy tales offer the child-reader models of successful behavior. In the tales the heroes venture into the world, find "secure places" and meet their mates, with whom they can live "without ever again having to experience separation anxiety."[4] The youthful author, however, was not quite that optimistic. The prince is too weak to act on his own, and Rosebud makes no helpful suggestions. To resolve the stalemate, Pym borrowed a device from Gilbert and Sullivan. A member of the older generation steps in and saves the day. No wonder Pym had difficulty becoming autonomous in later life. Even in her imagination she found independence rather difficult.

The Magic Diamond is a childish effort, of course. Like her later work, however, it reveals a preoccupation with the topics of love and death. The young writer emphasized domesticity and human relationships rather than action.[5] In a similar fashion, the adult Pym would begin her plans for a novel with a domestic observation. From this starting point, she gradually felt her way into a story, in which her heroines would, like Rosebud, be preoccupied with the problem of finding and keeping a suitable mate. Of course, Pym's novels are far more subtle and indirect than her childhood effort, but the unresolvable problems of love and death, rivalry and power are deeply embedded in all of them.

In view of the persistence of these themes, we must understand how Pym developed her perspective. Little is known about her earliest years. Pym herself wrote Robert Liddell on April 24, 1936, when she was twenty-three, that she could not remember very much of her early days, and what memories she had were hardly material for fiction.[6] As a result, unlike Liddell, who drew upon his past for several of his early novels, childhood as a topic is generally absent from her novels. Pym's characters, in contrast to the protagonists in the fiction of Margaret Drabble and Doris Lessing, refer only briefly to their memories of their parents.

Pym, the elder of two sisters, grew up in Oswestry, Shropshire. Her father was a solicitor; her mother was the youngest of ten children of a successful ironmonger. The mother's family had the most obvious influence on the young writer. Pym's maternal grandfather was an inventor, as well as a businessman, who died early. By the time Pym came along, his widow was content with her lot. She inspired Pym to create several complacent widows, like Mrs. Wyatt in *The Lumber Room*, whose late husband, the gifted water-diviner, was dearer to her in death than he had been in life. According to Hilary Walton, Pym's sister, it was their mother who insisted that the two sisters be properly educated. Both went first to boarding school and then to Oxford.[7]

Mrs. Walton was most helpful in answering my questions about growing up in Oswestry, but she had little to add to the memories of youth that she recorded in *A Very Private Eye*. Her recollections are not much more extensive than her sister's. The Pym family apparently did not indulge in much personal introspection. According to Mrs. Walton, childhood had been a happy time for both sisters, but, on the whole, they did not reminisce about their early days very often. The silence, however, was not the result of an absence of feeling. Instead, the plot of *The Magic Diamond* indicates Pym's attachment to her parents.

The sisters shared an uneventful upbringing. Yet when Mrs. Walton began her research for her essay in *A Very Private Eye*, she discovered the startling fact that their father, Frederic, was of illegitimate birth. Both parents being dead by that time, it took Mrs. Walton several years to uncover the facts. Hazel Holt has described the process of discovery. After much effort, Mrs. Walton pieced together the story, beginning with the observation that Frederic and his daughters shared Crampton as a middle name. She gained access to some Crampton family notebooks, which described the unreliable behavior of one branch of the family. From this material

Mrs. Walton inferred that Frederic's mother, Phoebe, had more than likely been seduced by Fiennes Henry Crampton, a young man whose father had deserted his family for a bigamous marriage more to his taste. At the time Fiennes was sixteen years old, three years younger than Phoebe. A considerable social disparity also existed between the families. Phoebe's father was an illiterate agricultural worker. According to Mrs. Holt, Fiennes Henry's family "was well connected," but known for their irresponsible behavior.[8] Ironically, the story, of which Pym had no inkling, suggests that Pym shared her grandmother's taste in men. Throughout her life she repeatedly became infatuated with Byronic younger men. Several had social backgrounds more elevated than hers.

It is impossible to estimate the precise impact of such a guilty secret on the Pym household. The grandparents covered up the truth as best they could; they brought up Frederic as their own child. According to Mrs. Walton, in childhood the sisters had no notion that anything was amiss. Mrs. Walton also reports that her parents did not appear to discourage questions or to avoid troubling topics. The sisters never noticed the absence of their father's relatives, or speculated about the advanced age of his deceased "father." In conversation Mrs. Walton wondered if her father's somewhat diminished role in their family life could be attributed to his possible sense of shame.[9] Certainly the lack of secure parentage and close family members explains why Frederic Pym chose to marry a woman with many siblings. He willingly lived next door to her widowed mother and two spinster sisters for much of their married life. Furthermore, there is no doubt that Irena Pym was the dominant partner in the marriage. Having grown up in Oswestry, the Shropshire market town in which Frederic settled, Irena Pym found it easy to take charge and establish the direction of their family life.

Frederic Pym was not a strong-willed man. Mrs. Walton describes him as being good humored, kindly, and uncritical, uncommon virtues for fathers of his generation. She also declared that Pym was very like their sweet-natured father, who rarely picked a fight. Frederic acquired his compliant traits very early. He found it necessary to please the people who reared him with such ambivalent feelings about his very existence. Illegitimacy in his generation was considered a disgrace. Although no doubt grateful for the help of a well-placed local family, who nearly adopted him, he must have felt the burden of emotional debt. Frederic passed on the habit of compliant behavior to his older daughter, Barbara, whose sensitivity and intelligence made her extremely receptive to the subliminal messages of her parents.[10]

As an adult Pym was unable to express her anger and disappointment directly. Chronic anxiety, like that glimpsed in *The Magic Diamond*, had long since modified her rebellious instincts. According to the psychoanalyst Karen Horney, our characters are set in early childhood, the time when we should learn to conduct ourselves with appropriate flexibility, moving when necessary "toward, against, or away from others." As an adult, Pym often responded to men in an excessive or rigid fashion. In Horney's terms "affection . . . becomes clinging; compliance becomes appeasement."[11]

Some of Pym's problems stemmed from the unavoidable fact that she was far more creative, literary, and sensitive than any other member of her family. Early in childhood she began to remake the world in which she lived. Pym's names for her parents, aunt, and sister were adopted by both family and close friends in deference to her ingenuity. Thus she experienced a heightened sense of creative power, as well as a strengthened sense of being an outsider, a position that helped shape her literary sensibility. Having a remarkable imagination can be a mixed blessing. Pym, like her heroine Wilmet, was "observant beyond her emotional means." Her parents were unable to meet her special needs despite their pride in her literary talent. Creative and sensitive children are never easy to rear. The budding artist clearly felt like a changeling in her parents' household, devoted as they were to a comfortable round of work, bridge, golf, and amateur theatricals.[12] The early manuscripts shed light on Pym's conviction that she was unlike her parents.

, Of course, the young writer noted the disparity between her father's gentle but ineffectual nature and her mother's managerial competence. Her father lacked her mother's drive. Her mother made most of the important decisions regarding their daughters' education. Luckily Irena Pym was no tyrant. Unlike the repressive older relatives in Charlotte Yonge novels, which Pym later admired, who are determined that their female relations shall exhibit all the feminine graces, Mrs. Pym was tolerant. She ran her household smoothly enough and entered into the women's work of the community, but she preferred golf to cooking. She threw on clothes without regard for her appearance and demonstrated her adventurous spirit by being photographed riding a motorcycle, sometime before her early death in 1945.[13] In reaction, Pym tried hard to conform in matters of dress and deportment. Still she was clearly attached to her mother, Men in general and fathers in particular do not fare as well as mothers in Pym's manuscripts. Aside from the clergymen, Nicholas Cleveland in *Jane and Prudence,* Canon Palfrey in *Home Front Novel,* and the vicar in "The Vicar Floating By," the men are either fatuous, slightly unfaithful to their bored wives, or easily manipulated. The women experience little difficulty in managing them to their own satisfaction. Even the few eligible bachelors in her novels, who are fought over by spinsters and widows, seem slightly defective and hardly worth the effort.

Although Pym cherished her mother's eccentricities, in general she attempted to live up to those few domestic ideals that Mrs. Pym *did* espouse. Despite Irena's casual housekeeping, she derived much pleasure and stability from her immersion in everyday life. As a young woman, Pym also took great pride in her own domestic skills, especially cooking and sewing. Yet in girlhood she showed little interest in dolls or children. Like Dolly Arborfield in *An Academic Question* who loved hedgehogs, both sisters as children seemed to have preferred animals. This tendency became more marked in Pym in later life. Furthermore, whenever following her mother's lead meant sacrificing the chance to write, Pym felt severe conflict. Rather than rebelling or making demands, she noted the problem in her diary or complained mildly to a friend.[14]

Pym's novels suggest that in childhood she acquired a realistic if unconventional view of women, while gaining relatively little useful expectations about men. Even her early fiction and diaries indicate that she overvalued men, provided they were more forceful than her gentle father.[15] In contrast, she was always more realistic in her appraisals of women. The hierarchial social life of Oswestry influenced her greatly. Pym became adept at the art of social observation and cultivated this technique to enrich her writing. Few contemporary writers are as capable of incorporating into their writing the tiny nuances of behavior that make Pym's characters ring so true. Her habit of observation and assessment became an almost unconscious response.

The Oswestry matrons, unfortunately, also bequeathed to Pym their ambivalent feelings about men. Busy, bossy women dominated the circle in which Mrs. Pym moved, and her precocious child absorbed the implications of their mixed messages about the value of men. In traditional societies, women exercise a potentially subversive power in exchange for shouldering the domestic and child-rearing responsibilities. Behind the scenes they control the society they have created by their hard work. Pym's early manuscripts describe the activities of such matrons. She learned in childhood that without her mother and her mother's friends daily life in Oswestry would have been far less comfortable. At the same time those women indicated by their words and actions that they believed marriage to be essential for the happiness of all women. Even competent women disparaged the role of spinsters; husbands conferred social status. They were needed to protect hapless females from the absentminded exploitation of vicars and curates, who specialized in beguiling spinsters into lives of pointless servitude in exchange for well-timed words of praise.[16]

As it happened, the literary tastes and fantasies that Pym developed in her post-Oxford years, when she returned to Oswestry to live once again with her parents, suggest that she had been troubled by some aspects of her upbringing. Feeling worried about her future, and as ambivalent about men as the Oswestry matrons had been, she attempted to resolve her confusion by exercising her powerful imagination. The following account of one of her favorite inventions highlights some of the forces that engendered her creativity. For most of her childhood Pym lived next door to her maiden aunts, her favorite being her Aunt Jane, whom she had nicknamed "Ack." Hazel Holt describes Ack as an energetic, lively woman, "a splendid example of how it was possible to be unmarried and still have a 'rich, full life.'" Although Pym was very fond of her aunt, she also wondered why loveable Ack had not succeeded in finding a husband. Pym pondered if such a fate would be hers, but she evolved her own methods of displacing fear. In her early twenties just after she left Oxford, she began describing to her sister, Hilary, the adventures of Miss Moberley, an aristocratic and managing spinster who delights in being dictatorial.[17] Creating a literary character who makes a virtue out of what others might regard as a disability reduced Pym's anxiety about the future. At the same time, the inspiration contributed to the development of her unique voice. Miss Moberley foreshadows some of the strongminded eccentrics of her fiction, like Edith Liversidge in *Some Tame Gazelle*, Dolly Arborfield in *An Academic Question*, and Marcia Ivory in *Quartet in Autumn*. Telling her sister stories about Miss Moberley kept the character alive until Pym was sufficiently ready to use the doughty old spinster in a manuscript.

Throughout her adult life Pym suffered from intermittent mild depression and expended entirely too much energy in suppressing her negative feelings—particularly her anger. She habitually put her faith in men who were most unlikely to return her affection. It is hard to determine what caused this disturbance in her development; probably Pym's sadness resulted from the discomfort she felt when experiencing the normal but negative feelings that most of us have. According to the psychoanalyst Alice Miller, patients who are especially gifted as children tend to have correspondingly greater difficulty being appropriately rebellious as adults. Like Pym they seek to ignore their anger, sense of loss, and other negative feelings. There is no simple explanation for Pym's inhibited life. Her parents by all accounts had never been particularly intrusive or demanding. Instead they allowed their intensely emotional daughter consider-able leeway in the expression of her feelings and tolerated her ex-cesses. Yet for all their forbearance, Pym's life and work seem to have been deeply affected by anxiety. In the personal realm, she became too self-effacing; in the artistic realm, she sought security at all costs. Rather consciously she clung, like Charlotte Yonge, to the rituals of daily life.[18]

Pym's deep longing for security appears much later in a story, "The Vicar Floating By," probably written around 1941 when she was twenty-eight. It is about the two Pomfret sisters, who are vil-lage spinsters, and it features the same pattern of paternal rescue as *The Magic Diamond*. The plot mixes typical Pym subjects with other issues that appear nowhere else in her work. The Pomfrets, two gen-tlewomen who paint watercolors, want to raise money for the church roof. They read an article in the newspaper about surrealism and decide that they will create surrealist paintings to earn the neces-sary sum. The task is surprisingly easy. They insist that surrealism merely involves using one's unconscious fantasies, glimpses of a buried life.[19]

Julia, the sensitive and talented sister, produces a painting, "The Vicar Floating By," which is based on a dream. It depicts a flood with objects floating by, of which the last is their vicar. The exhibit is successful, and the Pomfrets quickly earn the necessary money. According to Pym, however, the life of an artist has its pitfalls. Although the sisters break free, freedom ends by frightening them. They move to London and lose touch with the village. Of course their sheltered background guarantees that they will feel displaced in the London artistic world. In reaction to their sense of isolation, their work becomes alarmingly simple and comically bizarre. Julia begins a sketch of a head emerging from a toilet bowl. Agatha, the less imaginative of the two, paints fried eggs everywhere. She even shoplifts frying pans from Woolworth's for use in her collages. Julia begins to worry that Agatha is going crazy. She writes their vicar to ask him to rescue them. Like the father in *The Magic Diamond*, he obliges. He arrives, and in no time Agatha is talking normally about village trivia. Soon the sisters feel safe. They are able to talk of surrealism with complete detachment. They return to the village and resume painting watercolors. Only the painting, "The Vicar Floating By," testifies to their disturbing past.[20]

The story suggests that Pym was afraid of losing her way in her fantasies. She placed her faith in powerful men—father-substitutes like the clergy—and in the church as an institution. This conviction had an important effect on her life and work. At times Pym took refuge in the familiar, thereby resisting the experimentation and change that her novels required. Even more important, the whole episode suggests that she had little confidence in her ability to stand alone.

Oswestry had a permanent influence on Pym's life. Her view of village life enhanced her writing and provided her with material for much of her career. At the same time Pym absorbed many conservative and negative attitudes about men from her upbringing. She was extraordinarily sensitive to atmosphere, of course. Her sister, Hilary, did not emerge from this background with so many mixed emotional messages. (Indeed after reading a draft of my article, "Ellipsis, Eccentricity and Evasion in the Diaries of Barbara Pym," Mrs. Walton pointed out with some asperity that Oswestry was not a village, but a country town.[21] Obviously she did not share her sister's fantasy.) Whatever might have been the exact cause of Pym's difficulties, by the end of her childhood she had not developed a secure sense of her feminine identity. A fear of uncontrollable emotions certainly marks her mature fiction. These same feelings caused her much suffering in youth. By the time Pym left Oswestry for boarding school, she was well on the way to becoming both a writer and a romantically doomed spinster.

During Pym's final year at boarding school and her Oxford days, she was greatly influenced by the novels of Aldous Huxley. At first, the effect was beneficial; reading Huxley encouraged her to become a writer. At Oxford, however, she began to imitate a Huxley character in her daily life, thereby becoming once again the star of her own play. This time the drama had neither a happy nor a conclusive ending.

The writing from Pym's last year at school is worth analyzing at some length. It contains the genesis of certain techniques that she used throughout her career. At sixteen, Pym had developed the kind of detachment and humor that marked her later fiction. She had already begun her lifelong habit of converting unpleasant memories into funny stories, thus warding off distress. Huxley's example encouraged her to reexamine from a new perspective the subjects of love and death, which she had first addressed in *The Magic Diamond*.

Huxley's influence explains why Pym's adolescent stories feature male personae. Instead of ruminating about the misfortunes of vulnerable women—the spinsters, clergyman's daughters, and companions that populate much of her fiction—she portrayed independent and artistic young men and women, all of whom led autonomous existences. These characters are embryonic writers, who are both startled and gratified by their own capacity to convert their miseries into fiction. Furthermore, her heroes' romantic setbacks do not interfere with their enjoyment of life. Despite the momentary pain of rejection, they cheerfully anticipate the prospect of growing up. Thus they differ from the passive protagonists in *The Magic Diamond* and the diffident heroines of Pym's mature fiction.

It is not surprising that Pym was fascinated by Huxley's work. His novels startled the literary world of the 1920s. Despite his advanced ideas, however, Pym's parents made no attempt to censor their sixteen-year-old daughter's reading. For a time Huxley's writing dramatically altered her behavior, while expanding her notions of what subject matter would be suitable for social comedy. Huxley depicted an upper-class world, considerably less socially constrained than Oswestry. In his early novels he wrote nonchalantly about a society in which the usual rules of decorum have been suspended, and very little is accorded serious treatment. For example, politics are important in *Point Counter Point* largely because fanatical leaders exercise some mysterious sexual attractiveness. Otherwise the rise of Fascism is subordinated to the importance of personal relations, just as political matters tend to be in Pym's novels. To a young girl schooled never to discuss religion, politics, or sex in polite society, Huxley's sophistication was irresistible.[22]

Under Huxley's influence, Pym's adolescent effusions failed to reflect an especially feminine point of view. Like many young artists, she was preoccupied by thoughts of the opposite sex and the momentous discovery of her talents. Pym identified with Huxley's youthful heroes, many of whom aspired to be poets. Through their eyes she explored the different sensibilities of authors and more ordinary folk like her parents.

Of course, a feminist critic like Judith Fetterley might say that reading male authors like Huxley "immasculated" female readers like Pym. According to Fetterley, canonical literature written by men teaches women "to think as men, to identify with a male point of view, and to accept as normal and legitimate a male system of values, one of whose central principles is misogyny." Yet in Pym's case, Fetterley's worst fears were not realized. Huxley's male heroes empowered Pym; they encouraged her to dream of a career as a writer.[23] Selecting a male mentor temporarily extricated her from inner fears about her own helplessness. Despite the usefulness of the tactic, however, Pym's adaptation of a male persona was neither permanent nor entirely successful.

Pym's schoolgirl narratives provide a revealing glimpse of her emotional life in that period. Ordinarily adolescence is a time of strain for young people, a moment when they begin to redefine themselves in relationship to their families and society. The comfort of their childhood identity rarely proves adequate to their needs. For instance, the developing young artists in the bildungsromane of James Joyce and Thomas Mann are almost totally preoccupied by sex and their conflicts with family and society. In contrast, Pym's characters seem both less troubled and more childlike, reflecting her conditioning as an educated, middle-class female in a traditional society. Of course, Joyce and Mann were looking back on their childhoods, whereas Pym was still an adolescent. Nonetheless, her stories reveal both her intellectual precocity and her protected life.

The relative serenity of Pym's imaginative world suggests that the young writer cherished her sense of familial belonging. Her parents might no longer seem as powerful as the king in *The Magic Diamond*, but they still provided an important sense of security. Of course the young woman looked forward to the freedom of Oxford, but the constraints of school eliminated the necessity of making difficult decisions about her conduct. As a result, her final year at boarding school was a time of expansiveness and creative promise rather than of emotional struggle. But Pym's contentment depended on the protection offered by her environment and did not long survive her ventures into a more competitive arena. In fact, later events suggest that Pym had no clearly developed, personal code of sexual behavior. Instead, she took advantage of the dispensation society offered young women of her era to postpone thinking about such matters until marriage. She displaced her sexual preoccupations. Rather than confronting her anxieties and fantasies directly, she intellectualized and dramatized them. Writing stories disengaged her from uncomfortable feelings that she longed to obliterate.

According to her sister, Hilary Walton, Pym and her friends were more sophisticated and preoccupied by men than the other girls at school. They bypassed the usual adolescent crushes on older girls or attractive school teachers in favor of some advanced talk about sex. Pym's talk, however, was deceptive. Her emotional maturity lagged behind her verbal skills, and no amount of novel reading could bridge the gap. Her schoolgirl stories and poems clearly delineate the distance between her intellectual and her emotional development. Even when writing of unrequited love and early death, her tone is buoyant and cheerful. The suffering she describes had no reality to her. Thus her adolescent work, according to her own later commentary, reads like the production of a precocious child for whom adult feelings are not yet credible.[24]

Take, for example, the absurd romantic adventures of her first hero, Denis Feverel, in *Young Men in Fancy Dress*. Pym's hero is based on Denis Stone, the protagonist of Huxley's *Crome Yellow*. Denis proposes marriage to a famous poet, Marguerite Duval, after an acquaintanceship of half an hour, and then feels devastated when she rejects him. For a short time he indulges in thoughts of suicide. The idea of revenge appeals to him despite his upbringing, which discouraged such thoughts. In despair he turns to his parents, who take him to a nightclub. By the next morning he has fully recovered, indeed has almost forgotten his unhappiness. As a result he feels embarrassed when the now abject Marguerite proposes to him.[25]

Denis recuperates quickly. Like his young creator, he is easily distracted from dwelling on his feelings. He has the gift of detachment, allowing him to view his actions from afar as if he were an actor in a play. At humiliating moments, he is aware that the drama brings him pleasure although it is too soon to begin converting the episode into fiction. Of course, Denis's reaction is quite typical of self-conscious young writers.[26] Still, too much distance can interfere with emotional development, as Pym's later history reveals.

Another curious feature of the novel is that it ends inconclusively. Denis is rejected by another attractive young woman, but he is undaunted. Considering that Pym had not yet experienced unhappiness in love, her insistence on its unrequited nature indicates some innate pessimism, despite her comic tone. She accepted without question Huxley's contention in *Crome Yellow* that love relations are almost always doomed to misfire. Like him, she describes a social world in which mutuality is impossible. As a result this early novel avoids concluding with an engagement or a marriage, the traditional ending of romantic fiction and social comedy. Instead,

Pym emulates the more complicated and indecisive model found in Huxley's novels. The festive mood, however, is not marred. The protagonists are far too young to give up their search for suitable mates.[27]

Pym's other juvenilia exhibits the same jaunty good spirits while addressing the issues that preoccupied her at the time. In all of her early stories the protagonists attempt to define their artistic roles. Apparently, the young author was already worried about whether she could reconcile her creative instincts with her love of food and comfort. At this point Pym approached the dilemma with humor. In one of her early stories, "The Sad Story of Alphonse," the narrator explains why he chose to become a novelist rather than a poet. Poets are really ghosts, so by definition they cannot eat.[28] For all the humorous absurdity of the story, Pym understood that asceticism was not to be part of her artistic personality.

The difficulties of literary fame also absorbed Pym's attention at this time. One story suggests that privacy and fame are incompatible. In "Henry Shakespeare" literary lion-hunters destroy the peace of mind of an ordinary young bank clerk, who is unfortunate enough to have the surname of the famous playwright. An acquaintance assumes that diffidence is proof of the hapless clerk's poetic nature, even though the young man's idea of ecstasy is to complete the year-end balance sheet. Overwhelmed by invitations, the shy clerk is forced to cower in the dark. (Some curates in Pym's later manuscripts hide the same way to avoid the advances of man-hungry spinsters. Eventually they marry to escape the pressure.) Finally in despair the clerk accepts a transfer to Wales and changes his name to Lloyd. As Pym wryly comments, someone once asked him if there was any possible connection to the famous bank but luckily allowed the matter to drop.[29] Clearly, Pym's sense of narrative distance and her delight in humorous or absurd behavior developed early.

These stories appeared in Pym's school literary magazine, which she edited. The summer before she left for Oxford she also wrote a series of private poems about a bank clerk. Pym's analysis of the clerk's character in "Midland Bank: A Poem dedicated to JTLI with the Author's Fondest Love (But without his Permission)" reveals her sharp eye and her critical powers, as well as her attraction for difficult men. She praises the clerk in the same backhanded fashion she later applies to her Oxford friend Henry Harvey. The narrator insists that unlike his coworkers, this clerk has a soul. Those who criticize him are insensitive and imperceptive fools. Indeed, she admires him for his self-absorption and his disdain for others, hardly admirable qualities. In contrast, Pym was far more cynical about the pretensions of a young curate whose behavior she carefully depicted. In "Satire," a self-conscious imitation of Alexander Pope, which features young men that she knew, she pokes fun at the curate's custom of lacing his sermons with poetry, a habit shared by Archdeacon Hoccleve of *Some Tame Gazelle*. The Archdeacon positively delights in quoting obscure and difficult poetry in his sermons.[30]

Pym takes for granted that she should be entranced by such men but also stands apart from her objects of desire. By writing the poems she gains the upper hand. Her analytical skills give her a feeling of superiority, despite her schoolgirl status. For example in "Tame Donkey, Sequel to Midland Bank," another poem dedicated to the aloof bank clerk, her hero is a donkey who transforms himself into a unicorn. The sexual overtones of the poem are obvious. Equally important is the mixture of hero worship, condescension, admiration for the quality of his aloofness, and fascination with death. Pym assumes that becoming sexually active inevitably includes falling from grace but hints that such a fate is preferable to remaining drearily innocent.[31] At sixteen, however, she had not yet tested any of her ideas.

A commitment to her craft transcends the peculiarities of "Death of a Young Man," which she wrote shortly before leaving for Oxford. In this story Gerald, a poet suffering from writer's block, meets a famous novelist, who needs to kill someone to provide the ending for his next work. Admiring the writer's ability to capture his readers' feelings and frustrated by his own inability to find the right words for his poems, Gerald is more than willing to make the sacrifice for art. In the end, he dwells contentedly in heaven. There he is able to write the poetry he had always longed to produce, bothered only by his inability to read the novel for which he has prematurely ended his life. This story reveals the strong influence of Huxley's "distancing" narrators. Huxley's fictional voice accentuates the distance between himself and the reader and makes no effort to dissolve the barrier. Pym's later novels more often employed an "engaging" narrator, to borrow Robyn Warhol's useful terms. Unlike Huxley, Pym's typical narrative mode encourages readers to identify with her goals and desires.[32]

Before failures in love darkened Pym's comic vision, she wrote in a cavalier fashion about subjects that seriously preoccupied her later on. Her characters may fail to experience the mutuality of love, but their youth gives them hope for future happiness. She does not show any special interest in or sympathy for female characters. Instead, she identifies with artistic young men, thereby projecting, as Carolyn Heilbrun has suggested, "the ideal of autonomy onto a male character."[33] But despite Pym's lack of interest in the women in her early fiction, even in this early work they turn out to have hidden power.

Marguerite Duval is a case in point. Pym features her in both *Young Men in Fancy Dress* and "Adolphe," a story she wrote the summer before Oxford. Although Marguerite seems to have a marginal role in "Adolphe"—women in Pym's juvenilia generally provide the stable element against which the insecure young men react—her power over the titular hero is destructive and complete. Adolphe, in real life a bank clerk named Arthur, is an ordinary young man. He becomes part of a poetic circle after Marguerite, a talented and established poet, renames him Adolphe, the sort of romantic name that Pym favored.

The story has some elements in common with Pym's more mature work. First, the reappearance of Marguerite indicates that Pym began her habit of recycling her characters very early. Second, the plight of Adolphe foreshadows the disparate relationships between young men and older women in her later manuscripts and in her personal life. In this instance, however, the woman writer clearly has the upper hand, whereas in Pym's later life and fiction the situation is often reversed. Adolphe is transformed by his friendship with Marguerite. He becomes an intellectual, as well as her private secretary. In the process, however, he loses his sense of self.[34] The rechristening of Adolphe suggests that he represented a surrogate for Pym. The following autumn she renamed herself "Sandra," a character much like Lucy Tantamount, Huxley's femme fatale in *Point Counter Point*. Given the disparity between Pym's natural timidity and the pressures of that role, the resulting disasters were sadly predictable and probably explain why Pym never created a character like Sandra, except in a very faded version, such as Viola in *No Fond Return of Love*.

In later years, Pym remembered Oxford as being a golden time in her life, but a more dispassionate observer would disagree. In retrospect, Pym's decision to become Sandra was a measure of the apprehension that going up to Oxford aroused in her. Until that stage of her life, neither boarding school nor her family had given her the opportunity to act. Advanced talk aside, she knew little about men. Yet as long as she was protected by chaperons, she could safely

aspire to attract men without paying the consequences for such
behavior. Now that freedom was possible, the young woman took
refuge in a fictive personality.

To a degree, Pym had developed the qualities psychoanalysts
identify as belonging to an "as-if" personality. This kind of person
is unable to develop authentic feelings and interests but by an
unconscious process of imitation behaves normally. Pym's assumption of a fictional role was, of course, more deliberate. In fact her
school story "Adolphe" indicates that on some level she was aware
of what she was doing. Yet the repercussions from her action were
no better than if she had been completely oblivious. Behaving in an
inauthentic fashion dramatically increased the observant, detached
side of her personality. In consequence, she found it impossible to
master the emotions stirred up by Sandra's flamboyant behavior.[35]

The story contained in her diaries is sad, and the style of composition offers little indication that its author would eventually write
witty, eccentric fiction. Pym presents herself as a heroine of a mock-
heroic adventure. In the self-referential plot, the heroine, disguised
as an ebullient Sandra, arrives with a plan to take Oxford by storm.
Even after her second year, as late as July 1, 1933, Pym still clung
to her fantasy that Sandra was the most daring of the Pyms. Ironically her pose had roots in her family history that were quite unknown to her. According to Hazel Holt, the family of Pym's paternal
grandfather, Fiennes Crampton, had a reputation for being "decidedly wild."[36] In Pym's case, however, playing the role of a heartless coquette, like the Huxley heroines who had fascinated her,
never suited the romantically intense, innocent, and gauche young
woman. Instead her unbridled pursuit of romance stirred up strong
feelings of passion and melancholy that sometimes threatened to
overwhelm her.

Moreover, assuming a fictional identity rarely provides the surest
path to self-knowledge. Pym was by nature a chronicler, rather than
an introspective thinker. Whenever she recounted events, she tried
to be entertaining. She rarely questioned the events she recorded or
pondered their inner meaning. At times she expressed embarrassment for her ineptness. Yet her feelings reflect more consciousness
of shame and humiliation than of guilt and self-doubt. Indeed, one
of Pym's favorite quotations is "Social Success," from Logan Pearsall Smith's *Trivia*. Smith describes a self-conscious person who
becomes mortified by the memory of his extroverted behavior of the
day before.[37]

Pym's diaries seem underdeveloped for a combination of technical and psychological factors. Of course she wrote to express herself, not to make sense for a reader. Thus she described "daring" remarks made by young men or Sandra's outrageous behavior without explaining the context of the situation or the identity of the man in question. Her off-hand, elliptical style is bewildering, but Pym wrote as an actor in the drama. The structure of her writing, however, helps to illuminate her psychological state at the time. The pressures of her social life encouraged her to revert to an earlier, more egocentric, stage in her writing.[38] As a result, not only are Pym's diaries elusive, but they seem naive. After all, laundry lists of names of young men hardly offer proof that Sandra was a sophisticated young woman. Moreover, Pym's boasting and provocative talk obscured the real problems that she faced. Her extroverted behavior prematurely encouraged the advances of young men. They expected her to be able to live up to her self-reported dreadful reputation, when in fact she could not do so.

Actually, by modern standards Pym's deportment was refreshingly innocent. She did not drink, gamble, take drugs, or have serial affairs with men. Her flirtations with illicit conduct—the henna rinses, low-cut dresses, bright lipstick, orchid nail polish, and cigarette smoking mentioned in her diary—seem like tame gestures to us. They represented rebellion to her. The same conflict between innocence and rebellion is apparent in her sexual activities. Pym often reacted to the advances of young men in a prim and inhibited manner despite her efforts to attract their interest.[39]

Throughout Pym's first year at Oxford, she behaved like a starstruck young girl. Her diary entries abound with references to the attractive men that she saw, some of whom she gave nicknames. Whenever she discovered a new man, she would attempt to find out his name. She would follow him to his lodgings and, if necessary, look him up in the Oxford calendar, a list of undergraduates. Quite clearly she did not expect the man to pursue her. Her tracking behavior might have been unusual for an Oxford female undergraduate, but her friends did not reject her despite her curious obsession. In fact, her excesses provided a source of excitement and a focus for their lives. University students, whose own sense of identity is by no means secure, often find such behavior appealing. She acted out the confusion they felt. Pym's friends willingly abetted her efforts to track the man of the hour. Eagerly they reported their sightings of her chosen prey. Her fantasies also had a powerful effect on her friends. For instance, Mary Sharp, an Oxford contemporary, recounted a dream about the death of Pym's friend Robert Liddell.[40]

As Janice Rossen has suggested, Pym's frivolity did not help her academic standing. No doubt her dissatisfaction with Oxford's rigid curriculum had the indirect effect of encouraging her to continue with the absurd pose. Like many creative people, Pym found Oxford's scholarly approach inappropriate to her needs. Like most women she was inclined to blame herself.[41] The curriculum emphasized literature, an area of real interest to her, and linguistics. Lacking the requisite interest in Old Norse Sagas, Beowulf, or Old English, Pym could not expect to earn a first-class degree. Yet she spent much time absorbing literature that had some personal meaning to her. Her knowledge of lyric poetry was impressively extensive.

Pym lacked the discipline necessary to concentrate on those things that seemed irrelevant. Instead of developing scholarly habits or indulging in a litany of complaints, she amused herself by man-chasing. Indeed her intrusive activities served two purposes. They distracted her from the frustration of an unequal competition and established a pattern of watchfulness, which ultimately provided some material for her books. These tactics, however, had mixed results. Her intense preoccupation with a series of young men helped her forget her uneven academic performance. Nonetheless, such diversions had their price. Without them she might have taken a better degree—she took a creditable second—or have tried to fathom the reasons for her predicament.

If Pym's relations with men had continued to be as limited as they were in her first year, the diaries would not be of much interest today. Eventually, however, she became entangled with two Oxford men who ceased to be merely the objects of fantasies. The feelings stirred up by Rupert Gleadow and Henry Harvey had a profound effect on her emotional and literary future. Therefore these relationships must be examined in some detail. Both men played important roles in her life. As Hazel Holt once declared, Pym's long but fruitless pursuit of Harvey permanently undermined her fragile self-confidence.[42] More important, the episode permanently affected the kind of fiction that she produced. Her earlier misadventures with Rupert Gleadow are equally consequential. They offer a revealing glimpse into both her sexual difficulties and her compensatory technique of converting emotional disasters into novels.

Of Pym's lovers, only Rupert Gleadow seemed to care about her personally. Before he took an interest in her, men in her life had either been distant fantasy figures, such as Geoffrey, a young man who read theology, or friends whose interest she spurned. Of course,

Pym was delighted by Gleadow's attention, but at nineteen she was incapable of a deep attachment. Being somewhat older, Gleadow was eager to have a mistress and repeatedly complained that Oxford rules made that difficult.[43] Pym, however, was entirely too cautious to succumb merely to please him.

As a result, Gleadow's attempt at seduction failed miserably. Whatever Pym wrote about the event no longer exists. She subsequently removed those pages from her diary, leaving only a poignant fragment of the original, "Today I must always remember I suppose. I went to tea with Rupert (and ate a pretty colossal one)—and he with all his charm, eloquence and masculine wiles, persuaded . . . ." Despite the absence of commentary from Pym, the incident troubled her. Indeed the complete absence of detail about subsequent meetings suggests that she was blotting out a painful memory. Twelve days after the event, the dutiful chronicler recorded that she could not remember how she had spent the afternoon with Rupert. She planned to check with him in order to keep her record straight.[44] Such amnesia testifies to her lack of serious interest in him and to her wish to forget past unhappiness.

In retrospect, it is apparent that Pym's friendship with Rupert Gleadow marked the end of whatever optimism she had about her relationships with men. From then on, she intensified her habit of collecting photographs and mementoes—what she called relics—of men who interested her. Her diaries are replete with references to shrines in honor of her lost loves. Sometimes she began constructing these shrines before she had really developed a solid friendship, let alone suffered from its rupture. Pym herself was aware of the melancholy nature of her memorials, but cherishing the items gave her much pleasure.[45]

In contrast to Pym's evasiveness about the event, and the impression she gives that their friendship trailed off gradually, Gleadow was more forthright. He wrote that he regretted the failure and emphasized his sexual interest in her. Obviously, he found it easier to face defeat directly. After all, he could blame it on Pym's unwillingness.[46] Gradually his letter writing tapered off, their meetings diminished in number, and by the next term Pym was infatuated with Henry Harvey, whose unkind treatment caused her endless anguish for the next few years.

Two subsequent matters suggest how genuinely important the incident with Gleadow was to Pym personally and what literary use she made of it. At the time, Pym told her sister Hilary about her "affair," a claim which was greatly exaggerated. Second, in 1940, when the incident no longer troubled her, she converted Gleadow's unsuccessful seduction into a comically portrayed fiasco in *Crampton Hodnet*. In it the repressed young woman scholar not only runs away in panic from an imminent sexual encounter, but she embroiders the incident when describing the details to her woman friend, as Pym did with her sister.[47]

Pym was conscious of her own literary methods and described the process in *The Lumber Room*. Beatrice Wyatt says that she places the memory of a past love into a lumber room (a storage room or attic). After a long period of avoiding the room, eventually she risks inspecting the shrouded object. She discovers that the once painful love has become what Pym repeatedly described as "mild, kindly looks and spectacles" (*JP*, 129). The object has lost its power to hurt. The lumber room acts like death; it reduces all feeling. This metaphor illuminates Pym's creative process. She did not try to learn from her failures in love. Instead she preferred to distract herself by pursuing other men. Her behavior spared her much pain, but in the process of denying her feelings, some of them became, to borrow Jung's metaphor, "glowing coals under grey ashes." Jung himself deplored the all too human tendency to abandon "aspects of life which should also have been experienced . . . in the lumber-room among dusty memories."[48]

Pym behaved in much the same fashion a few years later when her second, and far more painful, love affair with Henry Harvey collapsed. As a result, what she called the Saga of Lorenzo is not just a sad story of Pym's misfortunes in love but the origin of *Some Tame Gazelle*. Pym never wrote about the saga with such charm, even though the novel provides an example of Pym writing herself out of her sense of powerlessness and desperation.

The saga represents an unsuccessful romantic quest. In it Pym, no longer under parental protection like Princess Rosebud of *The Magic Diamond*, suffered from the pangs of love, typical of both the courtly love tradition and of the Biblical account of Jacob's long servitude for his beloved Rachel. Pym was quite aware of the literary sources and analogues to her situation. On July 15, 1936, she commented quite proudly upon her many years of service to Henry (*VPE*, 58). Luckily Pym's love of literary drama was quite genuine. She simply could not resist turning her adventures into a series of dramatic scenes. Often she blurred the distinction between life and fiction, just as she had when she first created the artificial role of Sandra.

The details of Pym's pursuit of Henry Harvey can be found in *A*

Very Private Eye. The few scraps that amplify that account suggest how little pleasure she gained from the physical part of their relationship. Just as with Gleadow, Pym cut out painful incidents on which she would rather not dwell, leaving a wistful comment, recorded in February 1934, that she would attempt to conquer her fear when she was with Harvey. No doubt she dreaded the subservient feelings he stirred in her. Moreover, Harvey, like most male undergraduates, was more intent on his pleasure than on hers. As a result, Pym began to feel that sex was what she gave in return for the pleasure of his company, a conviction which adds irony to the title of her lost manuscript from her Oxford days, "Still She Wished for Company."[49]

Early in March 1934, Pym recorded Harvey's passionate behavior, rather than her own. She seemed happier remembering the ensuing tea, a cozy event which after all was not embarrassing to describe. No wonder years later in *Jane and Prudence,* Pym has Miss Doggett say vaguely, " 'Men only want *one thing'* . . . as if she had heard that men only wanted one thing, but had forgotten for the moment what it was" (*JP,* 70). To make matters worse, Pym was aware that Harvey harbored no romantic thoughts about her. March 9, after she submitted to him, he began talking admiringly about Alison West-Watson, a student who resisted his blandishments (*VPE,* 36–37). Unfortunately Pym lacked the self-esteem to imitate West-Watson's example.

Misery drove Pym to seek a confidant, someone who knew Henry Harvey but would be willing to sympathize about his sometimes offhand treatment of her. In desperation, she turned to Harvey's flatmate, Robert Liddell. His feelings about playing that role must have been very mixed. Pym had been quite aware that her pursuit of Harvey had not given his friend much pleasure. On February 23, 1934, she even recorded his hostile glance at her. Yet her interest in Harvey included strong feelings for Liddell. In fact she referred to the mementos of her association with Harvey as the Harvey-Liddell relics.[50]

Indeed his friends provided a large part of Harvey's fascination. Pym was well aware that in some sense Liddell was her rival for Harvey's attention and that he opposed her attempt to win Harvey's heart. Rivalry, however, merely added spice to her pursuit. Pym's relationship with these two men created a triangular pattern of great importance to her. She competed vigorously for a desirable man, but whenever her beloved treated her unkindly, she turned for comfort to the very person she had sought to displace. Liddell was not merely a part of the world she sought to invade. Sometimes he seemed its emotional center.

Unfortunately, Pym had no idea that her feelings might have originated from some unresolved oedipal conflicts in early childhood. She lacked any insight into or curiosity about her early life. Carolyn Heilbrun reports that American women poets born ten to twenty years after Pym recognized that "confronting the relation to the father was the only way to female self-realization."[51] In contrast, Pym kept her memories of both mother and father locked firmly in her lumber room. As a result, she kept repeating triangular relationships throughout her life.

At first Liddell did not welcome Pym's intrusion in Harvey's and his lives. Yet, as he wrote after Pym's death, eventually he became devoted to her. At first he was irritated by her persistence but in time relished "her original and quaint" humor and habit of self-deprecation. Intellectually the two had much in common. He found her love for literature and "ecclesiology" very engaging and admitted that eventually they became confederates. His friendship with her, however, was based initially upon a mixture of pity and affection. Thus he never felt inclined to take her feelings for Harvey very seriously. He sympathized with her inability to manage her erotic relations satisfactorily but condescendingly remarked that her " 'affairs' (and they were hardly that) usually ended with tears."[52]

Years later in *An Object for a Walk*, Liddell created characters reminiscent of Pym and Harvey, who have an affair. After Flora (Pym) becomes Geoffrey's (Harvey's) mistress, she behaves as if "her conscience had stopped, like a watch whose spring had been broken." Flora was not meant to be a faithful portrait of Pym, but at certain moments Liddell captured the essence of Pym's situation. Flora behaves as if her newfound passion had blocked "many of her ordinary channels of thought and feeling."[53] As a result, she totally disregards the code of conduct by which she had been reared. Under the circumstances she finds it impossible to protect herself against exploitation. Furthermore, Geoffrey (Harvey) cannot tolerate so much intensity in a love relationship. He soon tires of Flora and moves on to fresh conquests, just as Harvey did in real life. Although there is no evidence of sexual delirium in Pym's account of the affair, Liddell sheds light on her inability to resist Harvey's advances, despite her awareness of his increasing interest in another woman.

In March 1934, when Pym was beginning to realize that her only hope was to follow Liddell's advice and obliterate her pain by hard work, she discovered new distractions—travel and foreign men. On a trip to Germany, she was delighted to receive the attentions of several Nazis, chief among them Friedbert Glück and Hanns Woischnick. Her behavior on this occasion was quite typical of her earliest days at Oxford when she cheerfully chased several men at the same time. The positive reaction of her German admirers pleased her. Before long she became romantically involved with them. Once again she later deleted the pertinent details from her diary, making it impossible to know exactly what transpired. Nonetheless, the excitement of being in Germany freed her from the sense of detachment that marked so much of her behavior. She reported that for once she was able to concentrate on the moment at hand, rather than observe herself thinking and feeling, a freedom from self-consciousness she too seldom experienced.[54]

Pym's fascination with the Nazis is difficult to evaluate accurately. Of course, her behavior was naive in the extreme and, in retrospect, regrettable even to her. Yet Henry Harvey's behavior had made her desperate for male admiration. To some extent the admiring young Germans helped her overcome the despair caused by Harvey's indifference. In May 1935, she declared in her diary that she did not agree with the politics of National Socialism, despite trying to do so for the sake of her friends. On one occasion she struggled to read one of Hitler's speeches, sent by one of her admirers. Jay Martin, a psychoanalyst and literary critic, has argued that individuals like Pym make intense but "transient identifications" with those who attract them. Robert Liddell suggests that Pym responded to the young Germans' good looks.[55]

Pym's more earnest friends were shocked by her lack of political sense. In response to her effusions, Rupert Gleadow wrote October 29, 1934, begging her not to be impressed by the despicable Nazis. He also commented that it sounded from her letter as if she had indulged in another love affair but closed by remarking that no doubt she was as chaste as ever. In some ways, Pym's interest in the Nazis was quite childish. She admired their uniforms and was absorbed by the trivia associated with National Socialism, rather than by its principles. In April 1934, she took real pleasure from making a scarlet box with a swastika on it and also bought a swastika pin. Years later in her Daybook, July 31, 1941, she expressed some regret for past excesses, but her self-condemnation never sounded entirely convincing.[56]

Pym's hints about her sexual intimacy with the two Germans offer no more conclusive proof about her behavior than do her accounts of earlier romantic entanglements. It is impossible to tell exactly how much sexual experience Pym actually had with any man. Pym deliberately obscured her accounts.[57] Moreover, when writing she often switched between reality and fantasy, at a sometimes dizzying speed, as if life and fiction were intertwined in her consciousness. She probably knew which entries were factual, but she rarely indicated which was which.

Two further matters are worth commenting upon: the first is that Pym's desperate need for privacy contended with her exhibitionist tendencies. The conflict sometimes caused her to behave unpredictably. For example, sometime after her relationship with Harvey became at least partly sexual, on April 18, 1934, she reported in her diary being furious that he had embarrassed her in front of Robert Liddell (*VPE*, 38). In the ensuing scuffle, she feared that the others had seen far more than she wished. The second point is that despite Pym's habit of confiding her troubles like an abject child, her closest friends never accepted her version of her love relationships. Robert Liddell consistently denied the gravity of her feelings for Harvey, perhaps for his own reasons. Even the loyal Rupert Gleadow, who continued to correspond until his first marriage, reported on August 3, 1935, that he had never credited her strong feelings about Harvey, regardless of what she had told him.[58]

Pym's friends observed her inhibited behavior and her tendency to exaggerate and romanticize her life. They, however, could not see her struggle to decide whether to reveal or conceal her thoughts and feelings. As D. W. Winnicott has suggested, many artists experience a conflict between "the urgent need to communicate and the still more urgent need not to be found."[59] On the one hand, Pym lived her love life in public, and all of her friends were privy to her latest adventure. At the same time, throughout her life she believed in keeping her problems to herself and presenting a pleasant demeanor to the world. In numerous diary entries, she commented proudly that she had hidden her anger from the person who had aroused it most intensely. As a result, there was much in her life that she refused to confide to anyone, including her diary.

In consequence, many of Pym's friends misinterpreted the meaning of her serenity and assumed that her emotional life was far simpler than it was. On May 22, 1985, Hazel Holt commented upon Pym's cheerful good humor. She felt that Pym's frivolity indicated that she did not experience much depression or regret over her life.[60] In actual fact Pym had so successfully removed her feelings to the lumber room, that to a certain extent they had ceased to exist. In consequence, even the people she cared for were oblivious to the misery that sometimes troubled her.

Yet, whenever Pym experienced sexual rejection, its reality was far more painful than she had once imagined. Her two-year effort to captivate Henry Harvey temporarily drained her of her courage and powers of detachment. The anticipation of completing her university career failed to compensate for the absence of plans for the future and the dreary prospect of returning home. Dejected, but still committed to being a writer, she returned to her parents to begin a long apprenticeship. Very slowly she learned to convert her suffering into a new kind of comic novel that would celebrate the experience of deprivation and self-restraint.

2

Pym's Moratorium

The patience of Barbara Pym's parents must have been sorely tried during the years that their creative daughter lived at home after attending Oxford. Not only was she sometimes moody and preoccupied with the absent Henry Harvey, but she found it difficult to launch her literary career. Disappointments in love had eroded the optimism that characterize her juvenilia. She could no longer write the sort of stories that had given her pleasure in girlhood, and for years she found no adequate substitute. Most of the manuscripts drafted between 1934 and 1941 represent a series of false starts. During her lifetime she managed to complete only one successful novel from them all, *Some Tame Gazelle*, and even that one did not come easily to her. Despite the difficulties, however, the tolerance of Pym's parents was eventually rewarded. These largely discarded pieces of writing represented a necessary stage in her development as a novelist. Composing them helped her regain the equilibrium that had been badly shaken at Oxford and at the same time develop her unique literary voice. Out of the unsatisfactory raw material of these manuscripts ultimately evolved the polished novels of her maturity.

At first, the return to Oswestry signified an ignominious defeat for the competitive young woman. Like many other lovers of Oxford, she hated leaving. In her diary, she reported feeling numb but was inclined to regard numbness as a comfort. After all, the final half of her university career had been a time of intense experiences, many of them bitter.[1] Going home offered much-needed privacy and an opportunity to reestablish some control over her unruly feelings.

Pym's decision to return to her parents, with only a vague plan of becoming a governess in Germany the following September, suggests how much her Oxford experiences had undermined her confidence. She obviously needed a tranquil environment in order to regain her equilibrium. On the whole she was happy with her parents, but understandably there were occasional eruptions. For example, on October 4, 1934, in her diary she declared that she was perfectly happy to live at home and work on a novel, but three days later she also recorded an uncharacteristic hysterical outburst at her mother (*VPE,* 45). In subsequent letters to Robert Liddell throughout 1936, her contentment was marred only by a sense that nothing much was happening in Oswestry and the nagging worry that she ought to be employed. Of course, a demanding job would have slowed the progress of her literary career, and Pym was very productive throughout the next eight years. She worked on eight novels and wrote many stories, often simultaneously. At the same time, she had obviously chosen to recreate the life of a Victorian spinster-writer, a role encouraged by Robert Liddell.[2]

Pym gained safety by her decision, but at a price. Oswestry was relatively isolated, both socially and intellectually. To make matters worse, going home represented emotional regression, a position from which she found it difficult to move forward again. Although she was able to save money by living at home, the primary motive according to her sister, Pym's frugality had its price. Cut off from people of her own age, she could not find adequate substitutes for her Oxford compatriots.[3]

Although Hilary Walton insisted that Pym's decision was quite usual for the period, it was hardly typical of her classmates. October 10, 1934, Rupert Gleadow wrote to express amazement at Pym's willingness to forgo the ritual task of hunting for employment. Moreover, according to the 1977 *St. Hilda's College Register, 1893–1972,* nearly every one of Pym's classmates for whom there is a completed entry either continued her education or took a job upon leaving Oxford. By refusing to follow the established paths of Oxford graduates, Pym was rejecting the accepted scripts of contemporary female behavior of her time—at least for those as highly educated as she. Carolyn G. Heilbrun in *Writing a Woman's Life,* points out that men have many possible scripts for their lives. In most cases, the exceptional women Heilbrun depicts find it necessary to break the bounds of societal restrictions. Yet Pym, unlike her Oxford cohorts voluntarily adopted an old-fashioned role. She returned to a milieu, in which she, like the heroines of female bildungsromane described by Elizabeth Abel, Marianne Hirsch, and Elizabeth Langland in *The Voyage In: Fictions of Female Development*, had to "struggle to voice any aspirations whatsoever."[4]

In retrospect, it is apparent that the aspiring author never planned to stay permanently with her parents. She simply lived from day to day, waiting for a better opportunity. Gradually the autumn stretched into the next year. Meantime she seized every opportunity to return to Oxford to continue her pursuit of Henry Harvey. Besides the Oxford expeditions and an occasional trip abroad, Pym also shared a London flat with her sister from October 1938–July 1939. Yet, when the war loomed, she, and not her sister who had a job, returned to Oswestry to help her parents manage the evacuees. She stayed there until 1941, when the need to do war work became compelling.

Pym's difficulty in making mature decisions, compounded by her literary problems, suggests that her lengthy sojourn with her parents reactivated some unresolved feelings from childhood, a sort of "symbolic regression," or an expanded moratorium, to use Erik Erikson's useful term.[5] In some ways Pym's situation was not that unusual for a gifted but unconventional person. The American writer, Nathaniel Hawthorne, had much the same experience. After college he lived at home, writing in seclusion for about twelve years. Like Pym's fiction, his novels have a strong old-fashioned element; but unlike her, he eventually married, at the age of thirty-eight.

Recently, Carolyn Heilbrun has argued that creative people need a moratorium in order to become the special kind of writer they have the capacity to be. A female moratorium, in particular, represents "an unconscious decision to place one's life outside the bounds of society's restraints and ready-made narratives." Still Pym's withdrawal from a more competitive arena probably slowed down her artistic development somewhat. Her two unhappy love affairs at Oxford had made it impossible for her to continue using the "distancing" narrator, the male voice of her juvenilia. Instead she began obsessively to explore themes connected with female dependency. Reflecting the helplessness she felt, she filled her manuscripts with spinster companions and governesses, like those in the Victorian novels she had begun to read with great interest.[6]

Like many creative young people, Pym's imaginings had usually been based on her favorite books, what A. A. Milne called "household" books. The odd part is that Pym, who had read Huxley as a girl, suddenly turned to old-fashioned adolescent fiction and poetry when she returned home from Oxford. When on November 17, 1935, Robert Liddell casually referred in a letter to rereading Charlotte Yonge's *The Heir of Redclyffe,* which he had first read at the age of twelve, Pym began reading her novels. She seemed captivated by the thought of a childhood spent in a country vicarage. In keeping with Liddell's clerical and social interests—which were powerfully reinforced by Yonge, who was herself a teacher and a devout churchwoman—Pym developed an obsession with governesses and high Anglicanism. She started an Anglo-Catholic datebook in which she recorded plot synopses of Yonge's novels, the founding date of a college for governesses, and the date of the Anglican poet Coventry Patmore's conversion to Rome.[7]

Charlotte Yonge's novels constituted a conservative choice for a university graduate in the 1930s. Yonge had been a pupil of the high Anglican vicar, John Keble. He encouraged her to mirror his religious attitudes in her novels, a task she cheerfully undertook. *The Daisy Chain* (1856), for example, explores "the danger of ambition" by expounding social attitudes that seem quite repressive to the modern reader. From Ethel, however, Pym discovered "the romance of missionary enthusiasm," and Yonge's respect for parish workers helped shape Pym's affection for what she later called "excellent women."[8]

Unfortunately Yonge's conservatism reinforced Pym's sense of helplessness. For example, Yonge's heroine in *The Daisy Chain,* the energetic but ugly Ethel May, who has more brains and ambition than most of her brothers and sisters, is forced in a poignant scene to abandon her study of Greek. Her family wants her to devote more time to the mastery of those ladylike skills she instinctively detests. Ethel tries to resist such blatant manipulation, but she is outnumbered by her older sister and father, who invoke the memory of her dead mother. Pym omitted that painful scene in her extensive plot synopsis; nonetheless, it left its mark on her thinking. It taught her that women have no defense against social pressure, a lesson which helps explain why so many of Pym's later heroines seem passive by contemporary standards.[9] Moreover, the slightly dated air of Pym's early novels and her fascination with Victorian village life (the time of her parents' childhood) can both be attributed to her affection for Yonge's world.

Although developing a story about substitute parents, a family romance, is a relatively common occurrence for a child, doing so in one's twenties suggests that Pym really was experiencing some emotional regression. More than likely, however, the fantasy had little to do with dissatisfaction with her parents. Instead it reflected her unhappiness with her social situation and her misery over the unattainable Henry Harvey. These fantasies affected both her emotional and her literary development. She was able to use them to generate stories, but her plots are unduly repetitious.

Indeed the old-fashioned flavor of Pym's writing indicates how she interpreted her favorite books. For example, Charlotte Brontë, one of her favorite authors, had energetic heroines who might have inspired Pym to do battle for her autonomy. Instead Pym absorbed from *Jane Eyre* a belief that powerless women must inevitably submit to their adored but aloof, Rochester-like men. The considerable number of references in the manuscripts to remote men and to vicar's daughters, roughly half of whom are orphans, makes clear how that novel affected her imagination.[10]

At this point in Pym's life, fiction imprisoned rather than liberated her. Phenomenological scholars of reading, like Georges Poulet and Wolfgang Iser, as well as cognitive psychologists like Victor Nell and Jerome Bruner, have argued that reading usually enlarges our worlds. Poulet, for example, states that books take us over and impose their reality on us. Nell defines fiction's "reality-changing experience of total attentional commitment" as a positive kind of entrancement. Bruner notes that some novels open up the possibilities of life, "trafficking in human possibilities rather than in settled certainties." Such open-ended narratives allow us to rewrite the story, thereby creating a world of our own. Like Roland Barthes, Bruner declares "that the writer's greatest gift to a reader is to help him become a writer."[11]

Unfortunately, Pym's reading of nineteenth-century fiction was a largely solitary act. She had only Robert Liddell to consult, and his view of fiction was idiosyncratic. His interest in childhood and the life of the church allowed him to produce successful fiction, but his ideas could not be transplanted successfully in Pym's imagination. Joanne Frye has pointed out that women have special problems with reading. Before the twentieth century, most fiction offered women limited roles. Until recent years both female characters and female writers could be entrapped "within outworn plots and outworn definitions." Pym's isolation made it harder for her to break free from these traditional bonds. Iser has commented that "we often feel the need to talk about books we have read—not in order to gain some distance from them so much as to find out just what it is that we were entangled in." Pym's chosen favorites—Charlotte Yonge's and Charlotte Brontë's novels—are powerful texts. In fact Iser mentioned a nineteenth-century male critic who admitted to identifying with Jane Eyre.[12] When Pym, however, became entangled in these novels, no one challenged her interpretations of them. Instead Robert Liddell, in whom she confided, was inclined to agree with her. As a result, Pym's immersion in Victorian girls' fiction became too deep for comfort. Her complicity made it even harder for her to imagine an independent life.

In consequence, Pym had trouble developing a personal sense of audience although her theoretical grasp was keen enough. On July 14, 1937, when she returned a freshly typed manuscript to Liddell, she complained that he never referred to any reader. (The work in question was a history of Christ Church College, in which he had little interest.) Applying such an analysis to her own work, however, was a different story. Russell Long has suggested that writers do not so much analyze their audience—assess their interests and adjust their writing to obtain their approval—as invent them. In order to write effectively, he suggests that the neophyte writer should ask, "Who do I *want* my audience to be?" and then adjust style and tone to encourage the kind of reader desired. This question alters the author's role "from . . . amateur detective to . . . creator," an important shift.[13] But Pym, who was by nature an amateur detective, had little idea how to create a loyal readership for herself.

In Oswestry, Pym found no mentor nor group of struggling writers. Throughout her lifetime she corresponded with Robert Liddell, who gave her good advice and moral support at every turn. In general his advice and support kept her going throughout the difficult period of her apprenticeship. Without his enthusiastic backing, Pym might have abandoned her efforts to become a novelist. Yet he repeatedly encouraged her old-fashioned tendencies to be Coventry Patmore's "the Angel in the House," the ideal writer who soothed the unhappy reader. In contrast, Virginia Woolf on January 31, 1931, had declared that professional women must abandon Victorian notions of ideal womanhood. Woolf declared that Patmore's "the Angel in the House"—the pure, sympathetic, and self-sacrificing woman—could not express her honest feelings about "human relations, morality, sex." Therefore, she insisted, "part of the occupation of a woman writer" was to destroy that ideal.[14] Pym's situation suggests that one literary supporter is not quite enough. Eventually she adjusted to working in isolation, but for most of her life she hovered, like the Misses Pomfrets of "The Vicar Floating By," on the fringes of literary circles.

Although the stories and novels Pym started represent an advance over the Oxford diaries, she still could not convert material of personal importance into something of universal interest. She had no sense of the direction she wanted her life to take. Norman Holland has commented upon the emotional transactions of texts. Successful literature "transforms our primitive wishes and fears into significance and coherence, and this transformation gives us pleasure." The writer draws on "deep personal feelings," but converts them from " 'something that's only of interest to yourself' to 'something that is worth something to everybody.' " In extending Holland's argument, Madonne Miner, a feminist critic, has suggested that books supply a place for readers to "reexperience and rework unresolved fantasies and fears that date back to earliest infancy."[15] Until Pym had worked through her hurt feelings, she could not produce publishable work.

The editors, however, to whom Pym sent *Some Tame Gazelle* and *Civil to Strangers* recognized her talent and tried to help her. They thought that for such a young writer, Pym had a refined sense of style. In response to an early draft of *Some Tame Gazelle*, Harold Raymond of Chatto & Windus suggested to her that her writing was too detached. He urged her to convey more of her own feelings and recommended that she treat her characters either with greater empathy or more spite, avoiding blandness at all costs.[16] Raymond could not have known, but might have guessed, that Pym's tentativeness was a way of denying her own strong feelings. Rather than voicing her complaints, she tried to suppress them. As a result, she developed a posture of sprightly detachment that denied her inner self. At moments anger breaks through the civility of her writing. But aside from flashes of annoyance, Pym never let down her guard completely. She was so preoccupied with her own needs that she could not develop a secure sense of audience for many years.

Luckily Pym's parents were forbearing. Her moods were sometimes hard to bear. Any concerned parent might have felt alarmed by the depressed tone and the bitter remarks about sexual intimacy that appeared in several short stories, especially "Mothers and Fathers" (1936) and "Trivial Rounds and Common Tasks," which was probably written about March 1938. Although the Pyms must have periodically worried about their daughter's future, they endured her excesses and allowed her to deviate from their more bourgeois pattern of life. As a result, Pym was able to chart a new course for herself and her writing without interference. She could not hurry up the process of healing. On July 15, 1936, she complained about how dull Oswestry was compared to her recent stay in Oxford, but the appearance of fresh strawberries and a Huxley novel, and a postcard from Harvey, she recorded, soon diverted her (*VPE*, 58).[17] The strategic retreat allowed Pym to handle her wounded feelings in private. In these early works one can trace her development as a writer. She evolved from a pathetic hanger-on to an artist who has been resurrected by the pleasure of the creative process itself.

The little that Pym recorded in her diary gives the impression of a life made up of negatives, the absence of feeling, of action, and of decisions, except for the busy war years. Hazel Holt in "The Home Front" describes Pym's life at that time. Under the guise of volunteer work, Pym spent a lot of time flirting with much younger soldiers at a nearby base. Unfortunately she was too old to find a suitable mate among the youthful soldiers. No wonder in maturity Pym specialized in writing about characters who realize, as Philip Larkin put it, "that the so called 'big' experiences of life are going to miss them."[18] Yet the very dullness of her life served its purpose. She had a lot of personal anguish to express before she could write to transcend her woes. It was a slow process, and emotional distress interfered with the development of her talents. Still, Pym had a genuine gift. Writing was more than just an outlet for her misery.

According to a September 1, 1934, diary entry, Pym started the short story that eventually became *Some Tame Gazelle* in July 1934, at a moment when she felt jealous of Harvey's attentions to other women (*VPE*, 44). Rather than dwelling on the intractable present, she projected her life and that of her sister Hilary, Henry Harvey, and their friends some thirty years into the future. At that point, Pym assumed that she would no longer be troubled by jealous passion. From the start, the idea of the novel was unusual. Few writers in their twenties employ middle-aged protagonists at all, let alone with such affectionate good humor. Still Pym had trouble making her concept work. She was in an impossible position, much too hurt to write convincingly about love. Yet from the days when she first wrote *The Magic Diamond*, she had been obsessed with the topic.

Unable to cut her ties to Harvey, Pym had not yet relinquished her feelings of immaturity and dependency. Thus in early versions of *Some Tame Gazelle* the heroine is far too entranced by Henry's rather feeble charms. A diary entry, September 1, 1934, in which Pym commented on the novel's genesis, reflects her confusion. She admitted that the narrative offered her "an excuse for revealing" some of what she felt for Harvey (*VPE*, 44). Even when discussing the work, Pym often shifted back and forth between "Barbara" and herself without much differentiation. Pym's manipulation of narrative distance was incomplete. She no longer used a "distancing" narrator but had not yet developed an "engaging" one. Her chief desire was to memorialize her university days, along with her trips to Germany. "Barbara" complains feebly about Henry, suggesting that he did not understand Spenser's Platonism and demanded submissive and humble behavior from her.[19] Still, on the whole Pym was too attached to the Oxford milieu to be very critical of Harvey or of "Barbara's" devotion.

Pym, who sent the story in installments to Liddell and Harvey shortly after beginning it, was fortunate in her readers. From the start Liddell and all their friends were unstinting in their praise. As a result Pym felt encouraged to improve her effort and convert it into a novel. She worked on the first draft of *Some Tame Gazelle,* throughout 1935, before submitting it to Chatto & Windus on November 23 (*VPE*, 53). That version makes a fascinating comparison to the published novel. Once again, the characters, now renamed Belinda and Harriet Bede, are described as being in the middle forties. (They are in their fifties in *Some Tame Gazelle*). Both are obsessed by men. Harriet specializes in curates, while Belinda dotes on the Archdeacon. Belinda is much less confident than in the final version of the novel. Harriet shares many of the qualities of Sandra, Pym's alter ego, rather than those of Hilary Pym. Harriet has Sandra's rapacious appetite, her willingness to pursue men, and mildly eccentric behavior.[20]

This draft is better than the original short story, but it lacks the energy and humor of the published novel. Pym had yet to achieve an emotional distance from her Oxford experiences. Rossen complains that Pym used the manuscript "to apologise for her demonstrative character by abasing herself." Belinda lacks confidence in herself. She feels so preoccupied with the past that she wonders if her memory ought to be seen to. Like Pym she is unduly proud of having once been intimate with a man. She even comments that she knows what size pajamas the Archdeacon takes, the sort of remark that Pym put in several short stories as well.[21]

At the same time, Belinda expresses jealous feelings about Agatha Hoccleve, the Archdeacon's wife, a character who was based on Alison West-Watson, Pym's rival at Oxford. At this point it does not occur to Belinda that by winning Henry, Agatha might be the loser.

In sum, Belinda is still as preoccupied with life at Oxford as Barbara is in the first story. Even news of structural changes at the Bodleian Library disturbs her. She is, however, a bit more independent than Barbara. At one point while darning one of Henry's socks, Pym's otherwise demure heroine sticks him, perhaps inadvertently. Once in her Oxford diary, Pym had also admitted to having accidentally burned one man and bitten Henry Harvey.[22]

In the novel, Belinda is a strong figure. For instance, she often makes witty asides that undermine Henry's sense of dignity. According to Laura Doan, most of her interior monologue mixes a "dutiful and subversive voice." In the early draft, however, Belinda seeks to justify her servitude. She admits that Henry converses about boring topics but illogically concludes that his overbearing nature makes him irresistible.[23] Pym was both attracted to and repelled by Harvey's self-absorption. She liked listening to him talk, but on May 30, 1935, she could hardly contribute to subjects such as travel in Finland (*VPE*, 50). Only in retrospect could she defend herself.

In the early draft, however, Pym experimented with methods of expressing her characters' inner thoughts and submerged passions. On three occasions, she ventured into melodrama. Once an Ivy Compton-Burnett touch jars her decorous plot. For a short time, Belinda worries that her old friend Count Ricardo is about to go crazy and may commit a violent deed. On another occasion, Pym suggests that Belinda's sexual feelings for Henry threaten to overwhelm her. She becomes muddled by Sibelius's music. Afterwards she feels guilty, even though it is by no means clear that Henry has kissed her. The final instance occurs when Bishop Grote overreacts violently to the thought that the Bede sisters may be husband-hunting. Belinda begins to wonder if he has any energy left over for his official task of converting Hawaiians.[24] In each of these scenes, Pym's heroine can only observe and comment upon masculine oddities. Yet in the published version, Belinda exacts a delicate revenge.

Ironically, Pym was saved later embarrassment when the novel was repeatedly rejected. The early draft is full of references to the Nazis, who are in exile some years in the future, and to her old lover Friedbert Glück. Her tone was light: she poked fun at the Nazis and at Belinda for being besotted by them. Pym's frivolity did not seem outrageous at the time. The director of Chatto who read the manuscript made no mention of the Germans at all. Robert Liddell, however, on December 22, 1935, after reading the complete novel for the first time, recommended that Pym remove all references to

Nazis. He argued on purely aesthetic grounds that if she projected the time into the future, the readers would expect elaborate inventions, which she was not prepared to provide. On January 27, 1936, after receiving Liddell's detailed criticisms, Pym declared that she would gladly remove the Nazis. She wrote that they were not essential for the story and had never been that important to her. Yet some traces of the German influence remained. On May 4, 1940, after reading the revised version of *Some Tame Gazelle*, Liddell once again told her to remove all references to Germans.[25] Despite the response of Pym's readers in the prewar period, had the early version of the book been published, her political myopia might well have cost her a postwar audience.

Her next manuscript, *Civil to Strangers*, has fewer comic touches. At the time she was writing it, Pym was reaching a point of desperation with Henry Harvey. When on May 15, 1936, she wrote him about the start of her second novel, she complained about his inability to see beneath her joking tone. She rejected Harvey's excuse that Robert Liddell's flippancy made it difficult for him to take her seriously. She disagreed, claiming that Liddell's habit of teasing her about her forthcoming marriage to Harvey helped salvage her dignity. (Indeed his jokes asserted that she had some rights to Harvey. Moreover, Liddell encouraged her to think of herself as a professional writer, a role which appealed to her ambitions as well. As a result, his letters provided a lifeline to self-respect.) Still from Harvey, she wanted a return of feeling, not more jokes. Realizing the impossibility of her situation, she struggled to explain herself. She ended by requesting him to recognize that she was "a real person as well as a 'flat' one," using E. M. Forster's famous terminology, in imitation of Harvey, who frequently used Forster's terminology (*VPE*, 56–57). Pym was caught in a dilemma for which writing fiction offered the only solution. Recognizing the uselessness of appealing to Harvey's better nature, she took the only available course. Cassandra, Pym's namesake according to Liddell, has the satisfaction of taming her caddish husband Adam, the Henry Harvey figure.[26]

Civil to Strangers temporarily restored some of its author's lost self-esteem, but it was not a success with the publishers. They complained that it was not distinctive enough to be marketable. For one thing, Pym used traditional comic stereotypes in a rather unconvincing fashion. To complicate matters, her anger affected her perspective. Adam is so unappealing that one wonders why the nearly perfect Cassandra tolerates him. Not only is he selfish, but he denies her love and reassurance. At one point, sexual deprivation even causes Cassandra to dream of a young lover. Furthermore, Adam is capable of petty violence. When the long-suffering Cassandra finally criticizes his latest novel, he hurts her.[27]

Real life events impeded Pym's artistic development. By August 1936, she was well aware of Harvey's interest in Elsie Godenhjelm, a woman he had met while teaching English in Finland. Yet the finality of the event itself was hard to bear. Robert Liddell wrote Pym's sister Hilary, December 6, 1937, asking her to break the news that Harvey's wedding would take place the following week. He typed the letter to avoid Pym's notice, knowing full well how painful such information would be. His previous letters had, however, given her ample warning of the coming event. For example, she knew that Harvey had traveled extensively in Europe with Elsie Godenhjelm, with only Liddell for a chaperon.[28] Still, given Pym's stubbornness and her transforming imagination, no doubt she had cherished unrealistic hopes that Harvey might still be won.

In her unhappiness, once again Pym turned to fiction and to Liddell for comfort. He was equally shaken by the long-awaited event. He mailed her a letter December 11, 1937, a pastiche of Ivy Compton-Burnett, in which he described the dire scene that he had imagined at the Pym household. Toward the end he remarked that he too felt Compton-Burnett was a great help in time of crisis, no doubt a response to a previous letter from Pym. Once again, their shared imagination helped both of them jolly themselves out of their gloom. On the wedding day itself, December 12, 1937, Pym even copied in her diary the quotation from Compton-Burnett's *More Women than Men* to which Liddell had referred. In the passage the protagonist, Josephine, dramatizes her role as widow when her husband dies unexpectedly. She proclaims that she will wear mourning clothes for a long time. She denies that she is merely having her own way, saying, "I have no way in the matter. It is settled for me from within, as it were behind my back." When Pym first read this book on September 15, 1933, she reported disliking its characters and lack of plot (*VPE*, 26). Now that she herself felt bereaved, Josephine's self-dramatization seemed very appealing.[29]

Pym's desire to please her friends by turning her rejection into a scene from fiction meant that Liddell and her other friends found it easy to underestimate her feelings. Years later Liddell insisted that she had probably "grieved," but had been too "sensible" to "feel aggrieved" when Harvey married. Liddell himself was understandably preoccupied by his own sense of loss. He wrote Pym on December 27, 1937, that he was recovering from a bout of nervous exhaustion and could no longer tolerate staying in Oxford.[30] In contrast, Pym had hidden her feelings. Still Liddell's detached and logical analysis does not do justice to Pym's response. Being in love with Harvey—even in an unrequited way—had increased her self-esteem. When he married, she ceased to be an actor in the drama. She hid her frustration as best she could but sometimes felt as if her emotions were not quite genuine.

Fortunately for her wounded pride, Pym had visited Oxford on December 3, 1937, just before she received the news of the wedding. She had met Julian Amery, an eighteen-year-old Balliol man, six years her junior (VPE, 62). Although she saw him no more than eight times for a total of twenty hours, his attention restored her self-respect. She began writing novels energetically again, even though she still had no adequate model of life to incorporate in her novels. From 1938 to 1941, her manuscripts were full of Amery-like characters. To emancipate herself from Harvey, she transformed the young man into one of the great loves of her life.[31]

Managing her feelings about Harvey in real life, however, was not as easy as in fiction. Pym could neither tame nor abandon him. Early in 1938, Pym wrote the newlyweds a series of letters imitating Stevie Smith's style. (Liddell and she had begun deliberately imitating Ivy Compton-Burnett and Stevie Smith in their correspondence once the wedding date was firmly set.) In a letter written jointly to Liddell and Elsie and Henry Harvey, Pym described herself early in 1938 as "this queer old horse, this old brown spinster" (VPE, 68–69). She wrote about herself in the third person. Harvey's wife must have found the arch style of the letters bewildering. She also may have been uncomfortably aware of Pym's exposed feelings. Luckily, within six months Pym felt better. By mid-1938, she had calmed down. She was looking forward to becoming a governess in Poland.

Even so, Pym had developed some bad habits for an aspiring writer. Troubled by her own misery, she forgot what suffering she had once cost her old friend Rupert Gleadow. Hence, she sentimentalized spinsters and vicars' daughters while assuming that most men were impervious to rejection. In addition, she entertained Robert Liddell's naive idea that only the young suffer from emotional frustration, which explains why her characters long to grow old quickly.[32] She suppressed her passions and forced herself into the straightjacket of a tepid spinsterhood to find some peace. She accentuated her ordinary qualities and overvalued the quotidian to the point of occasional banality, thereby cutting herself off from a potentially rich source of inspiration, her unconscious. Not only did she lose part of her creative power, which did not completely re-emerge until *Quartet in Autumn*, but she never learned to protect herself from hopeless entanglements with unsuitable men.

In the next few manuscripts, Pym struggled unsuccessfully to compensate for her loss of Henry Harvey. Some months before the wedding, on February 25, 1937, Liddell had written to encourage her to write about Harvey's adventures teaching English in Finland. In subsequent letters he sent her copy for what he called "Henry in Finland," perhaps in an effort to distract Pym from dwelling on Harvey's increasing attachment to Elsie Godenhjelm. At that point Pym was trying to finish *Civil to Strangers*, but by October 19, 1937, she had started writing the requested novel, borrowing many details from Liddell's letters.[33] According to a daybook entry, Liddell read and disapproved of *Gervase and Flora* on February 28, 1938 (*VPE*, 64).

Liddell had grounds for his disapproval. The thirdhand material, which originated with Harvey but was filtered through Liddell, is simply too sketchy to work. To make matters worse, the action represents a transparent wish fulfillment on Pym's part. Flora Palfrey, the companion of Miss Moberley, survives the engagement of Gervase Harringay, the Henry Harvey character. She becomes engaged to Ooli Ruomini-Forstenborg, a Finnish count and Julian Amery figure, who is socially superior to Gervase's bride. But Pym is not persuasive. Flora even admits that she prefers Gervase to Ooli, thus making it impossible to believe in her devotion to the Count. After accepting Ooli's proposal, however, she talks of showing off her fiancé at home.[34] (Pym was obviously pleased with Julian Amery's superior social position.) The most amusing moments occur when Pym describes the pretensions of the expatriate English community. This group is headed by the snobbish Miss Moberley, a sixty-five-year-old woman who looks like a sheep (*GF*, 177). She is a linear descendant of the Miss Moberley of Pym's earlier fantasy.

Pym apparently accepted Liddell's rejection of *Gervase and Flora*. On March 10, 1938, less than two weeks after he had expressed his disapproval, the resilient young author began *The Lumber Room*. In it she drew upon her friendship with her young friend Julian Amery, even though she had already parted from him. The novel contrasts two sisters, Beatrice, an Oxford don, and Frances, an embryonic excellent woman. Frances Wyatt is rather pathetic. She dresses badly, and her slip generally shows. She is reduced to doing all the disagreeable work in the parish, which is relegated her by the curate. But unlike Harriet Bede, who enjoys petting curates, Frances resents being given the tasks traditionally assigned to spinsters.[35] In contrast, Beatrice is sophisticated and supposedly a scholar, although Pym ignores that side altogether. Instead Pym focuses entirely on Beatrice's romantic attachments.

In truth, Beatrice's love life fizzles out, despite the presence of several interesting males. One is a don named Henry Grainger, the Henry Harvey figure, who years before had married another woman. The second is Gabriel Bone, a curate who marries an unsuitable young woman with Pre-Raphaelite beauty and no domestic talents. The third is Gerald Cleveland, the vicar's young son, the Julian Amery character with whom Beatrice has some agreeable meals and romantic moments. Although Gerald is charming, and Pym describes their friendship with nostalgia, he is a callow youth, incapable of understanding Beatrice's sentimental sympathy for a woman who looks like a spinster governess.[36] Very quickly, the flighty young man finds himself attracted to the curate's wife who fancies herself a painter.

Despite the amusing beginning, the manuscript trails off. The two unsuitable marriages unravel. Henry Grainger's wife dies and Gabriel Bone's leaves. Beatrice's old passion for Henry does not revive, however, even though in bereavement he turns to her. In fact, she discovers to her surprise that she is unwilling to forgo her newfound equilibrium. In the past she was forced to put the memory of her old love in a lumber room in order to contain the pain. Now that her feelings are under control, she prefers to keep the door to the lumber room locked. She is more than willing to take her place among the older folk.[37] *The Lumber Room* runs out of steam. Pym could neither believe in a really happy ending nor construct an alternative.

In October 1938, in order to escape from a war zone, Pym returned in haste from her abortive Poland adventure. According to a letter to Elsie Harvey, October 31, 1938, Pym began revising *The Lumber Room*, which she had first begun in March of that year (*VPE*, 86). Daily life, disrupted by what was then called the Phoney War—the period before Dunkirk when nothing decisive had occurred to the British in battle—became ever more complicated. A year later Pym's favorite aunt "Ack" was diagnosed with cancer in November 1939.[38] As usual, her niece handled the bad news by frantic writing. She drafted two novels and a short story simultaneously, *Home Front Novel*, *Crampton Hodnet*, and a Compton-Burnett-style short story about Julian Amery. Misfortune had a noticeable effect on Pym's plots. She found it increasingly difficult to write about love. The ingenue of *Home Front Novel,* again named Flora, is a subordinate character of little importance. Instead, Pym reveals her fascination for an older woman character, Amanda Wraye, who owes her creation to Pym's brief encounter with Julian Amery's mother.

Pym's addition of Mrs. Amery to her limited cast of characters reveals her ability to convert even impossible situations into dramatic fiction. According to her diary, she actually met Mrs. Amery, July 4, 1939, on the very day Amery told her that he had no further interest in her. In the entry Pym commented in her usual elliptical fashion about the pain of the meeting. She simply suggested that one would be better off avoiding such situations. At the same time she was delighted to enter the house and meet Mrs. Amery, "a splendid character for a novel." Instead of acknowledging her anger, Pym preferred to wax nostalgic. She declared that she would remember the "relics" and "jokes" and all the events including those that actually happened, "and didn't quite happen and might still happen." Her friendship had lasted merely twenty hours but would garner, she insisted, as many "years of memories" (*VPE*, 92).[39]

In actual fact Pym did not give up quite so quickly. Julian Amery's upper class, Balliol background made him worth an extended pursuit. She telephoned him on several occasions and wrote him letters, as late as 1941.[40] During that time Pym was seeing other young men, but she still hoped to revive Amery's interest. Subsequent manuscripts show a change in her feelings. After describing him as a charming, but childish, young man who pursues Beatrice Wyatt, other Julian Amery figures are notable for their selfish absorption in the world of politics and their heartless treatment of loving young women. The portrait of Simon Beddoes in *Crampton Hodnet* is particularly hostile.

Pym treated the parents unequally. Whenever she describes a character like Mrs. Amery, she uses a fond, forgiving tone. For example, Lady Beddoes in *Crampton Hodnet* talks in a friendly and voluble fashion to Anthea Cleveland, quite unlike other upper-class characters in Pym's novels. She is also extremely vague. A newspaper clipping that Pym saved for many years records that on one occasion Mrs. Amery took the wrong train out of London and never arrived at the garden party that she was supposed to open. In contrast, Pym seemed inclined to blame Mr. Amery for his son's fickle behavior. Her characterizations of him are unfailingly hostile although she never met him. In her novels men like him are consistently portrayed as being self-satisfied, pompous, and thoroughly weak. She even suggests that one of them, Lyall Wraye in *Home*

Front Novel, enjoys the company of young women, but his wife ignores such peccadillos because nothing comes of them.[41]

Thus, this minor episode provides a glimpse into the workings of Pym's creative process. Julian Amery's behavior clearly hurt her feelings, and versions of that encounter are given in *Home Front Novel, Crampton Hodnet*, and remembered in the *So Very Secret*. Yet the author expeditiously converted her personal discomfort into public humor. Her brief glimpse of the Amerys' house provided details of the Wrayes' home life in *Home Front Novel* and the Otways in *Something to Remember*. As time went on, Pym embellished those characterizations so effectively that one regrets that barely a trace of the family remains in the published work. Aside from *Crampton Hodnet*, the only remnants of Mrs. Amery and her son are in *Jane and Prudence*, where the village MP is a bachelor named Edward Lyall. His mother is believed by some villagers to harbor leftist sympathies because she is relieved by the simplicity of breakfast in postwar England (*JP*, 87 & 90).

Home Front Novel, Pym's next effort, is dominated by the war. For once the plot is thoroughly grounded both in time and place. Caught up in the excitement of the constantly shifting war news, she wove some of it into the plot. Consequently, the background is nearly as important as the characters. Pym, however, found a method of domesticating even foreign affairs. The war is viewed through the eyes of her characters and carefully filtered through their limited experience of it.

In many ways this manuscript is a transitional one in Pym's early work, inasmuch as the author reused characters from earlier fragments and developed scenes which later appear in published work. There are some amusing moments. One is the evening party where the obsequious Connie Aspinall listens respectfully to Lyall Wraye's sister, Lady Nollard, talk about her digestion, Lady Nollard being the first of Pym's absurdly snobbish, titled women (*HFN*, 267–69).[42] But Pym could not sustain the action. Realizing that she had written a series of vignettes, ultimately she abandoned the manuscript with regret.

Home Front Novel, however, remained useful to her. At various points in her career Pym raided the manuscript for choice tidbits. For example, in the final version of *Some Tame Gazelle* written just after the war, Connie Aspinall reappears. She even enjoys talking to the condescending Agatha, much as she had previously listened attentively to Lady Nollard. In an early manuscript of *An Unsuitable Attachment*, Lady Selvedge is called Lady Nollard, but by the time

Pym finished the novel, Lady Selvedge no longer resembles her forebear. In 1976, Pym returned to *Home Front Novel* once more, hoping to revise it for publication as a historical novel, but gave up the attempt. Then in her final novel, *A Few Green Leaves*, war memories abound. The story of an evacuee who smokes in bed in the *Home Front Novel* reappears as an important wartime recollection, tying together the past and present quite effectively.[43]

In contrast to the cheerfulness of the *Home Front Novel*, Pym used *Crampton Hodnet*, which she wrote simultaneously, to express her pessimism about the future. *Crampton Hodnet* has a dark side. Although it is set in the prewar period, its characters seem as deprived as Pym felt during the war. Despite marvelously comic moments, its underlying assumptions are quite bitter. Characters come close to caricature and the plot to satire. The author struggled to keep her sense of humor, but for once the miseries of war, combined with Julian Amery's rejection and the impending death of her aunt, were realities she could not dismiss. Under the circumstances, it is not surprising that at a few unguarded moments anger breaks through. For example, in one place Miss Morrow imagines asking Mr. Latimer in angry tones how he likes the dreary clothes that are her lot (*CH*, 31). Indeed, Pym often used clothing as a barometer to measure her characters' self-esteem. (Belinda Bede enjoyed gardening in sloppy clothes but hid when unexpected guests arrived.) During the war Pym went to considerable trouble to remake her clothes skillfully in an effort to look attractive.[44] In *Crampton Hodnet*, the combination of wartime austerity and Pym's anxiety about growing older without a husband in sight account for the passion behind Miss Morrow's outburst.

For the first time in her fiction, Pym balanced the activities of two interconnected, and equally important, households. Margaret and Francis Cleveland, with their daughter Anthea, live near Mr. Cleveland's elderly aunt, Miss Doggett. Miss Doggett bullies her downtrodden companion, Miss Morrow, who is described as "a thin, used-up-looking woman in her middle thirties." But Miss Morrow also has unusual powers of detachment and "a definite personality" (*CH*, 2). In Pym's earlier efforts, such companions either played minor roles or were quite young. This time, however, the companion, Miss Morrow, turns out to be far less pathetic than one might expect.

The plot attacks the subject of marriage with a vengeance. None of the characters is a romantic figure, but each is troubled by sexual fantasies. For example, Francis Cleveland, an Oxford don and older

Henry Harvey figure, is ordinarily much too preoccupied with his own creature comforts to be a philanderer. He has been well taken care of by his wife, Margaret, a busy middle-aged housewife, quite like Pym's unconventional mother and a long string of vicars' wives in her fiction.[45] Yet he becomes beguiled by the unexpectedly passionate look that his student, the beautiful Barbara Bird, gives him at the end of one of their tutorials (*CH*, 35). He drifts almost accidentally into a sentimental episode with the young woman when his wife eagerly encourages him to leave the house so that she will not be interrupted in her daily chores.

From this unlikely beginning a romance blossoms, encouraged by the interference of most of the Clevelands' older acquaintances. Indeed, Pym suggests in a sly fashion that all of the older generation are delighted to find a flaw in the ostensibly happy marriage of the middle-aged Clevelands. She also implies that despite the appearance of propriety, her characters harbor some quite primitive instincts. At times the sheer strain of behaving properly becomes too much. For instance, Mrs. Cleveland is expected to act like a perfect lady while each of the older women of her acquaintance intrudes upon her privacy to report scandalous gossip about her wayward husband. She succeeds admirably, but on one occasion she has to suppress a "jungle impulse." Enraged by the smugness of the elderly Mrs. Killigrew, who had just repeated some gossip about Francis, Mrs. Cleveland almost succumbs to her anger. She longs to destroy Mrs. Killigrew's hat, "to tear the bird off it and fling it into the unseasonable fire" (*CH*, 142–43). The bird on the hat, of course, signifies Barbara Bird, but Mrs. Cleveland never admits her true desires.

In the world of North Oxford, few relationships seem to live up to romantic ideals or for that matter even to ordinary standards of decency. Even though Mrs. Killigrew is a pale imitation of a Compton-Burnett familial tyrant, she exercises a remnant of the power exerted by the elderly upper classes in bygone days. Miss Doggett, whose role is more substantial, scarcely acknowledges that her companion has any rights at all. When a marriageable curate becomes a boarder in their house, it never occurs to the regal old woman that he might become interested in Miss Morrow. Miss Morrow responds to Miss Doggett's despotism by hiding her private thoughts, the only possible way of retaining her integrity. As a result she has no one with whom she can share her moment of triumph, the rejection of the curate's ridiculous proposal of marriage. Miss Doggett regards the boarder as "a finely tuned instrument" and Miss

Morrow as "a harp with broken strings, an old twanging thing that somebody might play in the street" (*CH*, 78). Thus the old woman would never have believed Miss Morrow's story.[46] A further irony is that although both Miss Morrow and the curate are exactly the same age, they are treated differently. Even the blurb on the dustjacket describes them as "a young curate and Miss Morrow."

Despite her isolation, having the opportunity to reject a man improves Miss Morrow's self-esteem. Mr. Latimer proposes in order to protect himself from idle gossip. He hopes that Miss Morrow will rescue him from the depressing world in which he finds himself. Timid and weak-minded curates had been a staple of Pym's work ever since girlhood. Several appear in her manuscripts.[47]

Love is equally problematical for the young Barbara Bird, but in her case the trouble lies within. To some extent, Pym was drawing on her own experiences in describing the beautiful scholar, and her portrait is psychologically acute. The young woman is sexually inhibited, just as Pym had been when Rupert Gleadow attempted to seduce her in 1932. Of course, the middle-aged Francis Cleveland makes a less than beguiling Lothario. Totally inexperienced at amorous intrigue, he allows the remarks of an elderly friend to push him into planning a trip to Paris with his young student.

The trip is doomed from the start. It rains so heavily that Francis and Barbara have to stop in Dover. They take refuge at a hotel occupied by elderly people. They make the young woman wonder "if they had been left there many years ago and abandoned" (*CH*, 88). Barbara becomes so terrified by the threat of sex with Francis that she has no will of her own. Then when Francis kisses her on the forehead, "The kiss seemed to have woken her out of the dazed calmness which had come over her in the lounge, and all her panic came rushing back" (*CH*, 89). She bolts and takes refuge with a nearby friend.[48] She disappears so completely from Oxford that two months later "it was difficult to realise that there had ever been such a person as Barbara Bird" (*CH*, 212).

Sexual love fails the Cleveland's young daughter, Anthea, as well, but her mother's powerful affection almost compensates for male inadequacy. In the beginning Anthea pleases her snobbish Aunt Doggett by falling in love with the socially eligible Simon Beddoes, the Julian Amery figure. But Simon is not capable of permanent love. Although his mother, the vague Lady Beddoes, is really fond of the young girl, the aspiring politician is too selfish and politically preoccupied to care very deeply for a social inferior. In contrast, Mrs. Cleveland really loves her daughter—Pym is very convincing on this point—though the harassed woman is helpless to protect her child from the pain of Simon's indifference. Miss Morrow notes with scorn that when Simon writes a letter to break off with Anthea, he mixes bad grammar with "parliamentary phraseology" (*CH*, 200–201). By the novel's end, however, the young girl seems reasonably sanguine about the future.

The bleak honesty with which Pym confronted human relations in this novel is unusual in her fiction. For once she entertained few illusions about the power of romantic love. Instead she celebrated maternal affection. Burkhart remarks that "the wit falters in the latter third of the book," buried under the weight of personal misery. As usual, when she was under pressure, Pym wrote to please herself and not an audience. She was troubled by life's drabness. For the moment she had no great love in the offing. Flirting with a series of young servicemen from the nearby base was no substitute for that.[49] In fact, Pym's evaluation of her men friends can best be summarized by the behavior of Anthea Cleveland. When the young woman is jilted by Simon Beddoes, his best friend Christopher attempts to take his place. Anthea enjoys herself but seems indifferent to Christopher himself. She noted that "Everything went on just the same in Oxford from year to year. It was only the people who might be different. The pattern never varied" (*CH*, 212).

In reaction to her own situation, Pym created characters who are all trapped by circumstances beyond their control. Mrs. Cleveland takes her husband back without any explanation in order to avoid making an unpleasant scene. She insists that "talking very seldom did any good." Of course, she cares more for her daughter than for her silly husband. But for all her affection, Mrs. Cleveland is really powerless to help Anthea. At the same time Barbara Bird, far from being a vamp, is an extreme case of the inhibited heroine that Pym liked to depict. Finally, Miss Morrow represents with a painful accuracy the author's pride and her fears for the future. Pym had no interest in the men who found her attractive.[50] At twenty-six, she was both old enough to feel slightly desperate, yet scornful of such a feeble character as Mr. Latimer. From Pym's perspective, Miss Morrow's rejection represents a triumph of survival. Yet she was well aware of its pathos. Obviously, Pym longed to escape but saw no hope in sight.

In the next two novels, Pym abandoned the theme of love and marriage to explore other relationships that might be substituted for those elusive desires. Pym's real interest changed in the course of writing *Something to Remember*. She moved from depicting the plight of her young heroine companion to a fascination with the middle-aged woman employer, Mrs. Otway, another Mrs. Amery. The heroine, Deborah Wilde, lacks training and money, and circumstances force her to fend for herself. Her plight is scarcely unique in fiction. Lucy Snowe, the heroine of Charlotte Brontë's *Villette*, one of Pym's favorite novels, also finds herself in the same predicament. Deborah, however, is a limp version of Lucy. She seems unable to act, having only just learned to stop railing against her fate. To her surprise and joy Mrs. Otway treats her kindly. The maid even offers her fish on Friday.[51] After all, she is a clergyman's daughter. But in *Crampton Hodnet* Miss Doggett leaves only the tough lettuce for her companion (*CH*, 119).

Unfortunately, the novel quickly peters out. For one thing, the Otway family are all very similar to other Amery surrogates in earlier manuscripts. Furthermore, Pym's humor seems both mild and unfocused. Hughie Otway has formed a new political party at Oxford, combining all parts of the spectrum including Fascism. His father has written a book with the arresting title *What Next?*, which turns out to be a boring economic treatise. Mrs. Otway reveals an unexpectedly furtive passion for ice cream, an idea based on a 1938 entry in Pym's diary. As Rossen points out, Pym used the story to rewrite *Jane Eyre*.[52] Obviously Pym had not yet found an appropriate plot for her deprived and languid heroine. Perhaps her pseudo-Edwardian plot lay close to private fears that were not fully available for novelistic purposes.

On the other hand, the next novel, *So Very Secret*, makes quite delightful light reading. Returning to the perspective of *Some Tame Gazelle*, Pym abandoned young heroines for a study of a middle-aged character. The heroine, Cassandra Swan, is a prototype of Pym's excellent women. She certainly leads "a full life," a phrase which became the first title of *Excellent Women*.[53] She is both a spinster and a vicar's daughter, who in late middle age lives alone (*SVS*, 273). She becomes embroiled in a cloak-and-dagger thriller when her friend Harriet Jekyll disappears under mysterious circumstances.

Cassie's fond memories of her Oxford flame, Adrian, gave Pym an ingenious opportunity to acknowledge her early affection for Julian Amery while at the same time suggesting that he would become stuffy and smug. She divided her Amery surrogate into two characters. One is a young man named Hugh, who reminds her of Adrian, making Cassie regret the passage of time (*SVS*, 294). The second is the aging Adrian, whose house in Eaton Square Cassie invades. He fails to recognize his former love, who gets back at him by describing him as having "a certain facile charm, which could be switched on and off as required." (*SVS*, 301). Considering Pym's lifelong penchant for younger men it is not surprising that the energetic Cassandra enjoys Hugh far more than she does pompous Adrian.

The plot offers the heroine ample opportunity to use her talents as a detective. In fact, several of Pym's characters take great pleasure in spying on interesting men. In *Some Tame Gazelle*, Belinda enjoys roaming the village streets in an effort to bump into the Archdeacon (*STG*, 84). In *Crampton Hodnet*, Anthea Cleveland walks from Bayswater to Chester Square just to catch a glimpse of absent Simon Beddoes (*CH*, 173). In *Something to Remember*, Deborah Wilde surreptitiously walks by the lodgings of the Reverend Bernard Hoad. Moreover, various characters appear in this manuscript, some of whom Pym reused in later novels. For example, Cassandra meets Father Julian and Miss Boulding, a celibate high churchman and his sister. Their genteel bickering is typical of Pym's later clergymen and their sisters. There is also a tall, thin woman, called Lolly, another version of Mrs. Amery, elegantly dressed in black. Her shoes are as inappropriate as most of Pym's eccentric women characters.[54]

Unfortunately, Pym never really revised the novel. She began it in September, just before the worsening war situation forced her to register for a post.[55] For a time her behavior was marked by an anxious passivity. She felt unable to decide what sort of job she should take. By December her parents were moving into a new house. After all the uncertainty and some overeating caused by anxiety, Pym was about to leave home for good. In September she reported with disgust that she weighed 10 stone, 13 (153 pounds), hardly outrageous for such a tall woman. About a week later she wrote Rosemary Pulling, an Oxford classmate, for advice about jobs, and after an interview she received her government post in November. As soon as her parents had finished making their move, about a week after Pearl Harbor, Pym left for Bristol to do war work. Under the circumstances she had to drop the novel until the war was over. By that time she had endured another disastrous love affair and some soul searching, matters which made her frivolous manuscript seem inappropriate.

Yet the novel represented a milestone in her career. Instead of writing to ventilate old grievances, Pym had finally begun to spin fantasies about her own future. Although Cassandra Swan reminisces about dear Adrian, she obviously thrives on her new role as a detective and reacts positively to all the challenges. For the first time since Henry Harvey's marriage, Pym seemed to have regained her sense of humor and to enjoy the process of writing. Although she hated making decisions, she realized that she had a new job to look forward to and her personal future seemed bright. Pym's misfortunes in love were not yet over, but at this stage in her life, she had developed the inner reserves and confidence in her talent to survive, even though she still longed for a happier fate. The years at home had helped her to recover her sense of balance and to find her literary voice. In the future no amount of bad luck with publishers or changing popular taste would stem her productivity. Her apprenticeship had finally come to an end; she was ready to move on to stimulating new surroundings and to another set of attachments.

3

Transitions of War and Deconstructing Comedy

When Pym left Oswestry in 1941 for war work in Bristol, she was still a relatively immature and dependent person. By the end of the war, however, she had found her true vocation as a writer. Nonetheless, the process by which she matured was painful. It took another disastrous love affair and enlisting in the Women's Royal Navy Service (WRNS; also called the Wrens) before she was ready to abandon her romantic expectations and start writing in earnest. Like the youthful patients of Erik Erikson, Pym had to encounter despair before she could find "that immutable bedrock on which the struggle for a new existence can safely begin and be assured of a future."[1]

Gordon Glover, the man with whom she became romantically entangled, was also the estranged husband of Honor Wyatt, one of Pym's housemates in Bristol. The two women got along very well. Pym instinctively found the motherly Wyatt to be a good substitute for her parents. Yet, in 1942, about a year after she moved in, Pym was plunging into a short-lived romance with Gordon Glover before his divorce was final. By that time Wyatt was so preoccupied with her new fiancé's survival in the war that Glover's flirtation could not damage her self-esteem. But watching the naive and inexperienced Pym become badly hurt was not a happy sight. Wyatt did everything in her power to help her friend manage the ensuing distress.

Pym never realized that her tangled relationship with Gordon Glover and Honor Wyatt repeated her equally confused bond with Robert Liddell and Henry Harvey. She promptly wrote Harvey a naive letter on November 10, 1942, reporting the beginning of "a kind of love affair, not exactly of my choosing" (*VPE*, 111). Glover even reminded her of Harvey, something which she had not thought possible. (As it happened, Glover also sounded somewhat like her father, being attractive and attentive to women, but not entirely reliable.) Far from speculating that her friendship with Glover would last, Pym predicted cheerfully that she would probably end up with her sister, Hilary, even though at that time her sister was engaged to be married. Pym obviously hoped against all odds that the two of them would duplicate the relationship of Belinda and Harriet Bede.

In retrospect, the shortness of the romance was predictable. Glover ended the relationship at Christmas, using the pretext of having to supply evidence of adultery for the divorce.[2] Pym could not be expected to play the role of a divorce co-respondent. Of course she felt betrayed. She had valued Gordon's consideration and charm. According to a March 23, 1943, diary entry, he shared her taste in books and, like her, enjoyed strolling nostalgically through graveyards (*VPE*, 118). After a period of melancholy, she turned to Honor Wyatt for comfort. For some time Pym procured advice and support from Wyatt while she struggled with her anger. To some degree she even treated her friend like a mother, a designation that cast Glover in the role of betraying father. In some fundamental way, Pym felt Glover still belonged to his wife and two children. Hence, when she recorded some jealous thoughts, January 22 and March 27, 1943, she felt depressed by her reaction (*VPE*, 115, 119).

This time, however, Pym's failed romance proved a turning point in her maturation. She was extremely fortunate in her confidante. Honor Wyatt's maternal qualities made her a more effective adviser than the men Pym customarily chose as comforters. After all, Wyatt felt more loyalty to her fellow woman than to her philandering husband, whereas Robert Liddell's feelings toward Pym and Henry Harvey had always been more conflicted. Not only did Wyatt tell Pym the unvarnished truth about her husband, but she allowed her friend a reasonable period of grieving. She never simply dismissed Pym's attachment to Glover as a fantasy. July 14, 1943, Pym acknowledged that she had benefitted from such sympathetic listening (*VPE*, 146).

More important, however, Pym gradually learned to develop an emotionally equal relationship with another woman, rather than continuing to ask her friends for one-sided advice and support. At first Wyatt sympathized with her devastated friend and gave much good advice. After a few months she began telling Pym about some of Glover's more outrageous behavior. Very gently, Wyatt urged Pym to abandon any false hope of winning him back (May 3, 1943, *VPE*, 128–29). Luckily, Wyatt needed a sympathetic ear in exchange. Gradually Pym learned the pleasure of mutual exchange, what the linguist Deborah Tannen has called "troubles talk."[3] No doubt, Pym's newly won maturity gave her the courage to enlist in the WRNS in 1943 and later to volunteer for overseas duty in Naples.

Pym was not by nature introspective. Instead she was the sort of person who, according to the American novelist Gail Godwin, specializes in an "elegiac mourning for the loss of a world that never had been." Pym's sadness "provided the tempo and structure" of her existence. For that reason, as Carolyn Heilbrun puts it, Pym "avoided marriage with an assiduousness little remarked but no less powerful for being, often, unknown to the woman herself." Fortunately, during the later war years, Pym found that writing could substitute for the human relationships that evaded her grasp. Creativity was essential to her well-being, as it is to other writers, such as the Chicago-based Saul Bellow. In 1987 Bellow told an interviewer that he wrote to find his way. He could not offer a complete explanation "any more than birds do for bird song."[4] Of course the war made full-time writing impossible, but Pym kept a journal during those years. Like the manuscripts of her apprenticeship, the journal offered her an outlet for her anger and hurt. This time Pym, however, saw the absurdity of her position. At twenty-nine she could no longer continue to act like a nineteen-year-old. In consequence, the diaries chronicle her long delayed coming of age.

Several quiet allusions to *Crampton Hodnet* suggest that Pym recognized that life could be more painful than fiction. "After Christmas," Pym's record of the months after Glover's desertion, could well have been written by an older and wiser Barbara Bird. March 29, 1943, Pym remarked that the weight of her memories burdened her just as bad dreams disturb Mr. Latimer in *Crampton Hodnet* (*VPE*, 120; *CH*, 64). In a letter to Henry Harvey, May 11, 1943, she also noted that experiencing a "Victorian renunciation" is not as pleasant as inventing one for Barbara Bird had been (*VPE*, 131; *CH*, 190). Fortunately, Pym had a remedy at hand.

Gradually Pym's love for words and ambition to be a writer

crowded out the self-pity. May 26, 1943, after listening to one of Glover's radio plays, she decided to write one too (*VPE*, 134). Her play, "Something to Remember," was broadcast in 1950 (*VPE*, 184). On September 17, 1943, a few days after listening to another of his plays, Pym talked of finishing her radio drama and revising *So Very Secret*, her spy novel (*VPE*, 157). After the war was over, she created a Gordon-like character in *Jane and Prudence* named Fabian Driver. Fabian has so many affairs that his wife, Constance, begins inviting the women home to spend the weekend with them, creating a triangle much like Pym's relationship with Gordon Glover and Honor Wyatt. In the novel, the two women usually have such a "cosy" time that Fabian feels left out. A great deal of anger and suffering generated that absurd portrait of male egocentrism and female subversion.

As a result of the Gordon Glover episode, Pym's style began to change. Despite her wretchedness she started to look outward to her audience. February 9, 1943, Pym asked the reader directly in Victorian fashion—"what exactly, may Posterity ask, *was* all this 'struggle' about?" (*VPE*, 122)—and on August 13 queried her own use of naval jargon (*VPE*, 154). Of course she had, on May 27, 1935, referred to the reader rather flippantly in her Oxford diary (*VPE*, 47). In the 1943 entries, however, Pym is concerned about the reader's needs. Stilted though such passages seem, they indicate her growing awareness of others. At the same time, they are part of a new and complex role: the author writing for a reader and re-creating the history of the novel in her own developing "history." In effect Pym substituted the reader for the lover whom she hoped one day might read her diary. John Bayley has remarked that as a diary writer Pym "is better than almost anyone at the *feel* of being in love, which is a solitary matter shared with the diary self." Part of the pleasure of diary keeping, he insisted, is to imagine the lover reading the entry.[5] In time Pym refined her technique. She reread the later drafts of her novels carefully and wrote notes in the margins that demonstrate a vigilance for her readers' needs.

At nearly thirty Pym realized that she had to make a life for herself without waiting for a man to rescue her. She had always been a pessimist about love. At the beginning of her pursuit of Henry Harvey, she confessed that she found it difficult to imagine a happy ending for the two of them.[6] She had felt equally unsure about Glover. Of course, she recorded April 6, 1943, that she disliked making solitary plans (*VPE*, 121), but doing so gave her a new sense of self-esteem. Thus, the quality of the writing picks up in "After

Christmas II." Pym could look at herself more objectively. After four months in the WRNS she began to reassess her previous habits. To her dismay, October 12, she realized with a pang that if in future she reread this diary, she would have no idea that a war was raging (*VPE*, 160).

Very little from the war years ever appeared in Pym's novels. The adolescent quality of that life simply was inappropriate to the post-war era. At the same time, most of her experiences challenged her prewar pose of giddy exuberance. July 13, 1943, Pym frolicked with the younger WRNS officers but felt too old for such games (*VPE*, 146). Under the stress of war everybody played at love, but Pym's attempts were decorous indeed. She had a series of minor romances with an assortment of much younger men, including an enlisted man she called Starky. She revelled in the attention, but she wrote about her male friends with some coyness, once again skipping the salient details. The only point she emphasized was that most of the men were unsuitable.

After Naples, from June 14, 1945, to January 11, 1946, Pym received nine letters from a fellow naval officer named Alan Davis. His chatty epistles contain much naval gossip and gratifying concern for Pym as a person. Her entries in the 1945 daybook suggest that she longed to cast Alan in the role of suitor, but his letters were much too proper to encourage her. Nonetheless, Davis had great respect for Pym's quick wit and amusing company. He willingly reported the latest news about an affair between a notorious major and his wife's friend, a story which appeared in a manuscript of *Excellent Women*. Their correspondence lasted a shorter time than Pym desired; he brought it to a close in January 11, 1946, shortly after returning to his wife and baby. In his final letter on January 11, 1946, Davis wrote that he looked forward to her projected "Silence at the End of the Table," a story she never wrote, the germ of which was inspired by their letters.[7]

Although Davis never gave his wife any cause for jealousy, he showed real concern for Pym's welfare. In an earlier letter of August 31, 1945, he responded with real distress to the news of the failing health of her mother, who died of cancer ten days after he wrote his letter. On that occasion he recalled that when Pym was sent home on compassionate leave, no one had warned her how ill her mother was.[8] He understood how shocked she must have felt to discover her mother was terminally ill.

Although Pym grieved over her mother's illness and premature death, she took pride in the knowledge that her own career was just about to begin. Despite the many rejection slips, she had never given up hope that *Some Tame Gazelle* would be published. In 1943 she had begun some extensive revisions. In the summer of 1945 when her mother was dying, she worked hard on the novel to distract herself from her mother's unalterable condition. The notes to the final revision indicate a great change in Pym's viewpoint, signaling an increase in self-esteem. This time the women have the advantage over men. The author contemplated making Mr. Mold a philanderer but resisted the impulse. (He was based originally on a young man at the Bodleian whose antics Robert Liddell reported to Pym in 1934.) Instead Harriet dismisses him in a commanding fashion. Ideas spiralled as the writer gained confidence. A marginal note, inspired by Robert Liddell's tentative suggestion, asks "Can the Bishop propose to Belinda?!," an idea that required yet another revision of the plot.[9]

Some Tame Gazelle took a long time to be perfected. Events moved quickly. Irena Pym died September 10, 1945, and according to a letter Pym wrote Henry Harvey on June 5, 1946, her father remarried within the year (*VPE*, 180). Her mother's death at that juncture indirectly had a positive effect on Pym's move toward independence. Oswestry no longer held any charm. When the family broke up, Pym ceased to retreat there. She continued to work on the novel over the next four years. She could not easily liberate herself from anxieties about the future and a sense of inferiority to men. Luckily London and life with her sister offered a change of scene and a new environment to observe.[10]

During Pym's early years in London, for the first time she found a positive version of adult life to substitute for her girlhood romantic dreams. Being a spinster in the 1950s was less frightening than she had once feared. After all, the postwar period was a time of massive displacement. Many wartime marriages were dissolved by death or divorce. According to a letter Pym wrote Henry Harvey on June 5, 1946, her sister, Hilary Walton, had undergone a divorce as well (*VPE*, 180). The widespread character of the disruption made it easier for Pym to accept the limitations of her own life. To her great satisfaction, she and her sister were able to settle down to what social scientists call "a lifelong coresidence." Pym's new independence, gained in part by working at the International African Institute (I.A.I.), affected her final revision of *Some Tame Gazelle*. At last she was able to express more of her own emotion, as the Chatto & Windus editor had recommended so many years before.[11] For the moment life offered endless possibilities. Of course the anxiety that her sister might remarry and leave her also left its traces on the plot, but such fears were not enough to disturb the novel's comic tone.

Pym had always enjoyed her sister's company. On October 31, 1938, she had written Elsie Harvey that she was sharing a flat with her sister. Her happiness reminded her of her first year at Oxford (*VPE*, 86). That kind of euphoria could not be sustained for the thirty-four years they lived together, but the sisters experienced an unusual degree of harmony in their daily life. Vera John-Steiner points out that many artists find it difficult to balance "their desire for loving attention and support from friends and family" and an equally compelling need to remain aloof from them.[12] Yet most of the time the sisters managed very well. Hilary Walton offered her elder sister moral support and the privacy she needed to be productive. Moreover, Mrs. Walton was more decisive and independent than Pym. She took charge whenever they needed to make a move. In contrast, Pym hated to be uprooted, even though a change of scene often improved her fiction.

Finally, after a gestation period of fifteen years, Jonathan Cape accepted the novel on March 29, 1949. Robert Liddell, who had patiently reread the novel and offered specific and useful suggestions, rejoiced in Pym's success. April 12, the Tuesday before Easter according to his habit of dating many letters by the church calendar, he sent his hearty congratulations, noting that success could compensate for prior infertility. His biological language suggests that, in his life at least, books compensated for family life, and he assumed that Pym felt the same way.[13]

The published version of *Some Tame Gazelle* reflects the serenity that Pym gained from her sister's company, as well as the satisfaction she found in her new role as a wage earner. Its plot is funnier than the manuscript versions. Nostalgia is balanced by Belinda's joy in the diversions of everyday life. As a result, Pym dared to make fun of some of the tenets of comedy itself. Traditionally the comic heroine is quite young and beautiful; the hero worthy of winning her hand. Pym subverted these conventions. The Bede sisters are the most unlikely heroines. They are in their fifties, and Harriet is undeniably plump. Yet their interest in men is neither absurd nor pathetic. In fact Pym purged the manuscript of all traces of self-pity. Instead of emphasizing Harriet's pursuit of the Bishop, a conventional idea at best, the elderly sisters reject a series of unlikely suitors. The Bedes cease to be victims. They are convincingly charming and understandably attract the somewhat dubious men with whom they are acquainted.

Undiverted by the novel's good humor, Robert Emmet Long claims to have identified a theme of "inanition . . . and diminishment of life in the present." The male characters lack "personal force." If, however, the men were energetic and attractive, the sisters' behavior would seem misguided. Pym wished to celebrate her life with her sister. By having the Bedes spurn absurd offers of marriage, she could do so. At the same time, as Barbara Bowman has pointed out, Belinda's wry unspoken thoughts challenge the validity of patriarchal values, which are the ones that comedy has traditionally endorsed. Indeed the novel's plot violates the chief tenet of social comedy, the desirability of marriage. Instead the author asserts that the spinster's life has many advantages over the matron's. The action of the novel, as Long observed, is a "parody of romance."[14] Pym makes fun of all marriages, both those that have endured and those that are solemnized at the end.

No sane woman could long for a husband like Henry Hoccleve, who roars at his wife when a moth gets into his suit, and Belinda's observations deflate him expertly. Nor could one languish for suitors as inept as Mr. Mold, who drinks before lunch (STG, 100), or Bishop Grote, whose sheeplike expression makes him look like a descendant of Miss Moberley of Gervase and Flora (STG, 162). The curate might be eligible, but when he first appears at the Bedes' house, "his combinations [long underwear] showed" (STG, 7), a sure sign of absurdity. In the Bedes' village, men make good friends, but marriage is a doubtful joy at best. Still the novel's old-fashioned flavor obscures the fact that Pym has deftly punctured cherished beliefs. Of the few critics who have noticed that Pym mocked marriage in this gentle plot, only Diana Benet recognizes the scope of the subversion.[15]

Although the plot deconstructs the values of social comedy, Pym never developed a modern feminist perspective. She admired the writings of Virginia Woolf and was reading A Room of One's Own with great attention on October 3, 1943 (VPE, 159). Yet, unlike Woolf, Pym made a fetish of her love for Coventry Patmore's verse and never challenged his conviction that women were created to serve and comfort men. Far from rejecting Victorian family values, on May 11, 1943, she boasted to Henry Harvey of reading Patmore's poetry (VPE, 130). Even the stylish Prudence of Jane and Prudence is addicted to his work (JP, 45).[16]

Pym's obsession with Patmore's poetry helps to explain the development of her style. She lived by patriarchal principles but realized that few would be rewarded for such devotion. According to Barbara Bowman, when Pym's sense of outrage at women's victimization got the better of her, she "constructed an alternate system of linguistic codes." Her characters make wry asides that express their dissatisfaction. The poet Philip Larkin, who started corresponding with Pym in 1963, referred to Pym's bombshells.[17] They are unexpected statements with the same force as Mildred Lathbury's suggestion in *Excellent Women* to skip the ritual cup of tea. The churchwoman's hurt response tells Mildred that her question "had struck at something deep and fundamental. It was the kind of question that starts a landslide in the mind" (*EW*, 227). Pym's barbs start landslides, but the ladylike constraints of the plot limit their impact.

Pym wrote about women who are too polite for open rebellion. Thus Belinda instinctively does what is expected of her but is privately horrified by her acquiescence. For example, when the lazy Archdeacon refuses to stir himself, Belinda "much to her own surprise and dismay, heard herself offering to take on the organization and distribution of the boxes" (*STG*, 167). Pym could not let her characters, or herself, confront their situations more directly lest they lose their sense of humor. Instead the author mastered a variety of tones, from rueful self-effacement to occasional moments of sharp insight. She developed narrative strategies that shield her characters from uncomfortable self-scrutiny but allow for some expression of their true feelings.

At the time Pym's novels were first published, the reviewers missed the implications of Pym's approach. Her old-fashioned, accessible style lulled them into complacency. The story depicts the middle years of spinsterhood in their most attractive guise. The sisters and their friends create a community of "senior scholars." Burkhart declared, "It is a village that never was, any more than Cranford was; one wishes that it had been."[18] Almost every character is in late middle age. Most live comfortably without spouse, parent, or child. All of them are in good health, have adequate money and companionship; their network of friends counteracts any threat of isolation. As a result, the Bede sisters, Harriet and Belinda, are never tempted by their male admirers.

Still, Pym recognizes the power of sexual attraction, especially to forbidden objects. Despite Belinda Bede's age, she sometimes feels disturbed by complex sexual feelings. One time she charitably darns a hole in the Archdeacon's sock while it is still on his foot. Mending his sock is such "an upsetting and unnerving experience" that she barely responds when she accidentally pricks the Archdeacon with the needle. Harriet tries to "divert him with conversation" until he has "recovered his good humour" (*STG*, 77, 79). Yet not even the loyal Harriet really understands Belinda's position. Belinda muses about how she would feel if she were Lot's wife, who was turned to a pillar of salt for her sins, a comparison that reveals the proscribed nature of her response to the Archdeacon. Harriet is puzzled but quickly turns the conversation to more practical subjects (*STG*, 79). Later on she complacently talks about Belinda and the Archdeacon "as if she were giving her blessing to a young couple, instead of making rather a scandalous suggestion about a married archdeacon and a respectable spinster" (*STG*, 156).

Both sisters choose spinsterhood over marriage. Harriet likes being courted by Mr. Mold, a deputy librarian at the Bodleian. When he proposes, however, she begins to realize that a suitor "in the Prime of Life would be much more acceptable to her than a husband of the same description" (*STG*, 136). She wonders who would prefer "the unknown trials of matrimony" to "a comfortable life of spinsterhood in a country parish?" (*STG*, 136). Belinda is speechless with anxiety when she hears of the proposal. She had seen Mr. Mold at the front door but crouches in the bushes to avoid being seen. She even stifles an impulse to laugh, fearing to startle Mold with a "sudden burst of laughter coming out of a bush" (*STG*, 132). Fortunately, Harriet reassures Belinda that she has rejected Mold, and "the look of relief that brightened Belinda's face was pathetic in its intensity" (*STG*, 142). Belinda cannot think of an adequate substitute for her sister. Female friendship would be "a cold comfort" (*STG*, 160). The only person left to confide in would be Count Bianco. No doubt Pym was drawing on her own feelings about Hilary to inform this passage.

Harriet herself was no happier at the thought of Belinda accepting Bishop Grote. The proposal scene echoes the one in *Crampton Hodnet* when Mr. Latimer asks Miss Morrow for her hand but with some significant differences. Belinda cannot emulate Miss Morrow's calm demeanor. Displeased to be interrupted by the Bishop, Belinda regards his offer as "too fantastic and terrible to be thought of" (*STG*, 223), and she rejects him quickly. Unrequited love strikes her as superior to life with the Bishop (*STG*, 224). Then to her joy the smug Bishop tells her that Agatha Hoccleve, the Archdeacon's condescending wife, has been making vain overtures to him, thereby creating another triangle. Thinking of Agatha's disappointment makes Belinda glow with pleasure. The scene ends with the two sisters' happy acknowledgment that their lives will continue without separation or change, an uncomic attitude if ever there was one.[19]

The tone of the novel is good-humored and optimistic; the sisters' contentment is infectious. Thus the illusion of comedy is maintained. Pym could not eradicate her own longing for romance, but she could create characters who do not need our pity. In contrast to Miss Morrow in *Crampton Hodnet*, the Bedes are not dependent on a willful domestic tyrant. They have each other and enough money to be comfortable. Not only are they financially independent, but their many friends respect their independence. They live happily at the center of their social circle. Thus the mood of the novel is affirmative even if comedy's central idea has been rejected.

The positive assertions of the novel would not have been possible for Pym earlier when she had been living at home, watching her sister with what she described in 1941 as a jealous curiosity.[20] Now she was sharing her sister's life while her job introduced her to a new breed of interesting and strange people—anthropologists. Pym's diaries throughout this period are not very informative, but her literary journals, which she began in 1948, express a sometimes horrified fascination for the people with whom she worked. She wrote Henry Harvey, February 20, 1946, that she accepted employment at the I.A.I., partly to distract herself from the "Angst," which she claimed was bothering many people (*VPE*, 179).

At work Pym for the first time met individuals who were nothing like her parents' friends or her Oxford contemporaries. Editing the journal *Africa* exposed her to anthropological terminology and concepts. Throughout her life Pym rejoiced in the use and misuse of words. Anthropological jargon became a new source of amusement. She reported in "Finding a Voice," that she had consciously imitated her colleagues' detached way of looking at society. Field work, after all, was similar to sleuthing, one of Pym's favorite hobbies. As both Burkhart and Rossen have agreed, Pym's new job at the I.A.I. increased her cast of characters and her potential subject matter as well.[21] But most important, having a job offered security.

Pym had been writing *Some Tame Gazelle* for so many years that the influence of anthropology, a recent addition to her life, is less marked than in her next novel. Still she used her new knowledge to add some marvelously comic details. The Bishop has his seat in Africa, where most of Pym's colleagues did their research. In the manuscript his seat is in Hawaii. As a result of the change, Mbawawan hunting customs, habits of dressing, and a few bits of stray jargon enliven the comedy considerably. Pym punctures academic pretentiousness, poking fun at the Bishop's attempts to seem knowledgeable about Africa and ridiculing his efforts to share his understanding of culture and ritual with his audience. Not only does he know little about anthropology, but, as Long observes, he is uncomfortable when showing slides of his tribe.[22]

When Harriet sabotages his dignity by putting a slide of a strange musical instrument in upside down so that it looks like a phallus, the Bishop alone fails to see the joke. Despite giggling from the audience, he observes merely that the slide is inverted. (*STG*, 180). A few minutes later when the Bishop begins to play the instrument in question, Edith Liversidge knowledgeably murmurs, "Phallic. . . . Quite the usual thing."(*STG*, 181). Oblivious to everyone's reaction, the Bishop moves on to other demonstrations. But despite these comic bits, the influence of anthropology and African lore is minimal in this novel. In Pym's next, *Excellent Women*, two anthropologists play major roles.

Both Robert Long and Diana Benet notice how much Pym indulged in sexual innuendos. She developed this habit at Oxford after reading the Earl of Rochester's poems. She hid the jokes in the novels to avoid offending her genteel readers. Indeed, she had some reason to do so. In 1952 she received a letter from a woman complaining that *Excellent Women* mentioned bathrooms and toilet paper.[23] Given such responses, Pym had the right to exercise caution, but the absence of passionate feelings in her writing is altogether another matter.

Throughout her career, Pym deliberately limited her range of vision and choice of subject matter, developing a narrative style that had seemed somewhat dated as early as the 1930s. Her novels appealed to an audience who saw themselves as members of an endangered species. They constituted an ignored minority, being refined, well-educated, sensitive, and often eccentric women and men. Many of them were born into the upper reaches of society but found themselves excluded from its inner circles by temperament or marital status. In 1977, a woman wrote that she had been born upside down and had been like that ever since. Pym felt an affinity for such people. Their values and peculiarities were familiar ones. Besides, they provided a safe harbor for her after her disastrous attempts to enter the sexual arena at Oxford. To please them, Pym willingly suppressed the flamboyant side of her personality, elements of which had still been visible during her World War II naval career. After the publication of *Some Tame Gazelle*, May 31, 1950, Alan Davis wrote that he was startled by Belinda's naïveté. He had expected a more up-to-date and sophisticated novel from the WRNS officer he had known.[24]

In time, Pym paid a high price for her suppression of sexuality in her writing. She yearned for real popularity, which might have come to her had she expressed her love, desire, and anger more boldly. Eliminating volatile feelings from the range of her subject matter, however, made it difficult for her to attract a wider audience. Further, she could not keep up even the restrained euphoria of *Some Tame Gazelle*. Like everyone else, she was relieved by the end of the war, but she wryly acknowledged that postwar shortages included eligible men, as well as food and housing.

One of the unfinished stories, "A Wedge of Misery Tea Time," hints at Pym's primary desire. In it she describes a dim spinster whose good works take her to Africa. There she gets engaged to an anthropologist; anthropologists, in Pym's estimation, were about as dim as spinsters. The narrator, Belinda Marsh-Gibbons, joins the tea queue after spending many unhappy hours with a male friend at lunch. Accidentally, she ends up at the same table with the engaged woman, Hilda Gramp, Canon Gramp's daughter. To her surprise, mousy Hilda's eyes shine and her voice rings when she announces that she has become engaged to a man she met in Nigeria while teaching nursing. Belinda ends by wondering whether she would be as lucky if she went to Africa.[25]

Real life, however, was not so obliging. Pym's literary notebooks and manuscripts of 1948–1950 deal primarily with professional rather than personal matters. A few entries suggest that a trip back to Bristol in May 1949 stirred up old memories of Gordon Glover, leaving her in a nostalgic and saddened mood. On that occasion she contrasted her current visit with a wartime one, a time when the lights had been masked for the blackout, and there was "weeping in the Ladies" (*VPE*, 185). The sadness seemed to accentuate her single position. For a moment the sense of not belonging made her long for a husband. Then, in 1950, Glover wrote her a sad letter telling about his recent illness.[26]

Nonetheless, gloomy thoughts did not keep Pym from writing. If anything they acted as a stimulus. Her early notebooks are full of ideas for short stories. Once again, writing offered the chance of working through the discomfort she felt at her failures in love. Besides memories of Gordon Glover, Julian Amery, and Henry Harvey, she was saddened by the fact that peacetime had taken her away from Alan Davis, the naval officer she had fancied. Soon after the war, she considered writing "Silence at the End of the Table," which was to be about their friendship. In the plot synopsis, which Pym briefly sketched in a literary notebook on July 22, 1945, a naval officer incites his wife's jealousy by writing letters about a woman he meets in the WRNS. After he dies in an accident, his widow seeks out the other woman, only to discover that the two had not been that close. Imagining such unwarranted jealously apparently gave Pym some pleasure to contemplate.[27]

Over time, however, Pym's heroines become far more resourceful and successful than they had been in the early fragments, indicating that their author was no longer the insecure young woman who had retreated to her parents. Having survived a postgraduate course in suffering, Pym was eager to pass on her new knowledge. The plot of *Excellent Women,* drafted when Pym was in her middle thirties, describes the heroine's loss of innocent romanticism, an event that parallels the author's own bitter experiences. The beginning chapters reconstruct first Mildred Lathbury's prelapsarian world, followed by a delicate version of her fall. But Mildred is not as guileless as Pym was at the onset of her friendship with Gordon Glover. Instead Mildred has a sharp eye for masculine pretensions, and in general her character reflects Pym's new self-confidence. Pym deliberately chose to write in the first person. Then she could enlarge the comedy by contrasting Mildred's self-effacing behavior to her often subversive and independent thoughts. Mildred may behave like a kindly spinster who makes few demands on her friends, but her inner life is complex indeed.

Like the manuscript heroines Mildred is a vicar's daughter; her adult life has centered around the church. In many ways she is a tame character, even for the 1950s. Like Belinda Bede, she is overly concerned with her good reputation. Pym never completely outgrew her girlhood principles; at times her social attitudes were too old-fashioned for the mood of the times. In 1953, a literary agent reported that her story, "The Rich Man in His Castle," was almost too class conscious to submit to ladies' magazines.[28] The real difficulty was Pym's nostalgia for the world of Charlotte Yonge's novels. Luckily, Mildred has a forceful inner voice.

Indeed Mildred's penchant for irony belies her self-described role as a somewhat dim spinster. Her social isolation creates a discrepancy between thought and action. Here Pym was remarkably astute. She understood that sometimes single women are forced into social interactions that are so stereotyped or ritualized that their true characters become submerged. Pym knew from personal experience that having friends and acquaintances assume that one will marry the local vicar provides little comfort. In fact, it only rubs in the spinster's precarious position.[29] Nonetheless, Mildred falls in love with Rocky Napier, despite the presence of his wife. He is the only one who talks to her as an individual. By discussing her actions and possible motivations, he gives her value. The others are too busy discussing their own activities to notice her. Further, their egotism has the effect of limiting Mildred's range of possible responses. A series of bleak interactions make her feel like an unloving kind of person, whereas she is capable of deep devotion.

The divergence between Mildred's early conversations with Helena Napier and her later ones with Rocky demonstrates this point. Within a few minutes Helena has used "I" six times, and Mildred is forced to do so in response. Helena makes a series of off-putting remarks. She tells Mildred that "I don't suppose I shall be in very much" and informs her that "My husband will be coming out of the Navy soon" and "I'm just getting the place ready." She then goes on to say how disappointed she is with the flat: "Yes, I've had an awful time and this isn't really what we wanted. I don't at all like the idea of sharing a bathroom . . . and I don't know what Rockingham will say" (*EW*, 6–7). Helena asks Mildred very few questions and responds to Mildred's statement about growing up in a vicarage with a fantasy of her own but shows little curiosity about Mildred's past (*EW*, 8). Helena's lack of interest makes the spinster feel awkward. At one point Mildred feels "driven by curiosity" to ask a question. When she learns the name of Helena's husband "I snatched at the name as if it had been a precious jewel in the dustbin" (*EW*, 7).

On the other hand, when Rocky first talks to her, he immediately establishes a feeling of camaraderie.[30] In contrast to his wife, he addresses Mildred directly six times in the first eight sentences. He says "How very nice of you to come down." "It's lucky for me you were in. I think you must be Miss Lathbury." When asked how he knew, he replies "Helena mentioned you in a letter." By using his wife's first name, he immediately includes Mildred in the circle of his friends. When Mildred walks up the stairs with him to his flat, he asks her, "Don't you think they're [his chairs] beautiful" and then begs her not to go, "unless you have to" (*EW*, 30–31). No wonder Mildred falls in love with him.

Rocky teaches her that she is a person with rights and interests of her own. Mildred begins to change her self-defined role as helpful friend. At several points she resists the burden of helping others. Except for Rocky's temporary but kindly interest, she has no one like Harriet Bede in whom she can confide or who will encourage her to assert herself. Only the reader is privy to her thoughts; the other characters simply project their own feelings onto her as if she were a blank screen.

Sometimes reviewers and critics do the same thing. At least three of the early reviewers in 1952 compared *Excellent Women* to Jane Austen's novels despite the obvious differences. J. W. Lambert, wiser than most, commented upon its mixture of wit and sadness. Philip Larkin, who became a friend and advisor in the 1960s, showed the greatest insight into Mildred's plight. He commented in a letter, July 14, 1964, that *Excellent Women* depicted the "pain of being single, the unconscious hurt" everyone else regards as its natural state. Mildred suffers, and "nobody can see why she shouldn't suffer, like a Victorian cabhorse." Larkin knew the perils of being single first hand; he understood how vulnerable Mildred is, a fact which early reviewers overlooked. Yet he was equally aware that Mildred's acute eye makes her a formidable opponent. He remarked that "no man can read" Pym's novels and remain unchanged.[31]

One scene exemplifies Pym's techniques especially effectively. Mildred finds herself confessing inadvertently to her old friend William Caldicote that Rocky is "just the kind of person I should have liked for myself" (*EW*, 69). Alarmed by the idea that Mildred might want to marry, William forces her to deny any such desire. Then the relieved man picks up the bottle of wine, "judged the amount left in it and refilled his own glass but not mine" (*EW*, 70). Daryll Forde, Pym's boss, had made much the same gesture with cigarettes on June 7, 1946.[32] Any one who can so slyly depict the selfishness of her companion does not need our pity.

For all Mildred's acuteness, she is vulnerable to Rocky's shallow charm. The first time Rocky meets her, he gives her a china goat, the sort of present that Pym loved to receive (*EW*, 38). Like Pym, she observes his weaknesses but is captivated by his special gift for intimacy, the hallmark of Pym's unsuitable beloveds. Mildred's expectations are so few that she, like Belinda, prefers to cherish her unrequited love for Rocky, who treats her with breezy goodwill, rather than to concentrate on attracting the more attainable Everard Bone. He is an unromantic but solid anthropologist, who plays a role something like St. John Rivers in *Jane Eyre*.[33]

Toward the end Pym takes a risk. When a romantic ending seems imminent, she abruptly derails the narrative. Rather than proposing marriage, Everard unexpectedly offers Mildred the job of volunteer proofreader and indexer, which she accepts. Pym in "The Novelist's Use of Everyday Life," a talk she gave in Barnes in 1950, declared that the writer should attempt to end on a note of muted optimism. This time she stressed deprivation rather than allowing her heroine some self-determination. In protest, one of her astute friends wrote her April 15, 1952, that Mildred seemed to her a vitiated version of the writer herself.[34]

The ending of *Excellent Women* is unsettling. A number of critics have offered romantic or semi-romantic interpretations of the conclusion, suggestions that demonstrate how uncomfortable they are with Pym's assault on romantic and comic conventions. Burkhart declares that Mildred triumphs "in her growing relationship with Everard Bone," whose occupation and religious views make him as "appropriate . . . as the chastened and pious Rochester became to Jane Eyre." Long claims that Mildred is headed toward marriage with Everard but will find it as restricting as her previous life has been. Benet argues that Mildred has abandoned her role as excellent woman by the end of the novel. She believes that Mildred finds Everard attractive. Mildred's "happy ending is her decision to honor herself by making her best effort to fulfill her own desires and emotional needs." In contrast, Rossen correctly contends that Pym "displaced" the usual "happy ending" by having Rocky and his wife Helena reconcile.[35] She insists that learning about Helena's future happiness can not compensate for Mildred's dreary fate.

Pym snatched away the hope of romance to prove a point: unrequited love was preferable to the prospect of a safe but dull marriage. Yet Mildred's isolation at the end is even more poignant than it is in the beginning. Rocky has destroyed all of her old defenses, as Gordon Glover had Pym's. Before Rocky, Mildred could hide behind her spinsterly role and observe dispassionately the lives of others. Once she has a taste of even his rather superficial sort of intimacy, she feels an acute sense of loss. Thus Mildred may ultimately choose between serving the church as a spinster or serving Everard as a proofreader and indexer, a fate which Long projects, but her decision hardly matters. Neither option will satisfy the romantic feelings Rocky has aroused in her.[36]

A few years earlier, Pym had been a witness of the demise of her sister's marriage. June 5, 1946, shortly after her sister Hilary separated from her husband, Pym wrote Henry Harvey that Hilary was better off without her husband, who had been difficult. She added that the marriage had not been founded on passion. Left to herself, she would prefer a romantic beginning even if it faded in time. She concluded by suggesting that she would probably never change her mind, marriage being an unlikely event (*VPE*, 180). Pym preferred to withhold Everard's expected proposal rather than have Mildred pretend to care for the admirable anthropologist.

Despite the equivocal ending, many readers found Mildred a sympathetic character. June 7, 1952, a fan wrote that reading the novel helped her get over a depression. She had been an "excellent woman" in the village before her unexpected marriage. Her family was pleased by her new role, but to her surprise she found she almost preferred the old one. After the novel was serialized on the *Woman's Hour* (a regular BBC radio program) in April of that year, Pym's sales doubled those of her previous novel. No doubt its appeal was enhanced by two factors. On the one hand, the war-inspired shortage of men increased the appeal of a novel that showed respect for a spinster. At the same time readers liked the charming Rocky. Coincidentally he was a naval officer like the glamorous husband of Princess Elizabeth, who became queen the year the novel was published. The success must have been very pleasing to Pym. For the first time she had found a successful way to reconcile her cherished fantasy about being a vicar's daughter with the requirements of popularity in her own time.[37]

It is not surprising that Pym had chosen that moment to write about an isolated orphan, a vicar's daughter, like many of the ones who appear in her early manuscripts. After all, her mother had recently died. Only the failure of Hilary Pym's marriage rescued Pym from a fate similar to Mildred's. Indeed it was living comfortably with her sister that made it possible for Pym to avoid the traces of self-pity that had sabotaged some of her earliest attempts to write about vicars' daughters and companions. Mildred, however, is remarkably free from self-pity. In one extended scene Mildred's reactions to the visit of her old friend Dora (*EW*, 100–107) demonstrate that the solitary life is preferable to sharing a flat with the wrong person. Moreover, Daniel George, the reader for Jonathan Cape, convinced Pym to remove several references to the vicar's daughter and to ill-fitting WRNS's uniforms, thus removing the last vestiges of pathos from the text.[38] The success of *Excellent Women* made it look, for the first time, as if Barbara Pym's novels were headed for popular success.

Yet when Pym wrote her third novel, *Jane and Prudence,* she did not hold on to all of the new audience, attracted by the radio broadcast of *Excellent Women. Jane and Prudence* sold very well, but despite its captivating heroines, it began a downward trend in Pym's sales.[39] Perhaps the combination of passive male characters and an emphasis on the austerity of the postwar economy—both the shortage of meat and the shortage of eligible men—seemed too dreary for the euphoric mood that followed the accession of the young queen.

When writing the novel, Pym returned to old material, not only to characters and situations from her fragments but to sometimes stringent observations of her parents. She seized the opportunity to create negative fictional portraits of two men who had treated her badly in the past, Gordon Glover (Fabian Driver) and Julian Amery (Edward Lyall). Pym herself never recognized her hostility to men. When writing some notes for a BBC radio talk in 1978, Pym recollected that after *Jane and Prudence*, someone had commented upon her dislike of men. The author could still only respond weakly, "to quote a joke phrase, some of my best friends are—have been— men!"[40]

Jane and Prudence is full of fantasies and recollections that were of great importance to the writer. January 12, 1964, Pym wrote Philip Larkin that Prudence was one of her favorite heroines (*VPE*, 223). Therefore it makes sense to trace the plot back to its personal source. The central relationship in the novel is between two women, Jane, a kindly but fey individual, much like Pym's own mother, and Prudence, who had once been Jane's student at Oxford. Now Prue works at a place like the I.A.I. and specializes in unrequited affairs of the heart. The latest is Arthur Grampian, her middle-aged, unexciting employer, quite like Pym's boss. One of Pym's early notes suggests that Prudence is supposed to be Jane's unmarried sister, a favorite Pym device for generating a novel. Very quickly, however, Prudence becomes Jane's old college friend.[41] In the novel Prudence is Jane's ex-student and surrogate daughter (*JP*, 7–8).

Jane would be an anomaly in any society. She has much in common with early manuscript versions of unusual vicars' wives, who are very like Pym's mother. Jane's disregard for personal appearance and occasional bits of frivolity are very like Mrs. Pym. At the same time, Jane shares certain qualities of her creator. She has "insatiable curiosity" (*JP*, 106) much like Pym's. Pym, not her mother, was a writer and attended literary society meetings like the one in the novel. Of course in some ways Jane is a purely fictional character. After all, no one ever accused Pym or her mother of spending "a lot of time wandering around doing nothing," which is what Diana Benet says about Jane.[42]

Pym does not sit in judgment on Jane. Of course, Jane's love of people and her fascination with their hidden thoughts have distracted her from the kind of research that she was trained to do, "the influence of something upon somebody" (*JP*, 11). But, in Pym's judgment, being married is not the only hindrance to the productive life. Even Jane's dedicated English literature tutor has never completed her book (*JP*, 11). Although Jane often feels discouraged about her lack of tangible accomplishments, she is content with all her important relationships. In one of her notes, Pym commented that perhaps Jane's career has not been successful, but surely her happy marriage and child would be compensation.[43] Jane herself is unresentful and generally cheerful. She is well aware that her marriage no longer consists of an exchange of suitable or unsuitable Donne quotations, but to be able to say after years of marriage that "a husband was someone to tell one's silly jokes to" is a sign of contentment (*JP*, 10).

Jane's feelings for Prudence are a model of maternal acceptance. Her feelings for her daughter Flora are more contradictory, but here Pym shows exceptional insight. It is far easier to offer unconditional acceptance to one's friends than to one's children. Thus Jane is baffled by the young man Flora brings home but never makes fun of Prudence's penchant for unrequited love affairs. Jane is loyal to her friend. She has not given up hope even though the twenty-nine-year-old Prudence is at "an age that is often rather desperate for a woman who has not yet married" (*JP*, 7), the age when Pym herself lost Gordon Glover. Indeed, Jane shamelessly engages in matchmaking, hoping that one of the meager village men will turn out to be a good husband for Prue.

The character of Prudence also resembles several heroines from Pym's earlier work. Although Prudence is not an Oxford don like Beatrice Wyatt, her elegant attractiveness is very similar. Pym was older than Prudence when she wrote this novel—in 1939 she had been younger than her creation Beatrice. Therefore she was able to treat Prudence's efforts to attract men with humor and detachment. In one way, Prudence is much luckier than Beatrice. She has Jane's friendship, whereas Beatrice is not particularly close to anyone. Prudence is grateful for her friend although at times she observes all the inadequacies of the Cleveland marriage. In fact most of the complaints about the way the Clevelands live, the discomfort, poor cooking, and "the peculiar kind of desolation they seemed to create around them," are made by the fastidious Prudence (*JP*, 82).

Prue does not appear unhappy in her series of unrequited love affairs. She is clearly the kind of woman for whom marriage would be an adjustment. She enjoys her "solitary lunches" at which she reads Coventry Patmore and dreams about Arthur Grampian. As long as life offers her such solace, she feels content. This is just as

well. The village has only one eligible man, the rather moth-eaten
Fabian Driver, the Gordon Glover character, according to Pym's
literary notebook of 1950 (*VPE*, 187). Pym dramatizes his foibles from
the start. Before he even appears in the novel, Jane discovers that he
has placed "a large framed photograph" of himself on his wife's
grave, an act of vanity that should disqualify him from serious
consideration (*JP*, 27). Also Prudence, unbeknownst to anyone, has
a rival, Jessie Morrow, Miss Doggett's companion from *Crampton
Hodnet*. Pym has transplanted both of them from North Oxford to
the village to give the spunky Miss Morrow another chance to catch
a man.

About the time Pym was working on *Jane and Prudence*, she also
Jessie's role is worth investigating. Against all odds she defeats
the younger, more beautiful, and socially desirable Prudence. She
simply seduces Fabian. Pym alters her character considerably from
her earlier conception in *Crampton Hodnet*. In that work Miss Morrow is admirable in her isolation. Although being a companion is
clearly a thankless task, she is too sensible a woman to trade even
that unpleasant post for the hand of the reluctant suitor, Mr. Latimer. Apparently, Pym's view of her had changed over the years.

About the time Pym was working on *Jane and Prudence*, she also
wrote several versions of a story, "So, Some Tempestuous Morn,"
which provides another glimpse of the famous Sunday afternoon
tea party with which *Crampton Hodnet* opens. This time Miss Morrow is clearly "harder and slyer" than she is in the earlier novel.
Before the party begins, she attracts the attention of an attractive
clergyman, who waves to her as she looks out of her bedroom
window. Brief though the encounter is, it encourages her to make a
reckless remark to Miss Doggett. She declares after the rain that the
flowers look defiled—a word that worries Miss Doggett. The older
woman with rare astuteness assumes that the word itself is a dangerous symptom. Although the story ends inconclusively, Pym dramatizes Miss Morrow's predatory nature. When she is introduced
to the same clergyman, he has the vague feeling that he has seen her
somewhere before. Remembering all the details makes Miss Morrow feel superior. After everyone has left the living room to tour the
garden, the companion demolishes a piece of cake. Curiously, the
editors to whom Pym submitted the story ignored its imagery and
language. They rejected it on the grounds that the characters were
conventional.[44]

Although the plot of *Jane and Prudence* is quite thin, the character
of Jane gives the novel its charm and depth. In fact, Jane shares
some of the qualities of E. M. Forster's transcendent mother figures,

Mrs. Wilcox and Mrs. Moore, but Jane is treated in a consistently comic fashion. When Jane acts as if she were in some realm separate from daily existence, her inappropriate philosophical queries cause more mundane acquaintances discomfort, not the awed sense of being in the presence of some superior, otherworldly being like Mrs. Moore. Still the author invests her with considerable meaning. Jane represents the longing Pym occasionally expressed for a mother who would care about her fate. Like poignant moments in *Crampton Hodnet* when Margaret Cleveland tries to protect her daughter from knowledge of her father's infidelity, Jane's efforts to comfort Prudence after Fabian discards her are equally touching. Still it is hard to agree with one enthusiastic reader who described the novel as being a prelapsarian Eden.[45]

For one thing there is no Adam, for another, no fall. As Robert Long observes, "judging by this novel, men have grown small indeed." None of the men is a romantic figure. Nicholas, Jane's husband, is the direct descendant of Beatrice's old beau, Henry Grainger, in *The Lumber Room*, but he lacks energy. Unlike Archdeacon Hoccleve or Rocky Napier, both of whom are attractive despite their obvious failings, Nicholas is notable for his gentle and peace-loving nature. He complacently accepts the attentions of women even though he is "of a modest and retiring nature." His pleasure lies in the simple things in life—soap carved like animals or drying tobacco in the kitchen (*JP*, 51). On the whole, Nicholas is based on Frederic Pym, although a few incidents—the tobacco leaves for one—actually happened to someone else. Edward Lyall, the eligible MP like Julian Amery, is disappointing as well. Although the women all fuss over him as if he were a curate, when Jane finally has an extended conversation with him on the train, he does not know how to respond to her teasing (*JP*, 219). As for Fabian, the would-be Lothario, he never has a chance. Pym pillories his pompous attitudinizing and his self-indulgent behavior at every turn. Burkhart wittily commented that if these men had been kings they would have been called "Fabian the Vain, Nicholas the Mild, and Edward the Tired."[46] Indeed, depression almost subdues nostalgia in this novel.

Even though the details in the novel are quite different from *Excellent Women*, once again Pym repeated the strategy with which she ends the earlier novel. Rather than allowing Prudence the opportunity to choose between her comfortable life as a spinster and becoming a village matron, Pym permits the underhanded Jessie Morrow to capture her prey. But by using that particular twist Pym reduces the importance of whatever serious message the novel contained and diminished its effectiveness. Of course, it is obvious that Pym had no intention of competing with sociologists by offering a coherent analysis of the failings of modern marriage. She herself had not been trapped in an unhappy marriage, unlike Margaret Drabble, Penelope Mortimer, and Doris Lessing, all of whom have written about their problems. In fact during the next twenty years, they, as well as other important women writers, declared the institution dead while they dissected the corpse.[47] Instead Pym was an observer of marriage, a noncombatant who longed to enter the fray but only on her own terms. She still believed her girlhood romantic notions and longed to win the attentions of an aloof Mr. Rochester. That unsatisfied wish encouraged her to notice all the defects in the marriages around her, including her parents', her sister's, and her friend Honor Wyatt's, the people she had closest at hand. Lacking a long-term, satisfying encounter with a man, Pym never entirely abandoned her daughterly view of the world.

In many ways Pym's situation was not too different from E. M. Forster's, an earlier master of social comedy whose personal life made him feel an outsider at the marriage feast. In his middle period novels, he tried to avoid the required happy ending of social comedy. Instead he grafted Ibsen and Chekhov's romantic attitudes toward landscapes into his suburban world.[48] Pym was by nature a more conservative writer, and her personal situation was much less desperate than his. But she combined a lack of marital experience with a desire to be amusing and avoid unpleasantness at all costs. These factors affected both her own life and her approach to writing. She could only write about her characters' feelings at some distance. Rather than experimenting with new literary perspectives, she constantly struggled to balance an optimistic interpretation with her deeply felt pessimistic view of life. As a result Pym did not try new narrative strategies that could have modernized her plots in accordance with the evolution of popular taste.

Commercial success might have encouraged experimentation. Not only did the sales of *Jane and Prudence* decline slightly from that of her previous novel, but shortly after its publication Marks and Spencer's wrote a threatening letter claiming that a passage in the novel insulted their clothing. For over a month Pym and her publishers negotiated for a satisfactory settlement, while the threat of a lawsuit hung over her head. Clearly Marks and Spencer's had never heard of Bakhtin's idea that characters create their own "zone," rather than always representing the author's own perspective.[49] For all these reasons Pym was never able to feel wholly confident about her literary position. Although her will to create was strong and her next novel, *Less than Angels*, innovative, ultimately she became timid in her writing.

4

Playing Detective in Suburbia

Pym entered her middle years with increased literary expertise and creativity, but she was bedeviled with worries about her popularity. An ominous drop in her sales occurred in 1953. Then, in April 1954, six months before she finished the rough draft of *Less than Angels*, she was offered an unexpected opportunity. Graham Watson, a director of Curtis Brown, wrote the novelist that a Dutton editor from New York wanted to consider publishing her next book.[1]

At first Pym responded to Watson's news with delight. A year before she had been grateful for his attempts to place her short stories. In the ensuing correspondence with her publishers, however, G. Wren Howard, Cape's partner, told her that they had submitted *Excellent Women* to nine American firms and *Jane and Prudence* to seven, with no success. Ten continental publishers had turned down *Excellent Women* as well. Feeling humiliated, Pym declined Watson's offer. Rather than trusting his expertise, she insisted that Americans simply did not like her sort of novel. Watson appealed to her professional standards and tried to shake her faith in the competence of Cape's methods. Pym feared alienating the only publisher who had ever accepted her work. She refused to reconsider Watson's offer.[2] Unfortunately, Pym's refusal cost her a chance to broaden her professional horizons. Her loss of confidence also affected her writing style. Without realizing it, she gradually began to soften her tone from the stimulating astringency of the first three novels to a softer, less convincing, romantic note. Although *Less than Angels* shows few signs of a crisis of nerves, the two that followed display more.

Pym made no direct reference to her publishing prospects in *Less than Angels*, but its delicate interplay between good humor and somber events reveals that she anticipated a perilous future. On the surface, the novel is about the interaction of two disparate cultures—the anthropological world and the suburban—but its subtext concerns her own survival as a writer. Preferring to avoid unpleasant thoughts about future popularity, Pym concentrated on her heroine's problems in love. Besides providing a distraction from the specter of lost sales, Pym's choice of subject made good literary sense. More of her readers suffered from love than from lost royalties; and if the book sold well, she would no longer have to worry about her finances. By the middle 1950s, moreover, Pym's recollections of past romantic misery were no longer painful.

The novel is unusual in her fiction for several reasons. To begin with, after writing three works that challenge the importance of marriage, Pym reversed herself. *Less than Angels* ends on an optimistic but not entirely convincing note. On the other hand, the novel exhibits the influence of modern drama and narrative fiction for the first time. Echoes of Charlotte Brontë, Virginia Woolf, and Anton Chekhov abound. In addition, this novel is the first to be set partly in Barnes, Pym's new suburban home, and she manages to treat that habitat with the kind of affectionate scrutiny that is rare in modern fiction.[3]

Coming to terms with the suburbs, however, took time. One would never guess from Pym's early work that she and her sister Hilary had left Pimlico in 1949. Pym was then in the midst of writing *Excellent Women*, a novel that celebrated that district. Despite their affection for Pimlico's convenient location, the sisters wanted to settle down in the suburbs where they could make a comfortable life for themselves. Three years later, Pym finally began to write about her new environment.

Barnes was Pym's first taste of a locale that offered neither the anonymity of the city nor the community life of a small town. Yet she discovered that the suburbs mimicked aspects of her fictional village. As Pym's heroine remarks, suburbia provides a perfect place to watch one's neighbors. *Less than Angels* declares open season on that activity. In it the observer and the observed are often interchangeable, creating a sense of mutuality that is reassuring. One of the older residents, Mr. Dulke, spends almost as much time watching young Deirdre Swan as Deirdre's middle-aged aunt Rhoda does observing Alaric Lydgate, their eccentric next-door neighbor. Both are fascinated for much the same reason.

Determined to establish the similarities between Barnes and the kinds of places Woolf and Chekhov celebrate, Pym ignored evidence that Barnes had long since become part of the urban sprawl. Instead she manages to create a Chekhovian atmosphere by reconstructing the memories of its life-long inhabitants. Her poetic sense of place, however, was leavened by humor. She understood that it is difficult to share another person's nostalgia. Mr. Dulke bores Deirdre Swan, a young anthropology student, with his reminiscences about the old days when "the district was little more than a village" (*LTA*, 43). Yet nineteen-year-old Deirdre mourns self-consciously: "Ah, my childhood, my innocent childhood, she thought, remembering a Tchekov play which she had recently seen" (*LTA*, 38). Later on, when Deirdre hears the unexpected, muffled sound of rugs being beaten next door, she immediately compares it to the ring of the axe cutting trees at the conclusion of *The Cherry Orchard* (*LTA*, 44). Pym balances isolation and loss with literary echoes that remind us of the youth and energy of the characters. Catherine Oliphant asks Tom Mallow why men fear women who wear black, "Like Masha in *The Seagull*, in mourning for her life?" (*LTA*, 70). Catherine herself dressed so relentlessly in black that on one occasion a stranger asks her if she has been recently bereaved (*LTA*, 110–11). Yet she looks "like Jane Eyre or a Victorian child whose head has been cropped because of scarlet fever" (*LTA*, 7).

At the same time Pym paints an accurate and amusing picture of the anthropologists' arcane world (as she had done so successfully in *Excellent Women*). She views their activities with an outsider's detachment but an insider's knowledge. Thus, she goes beyond the obvious in explaining the dilemma of Alaric Lydgate, the failed anthropologist. He is the sort of perfectionist who writes fiercely critical reviews of his colleagues' books but is unable to write up his own field notes. In other hands, he might be treated as a stereotype or a mere joke. Instead, as Jane Nardin notes, Pym believed that men like Alaric "are the worst victims of the sexist society she portrays."[4]

Pym understood Alaric's pain. In the evening he sits hidden in an African mask, rather than risk dangerous social intercourse. Out of fear, he generally avoids looking directly at people, "for life was very terrible whatever sort of front we might put on it." The narrator comments that only the young or "the very old and wise could look out on it with a clear or untroubled gaze" (*LTA*, 57). Meanwhile the other academics compete fiercely for the paltry financial resources necessary to support their work. Their disputes, however, are comic rather than frightening. For example, Jill Rubenstein points out that the ridiculous contretemps between Miss Lydgate and Miss Clovis, two scruffy-looking academic women, leads to "forgiveness" and "a mutual understanding" that is rare in Pym's fiction.[5]

What is most remarkable about the novel is Pym's ability to exploit the linguistic paradox that communication rests on the listener's ability to interpret "a speaker's intent in performing a linguistic act."[6] At Oxford Pym had read English, not anthropology—which did not exist as a subject in her day. As a result, she often treated anthropological jargon as if it were a slightly absurd second language. She instinctively understood how ordinary people feel when confronted with unexpected vocabulary and concepts. She had no desire to make fun of the suburban household of the Swans (which consists of Mabel Swan, her two children, Deirdre and Malcolm, and Mabel's sister, Rhoda Wellcome). Without denigrating either side, Pym manages to create comedy out of the misunderstandings that occur when one world confronts the other. Refusing to accentuate the conventionality of her suburban characters, Pym concentrates her energies on recapturing their lives. As a result, the novel contains lively images of both dramatic scenes and still lives, much like genre paintings that depict the realities of daily life.

Accumulated details make certain pictures especially vivid. For example, Rhoda looks forward each evening to the return of her niece and nephew. She hopes to extract some "interesting little scraps of gossip and information about this and that" from them. When Malcolm arrives, however, she borrows his newspaper and "in common with a great many people in all walks of life" becomes engrossed in the account of "a nasty murder, or series of murders" (*LTA*, 36–37). On Whitsunday after attending the early service, where the organist absentmindedly begins playing "Hiawatha's Wedding Feast" by Coleridge Taylor (*LTA*, 79), her sister, Mabel Swan, sits in the kitchen, "listening to the happy sound of the meat sizzling in the oven" (*LTA*, 83). The others are at the Festival service. The dignity of that event is nearly spoiled. A young French anthropologist acquaintance of Deirdre, who treats English church services as informal field work, accidentally sits in Mr. Dulke's pew. He saves the day by unhooking Mrs. Dulke's kneeler for her, the kind of Gallic gesture that impresses Rhoda. She reports to her sister, "I don't

suppose you'd find an Englishman doing that" (*LTA*, 83). That afternoon Rhoda and Mabel bustle about setting up the tea things. They
choose the Lydgate side of the garden: "Who knew what they might
hear or see through the hedge on Mr. Lydgate's side?" The other
side is "dull and familiar" (*LTA*, 86).

Such details could well be used to poke fun at the sisters for their restricted but intrusive lives. Instead Pym extended her tolerance for eccentricity to the suburban scene, refusing to subject suburbia to the
easy satire or the sentimentality that it has so often inspired. She treats
all the characters as equally fallible and potentially amusing. As a
result suburbia receives its apotheosis in this novel while the interactions between ordinary people and academics are charted skillfully.

Janice Rossen has suggested that Pym inverts the conventions
created by Charlotte Brontë. She does the same in this novel. Catherine Oliphant, like Jane Cleveland, is a writer and a free spirit.
Catherine is an energetic and self-sufficient character, making it
easy to forget that she is an orphan, like Mildred in *Excellent Women*.
Unlike Mildred, who is forced to accept the inadequate attention of
Everard Bone, the St. John Rivers character, Catherine fares better
with her Mr. Rochester substitute. She liberates Alaric Lydgate from
his trunk full of field notes. Pym was quite aware of the parallels
between *Less than Angels* and *Jane Eyre*. In her notebook she wonders
if Catty and Alaric could reenact a scene from *Jane Eyre* in Alaric's
suburban backyard.[7]

As in many Pym novels, some of the characters are derived indirectly from her friends. For example, Tom Mallow was partly inspired by Peter Lloyd, a young anthropologist whom Pym met at
the I.A.I. and enjoyed sentimentalizing over. It was Lloyd's departure to Africa that enriched her scene of Tom's leave-taking. In
contrast, most of Tom's less attractive features stem from Henry
Harvey, Gordon Glover, and Julian Amery. Like Simon Beddoes in
Crampton Hodnet, Tom puts his career before his heart. Even in its
early days his love affair with Catherine is tepid. Their homelife is
based on the author's recollection of three magic weeks in June and
July 1936, when she helped her Oxford friend Henry Harvey complete his thesis (*VPE*, 57–59). Yet Pym ignored the temporary pleasures of continuous companionship, choosing to emphasize the desertion that followed. As John Halperin has justly commented, Tom
uses women who are devoted to him without showing "any recip-
rocal feeling." When one considers that Harvey blamed her typing
for any errors in his thesis, Pym's asperity is understandable.[8]

Initially, the author contemplated having Deirdre Swan—then

called Deborah like the heroine in *Something to Remember*—be a typical Pym representative. Eventually, however, Deirdre becomes a reader of anthropology at the University of London, rather than a husband-hunting Oxford graduate. At that point Catherine, the writer of romantic fiction, became the emotional focal point of the novel. Catherine is sophisticated but eccentric. She dispenses beauty tips in her articles but shows up at her own party in espadrilles, inappropriate shoes usually being the mark of Pym's fey heroines. (Pym herself loved collecting absurd tips from fashion magazines. In a 1955 literary notebook she joyfully recorded a fatuous *Vogue* extract that recommends drinking champagne while cooking.) Catherine represents Pym's view of the world. She shares her author's imagination, her amused reaction to anthropology, and her detachment. One of Pym's notes mentions how different her desires are from Tom's. Tom would rather help his Africans than make a woman happy, whereas Catherine longs to settle in a village where she could write, have a garden, and be surrounded by friends.[9]

Pym transferred her own methods of managing pain to her heroine. Thus she felt real distress when Robert Smith accused Catherine of being heartless. Smith was a young civil servant, sent to Pym in 1952 by Robert Liddell. Pym hotly denied Smith's charge. On October 24, 1955, she wrote him about her struggle to convey Catherine's complex feelings of loss. Indeed, all the women in the novel are greatly affected by Tom's death, indicating that in Pym's opinion women are more like the loyal Anne Elliot in Jane Austen's *Persuasion* than are most men. Of course, Catherine's art compensates for her romantic betrayal. Like Pym she detaches herself from the worst of her misery and later on makes literary use of her betrayal. After Tom's death she writes about his desertion. According to Janice Rossen, it is her first story that "flaunts the convention of a happy ending in order to write about pain or, literally, reality."[10] Of course, Pym herself had been subverting that convention in each of her first three novels. Neither Catherine's nor Pym's readers realized just how autobiographical their work was.

For the first time in *Less than Angels*, Pym skillfully borrowed some of the themes of Virginia Woolf and E. M. Forster. Pym had shown an interest in Woolf's literary style for some time. August 14, 1942, after finishing reading *To the Lighthouse*, she declared that Woolf's way of writing "commends itself to me" and felt that she had already used it "in a mild way" in *Some Tame Gazelle* (*VPE*, 107). She was reading Woolf's *A Writer's Diary* in 1954 while she was finishing her novel. The ending of *Less than Angels*, like those of *To the Light-*

house and *Howards End,* combines an affirmation of family loyalty
with respect for the power of evil. Tom's disloyalty to Catherine and
his subsequent death take the place of Beethoven's goblins and
elephants, the image that Helen Schlegel creates when she listens to
his Fifth Symphony in *Howards End.* Death, betrayal, loss of childhood innocence, and a nostalgia for the lost coziness of family and
village life permeate Pym's novel, but most of the characters have
the necessary strength and resilience to surmount obstacles. Nardin says that in this work Pym "tries to approach potentially upsetting topics such as aging, isolation, failure, and death without disgust or shrinking."[11] The characters may suffer grievous losses, but
they are given an opportunity to begin their lives again.

Less than Angels represents Pym's temporary triumph over despair. Despite the earlier difficulties with *Jane and Prudence,* her
humor still outweighs nostalgia. Daniel George, her editor at Cape,
reported with delight that the novel surpassed her earlier work.
Jonathan Cape not only praised the novel but promised to reprint
Jane and Prudence. Success seemed inevitable, despite the reduced
sales for her last novel. Luck, however, was not with her. (As late as
1963, *Less than Angels* had sold merely 3,657 copies; *Jane and Prudence,*
5,219.) According to G. Wren Howard, Cape's partner, the unexpected financial collapse of a wholesale bookseller reduced the initial subscription figures. Moreover, it could not have helped matters
when one of Cape's advertisements mistakenly said that the book
was about ornithologists rather than anthropologists. Wren Howard suggested merely that Pym should get someone to have the
novel read on "Woman's Hour," the BBC program that had helped
sell *Excellent Women.* No such miracle occurred, but a year later in
1956, Pym learned that at long last a New York firm, Vanguard
Press, had agreed to bring out *Less than Angels.*[12]

As it happened, finding a willing American publisher was not
enough to establish Pym's reputation in the United States. *Less than
Angels* did not sell well, even though Pym's novel probably would
have appealed to the upper-middle-class readers who enjoyed the
novels of Louise Field Cooper. Cooper, whose career spanned the
same thirty-year period as Pym's, wrote intelligent and witty novels. Some of them were Book-of-the-Month-Club selections, just as
Pym's were Book Society Recommendations. Unfortunately, Vanguard did not market it effectively. They printed an attractive brochure, but the précis of the plot sounded dull. Instead of soliciting
blurbs from American writers, Vanguard compared Pym to Angela
Thirkell, Nancy Mitford, and Evelyn Waugh, writers not that famil-

iar to Cooper's readers. Vanguard kept the novel in print until November 13, 1974, according to Jean Mossop of Cape who wrote Pym about the situation January 12, 1978. Unfortunately Vanguard sold merely 1,238 copies and never made back their original advance. Needless to say, the sporadic sales of *Less than Angels* discouraged them from publishing her next novel. Thus Pym had every reason to feel grateful when on May 29, 1957, Jonathan Cape willingly accepted *A Glass of Blessings* and sounded fairly sanguine about its prospects.[13]

With hindsight, subtle signs of Pym's discouragement are apparent in *A Glass of Blessings*. The novel is about failure. Its heroine, Wilmet Forsyth, combines every quality Barbara Pym admired. She is intelligent, attractive, well dressed, and married. Yet in spite of material comfort, from the beginning Wilmet is dissatisfied. To make matters worse, she discovers that Piers Longridge, the one man she finds appealing, is beyond her reach. Wilmet, as Jan Fergus has suggested, can be compared to Jane Austen's heroine Emma, but Wilmet has no hope of a glamorous future. Instead she must learn to abandon romantic fantasies, rise above rejection, and be grateful for her unromantic husband and restricted life.[14]

From its earliest conception, the novel centers around church life. In an early version called "Lime Tree Bower," the heroine shares an office with Piers. In the novel Wilmet is unemployed; her husband disapproves of professional women. Pym speculated in her notes that a curate and his wife might create a scandal by having marital problems, similar to the scandal threatened in *The Lumber Room* when Rosamond ceases to live with her husband, Gabriel Bone. Instead Pym decided that the marriage of a celibate clergyman would be sensation enough. The narrator of "Lime Tree Bower" begins as a "church crawler" of nearly forty and at various points is described as a widow, a divorcée, and a wife. Regardless of marital status, she, like Barbara Bird and Prudence Bates, finds sex distasteful. Wilmet catches a glimpse of a drunken printer's reader—Piers—at a service, which he attends in order to see a server. Then when platonic friendship sounds too depressing, the narrator contemplates becoming momentarily infatuated with Piers. She decides that he might have liked her better if she had achieved prominence by writing daring fiction, radically different from the novel Pym was writing.[15]

Pym's view of Piers did not change much from manuscript to novel. He is an attractive but seedy man, who makes a game of collecting license numbers, adding them up to see if they would

bring good fortune (*GB* 10). In the novel, however, Wilmet is transformed. She becomes a soignée, thirty-three-year-old woman. She
is married to a civil servant but frustrated by her lot. She makes
sharp comments about the men who make the mistake of taking her
for granted, and her remarks in the first chapter add a bitter taste to
the bland plot. In the early stages of composition, Pym stressed
Wilmet's professional life, assuming that these details would be
enlivening. Later, she frugally converted an early scene of office life
into a brief fantasy. Wilmet imagines female office workers unnerving their demanding boss "with their insolent detachment, so that
his wrath smouldered out like a damp squib and he was left floun-
dering and stammering" (*GB* 25).[16]

Such dreary ideas for a plot could not be expected to attract a
brand-new audience. But Pym's affection for Virginia Woolf's techniques improved these bare bones. For example, on a bus trip Pym
saw a woman crazily talking to herself. She commented, much as
Wilmet does in the novel, that Woolf would have made good use of
such a scene in one of her novels; "perhaps writers always do this,
from situations that merely shock and embarrass ordinary people"
(*GB,* 78). Pym went on to add that the woman could be added to the
blood-giving episode, and indeed Miss Daunt does appear, imperiously insisting that her Rhesus negative blood exempts her from
waiting in line.[17]

As in the earlier fiction, Pym drew on her own experiences to
shape her plot and characters. Her protagonists pursue their romantic goals within the confines of a church. Wilmet involves herself in parish life largely to stave off the pangs of ennui. Besides, she
might once again catch a glimpse of Piers at a service. Still, Benet's
suggestion that Wilmet's plan of "an extra-marital romance" is in-
consistent with her desire to "draw closer to the church" misses the
point. Wilmet is merely entertaining old-fashioned Victorian fantasies, like those of Barbara Bird and Barbara Pym. Eventually,
Wilmet gives up her fantasies about Piers without too much trouble—as Nardin says, in favor of "friendships with women, the
church, and marital affection." Sex plays little role in her interest in
the first place.[18] Throughout Pym's novels, attracting the attention
of men or finding a husband matters, not sexual relations. Therefore church is an excellent place for observing handsome men, both
in and out of the pulpit.

In fact, Pym's interest in her possible conversion of her character
Father Marius Ransome to the Roman Catholic church reflects aspects of her friendship with Robert Smith. September 8, 1955, she

recorded that she almost had a row with Smith about the Anglican church's South Indian church policy (*VPE*, 195). During the 1950s, the young civil servant visited church services and graveyards with Pym and lent her a novel called *The Call of the Cloister*, which gave Pym the idea of Mary Beamish's attempt to enter a nunnery. Smith also wrote Pym that a Father Morcom was to be instituted in July 1955 but to everyone's surprise would get married first. Pym turned those events into Father Ransome's marriage and installation. In another letter Smith mentioned a selfish vicar who would not put up a fellow clergyman, a story that Pym turned into Father Thames's refusal to house Father Ransome in the vicarage.[19]

Likewise, Pym's interest in Pier's homosexual relationship with his flatmate, Keith, was based on personal observations. Although it comes as a surprise to Wilmet that Piers is a homosexual, Pym had begun the novel with that idea. She was eager to incorporate observations of two young men who lived near her in Barnes and whose style of living fascinated her. Their unconventional unorganized lives marked the beginning of the counterculture, and Pym was usually intrigued by signs of social change. With her sister's help and the assistance of Bob Smith and Hazel Holt, all of whom enjoyed the challenges of the task, Pym unearthed a great deal of information about the young men. Burkhart calls those notes "the oddest pages in her diaries," perhaps overlooking their contributions to Pym's novels. At first Pym viewed the young men from a distance. For some time, they were not even aware of her existence, although she watched them nearly every day. Even after she learned their names, she often continued to call the taller "Bear," and the shorter "Squirrel" or "Treasure." Pym promptly made up stories about them based on her observations. After Bob Smith left London, she continued to keep him informed whenever she heard anything new. When repeating new gossip, she often delighted to note that it was impossible to keep straight what information she had learned legitimately and what surreptitiously. Once again, fact and fiction blended in her imagination.[20]

Squirrel, the chief object of her fascination, was years younger than she, but Pym often preferred younger men. His aloofness attracted her. In adolescence she had admired a haughty bank clerk, and later on her Oxford moderator, neither of whom paid much attention to her. Pym carefully recorded the various times when Squirrel snubbed or failed to notice her sister and herself. Over the years she developed a fantasy about her feelings for him—once she even wrote a sentimental little poem about him.[21]

Pym reacted to her sightings like an experienced birdwatcher. Far from taking her feelings seriously, she played at being in love with Squirrel. Later she used these emotions when she described Dulcie's confused feelings about Maurice Clive in *No Fond Return of Love*. Dulcie muses that their marriage would never have worked. She would have been "a little older and a little taller and a great deal more intelligent than the husband."[22] Still Dulcie does not deny her heartache. She concludes that "perhaps it is sadder to have loved somebody 'unworthy,' and the end of it is the death of such a very little thing, like a child's coffin, she thought confusedly" (*NFR*, 54).

Two implications of Pym's fascination with this homosexual household are worth noting. To a large degree the situation duplicated her Oxford habit of tracking men to their lairs. Of course, she still longed to invade what was clearly a sacrosanct masculine domain, but she had refined her methods over time. At nineteen, she had lived her life in public. All her friends knew about her yearning for Henry Harvey; her emotional anguish was common property. In middle age, however, Pym pursued her quarry with great discretion. She found it easy to exercise her powers of observation on the periphery. The men never knew they were under surveillance. For more than four years in careful field notes she recorded their comings and goings, their clothing, jewelry, friends, animals, cars, and other sundry details of their daily lives.

Although Pym speculated about their love lives, it was the accoutrements of her neighbor's existence that really captured her attention. Moreover, even though her friends and sister assisted her endeavors, she did not mention her sentimental attachment to Squirrel. They were oblivious to how much energy went into her careful notes. On November 12, 1956, about a year after she started her observations, Pym wrote herself a stern message that it was time she stopped. Despite the warning, she could not. Gradually the number of literary entries began to diminish.[23] Pym continued to pride herself on keeping her feelings secret although she knew she paid a price for her privacy. In *No Fond Return of Love* the narrator comments that "bereavement was in some ways the most comfortable kind of misery . . . the unhappiness of love was usually more lonely because so often concealed from others" (*NFR*, 101).

Pym needed this material for her novels. She lacked any other serious love interest. The misery she had experienced with Henry Harvey and Gordon Glover had long since diminished, and she lacked fresh experiences for her fiction. Watching Bear and Squirrel gave her new ideas, and she made the most of the opportunity. She often followed Bear to church, where he played the organ. She and her sister became active members of his parish, St. Laurence's. In time St. Laurence's became St. Luke's parish in *A Glass of Blessings,* especially its social gatherings.

Although none of her readers could possibly have suspected as much, *A Glass of Blessings* is as much a *roman à clef* as *Some Tame Gazelle.* Pym attributed characteristics of Bear and Squirrel to a variety of minor figures. She converted the organist Bear, who sometimes doubled as the server, into Bill Coleman, the head server at St. Luke's. Bear influenced the novel in other ways as well. When he moved out of Barnes in 1956 to set up a separate establishment in London with his friend Paul, Pym observed him at church and visited him at the florist's where he worked. She used Bear's relationship with Paul as the basis for Piers's affection for Keith. Later on Pym became their friend. On August 30, 1958, she and her sister visited their flat, but when she was writing *A Glass of Blessings* she drew on her imagination to describe their quarters. Squirrel's presence can be felt in various ways as well. He inspired a minor character, a friend of Bill Coleman, who teaches at a secondary modern school. More important, Squirrel, as well as Paul, contributed to Pym's characterization of Keith. Squirrel's name even appears in the early manuscript.[24]

Like most writers, Pym drew her protagonists from several different sources. Piers is an amalgam of several of her male friends and aloof ex-lovers. In an early manuscript draft, Pym suggests that he had been in the navy but was not an officer, a detail which recalls an old navy friend named Starky. (On her tour of duty in Naples during the war, Pym had a romantic entanglement with Starky. In her diary on September 26, 1944, she described him as being attractive but of a lower social class [*VPE*, 169].) In another note she contemplates the idea of Piers having the ruined good looks of her old friend, Gordon Glover. Wilmet and Piers's stroll through the park past the furniture repository was similar to one Pym took with Bob Smith on October 23, 1955 (*VPE*, 196). Furthermore, Hilary Walton suggested that Piers was largely based on Bear.[25]

To a surprising degree, Pym identified with her heroine Wilmet. On the surface, the elegant Wilmet seems most unlike her creator. Yet regardless of the obvious differences caused by marriage and a substantial income, Wilmet represents the kind of person Pym sometimes feared she was. In a literary notebook the author recorded on May 5, 1955, "The knowledge might come to me—and I dare say it would be a shock—that one wasn't a particularly nice person (selfish, unsociable, uncharitable, malicious even)" (*VPE*,

194). Pym habitually mixed personal statements with passages from works in progress, making it impossible to know exactly to whom she refers, herself, Wilmet, or both of them. The writer Joyce Carol Oates once told an interviewer, "My writing is full of lives I might have led. . . . A writer imagines what could have happened, not what really happened."[26] Pym's ambiguous remark, however, indicates her concern for the opinion of others. Although she literally invented Wilmet's funny but uncharitable comments about her acquaintances' clothing, speech patterns, and class behavior, she did not endorse all her protagonist's prejudices.

Yet some of Wilmet's habits and complaints about the shortcomings of men were typical of Pym herself. Wilmet muses at her birthday dinner that her husband Rodney and his friend James Cash will probably assume that the special dishes were "no more than was due to them" (*GB*, 13). That charge is very like the moment in *Jane and Prudence* when Nicholas eats his two eggs, happily oblivious to the fact that his wife has only been given one.[27] Wilmet also shares Pym's strong bump of curiosity. She is not above tracking down the man who interests her, even though in her case a plan for a stealthy visit to Piers's flat eventually falls through.

At this point, however, we need to put Pym's penchant for spying into reasonable perspective. Many writers and critics have urged writers to observe closely the actions of others. Henry James often commented that a writer must be observant and was aware that at times such observations could be intrusive. Elizabeth Bowen also developed a complex attitude toward spying in *The Death of the Heart*. More recently, the spy novelist John le Carré has claimed that a writer, like a secret agent, needs to maintain "a state of watchfulness." To that he adds, "A writer, like a spy, must prey upon his neighbors." Some literary critics would agree. Mikhail Bakhtin has declared that spying and eavesdropping remain the only efficient method of obtaining information about private life. He finds prying figures playing significant roles in the novel from the ancient Greeks to the contemporary picaresque. Patricia Meyer Spacks also connects the narrative of gossip to the novel.[28]

Snooping and spying played a complex role in Pym's life. She had, of course, first learned the pleasures of detective work in childhood from her family. According to Hazel Holt, the entire family enjoyed creating what they called a "saga."[29] Pym never lost her taste for the joys of the chase. Her vivid imagination and sense of fun allowed her at dull moments to recreate the same kind of excitement and pleasure that her family had shared. Not only did she enjoy collecting information, but the shared quest drew her friends together into a close family-like network.

At every stage keeping secrets and observing others were matters of great importance to her. Not only did Pym repeatedly track attractive men, but her manuscripts are punctuated with references to snooping, spying, and tracking. Discovering the secrets of her neighbors apparently provided an important emotional outlet for her, just as it did for Elizabeth Taylor's first heroine, Julia, in *At Mrs Lippincote's*. At the end of that novel, we discover that Julia has been prying into the lives of mere acquaintances to avoid facing the anxiety that her philandering husband has aroused in her.[30]

Pym sought reasons to justify her spying. She noted that anthropologists created a profession from the same activity, by analyzing the behavior of the people they observed. Reading the novels and journals of Denton Welch, who turned spying into an art form, further encouraged Pym's grand operation. He describes watching his neighbors to get material for his writing. (During Pym's lifetime his journals were published in a bowdlerized fashion in order to hide evidence of his homosexuality. What remained was his fascination with churches and graveyards and his penchant for spying.) October 5, 1955, Pym claimed to have become "besotted with Denton Welch," and she referred to him often (*VPE*, 192). His early death aroused her sympathy, and his hypnotically intense style entranced her. She immediately wrote Bob Smith of her new find in order to enlist his interest.[31] She went on Denton pilgrimages, in which she retraced his tours of country churches and graveyards. Encouraged by his example, she increased her efforts to write down conversations she overheard and to record telling details. Modelling her behavior on Welch provided her with ample justification for her own actions. She felt that his prose vindicated his fact-gathering techniques.

Still, spying suggests that Pym was deeply dissatisfied with some aspects of her life. Working at the International African Institute had lost its charm; she no longer revelled in recording odd tidbits about anthropologists like those in her earlier notebooks. The work continued to be demanding without offering the hope of promotion or a salary increase. The sisters' social life, like that of most middle-aged people, had become somewhat routine as well. Their circle of friends was no longer expanding, except for the welcome addition of Robert Smith. Pym had several other problems as well. Her books were no longer reliable sellers, and to make matters worse, her father went bankrupt in 1956. He had countersigned some second mortgages for clients who later defaulted. According to Hilary Walton, the sisters felt obliged to pay off his debts and support him, even though their means were limited. Pym's salary was especially meager; by 1974 she was earning only £1,764 per annum. She found watching her neighbors an irresistible antidote to her problems.[32]

Most important, Pym was running out of fresh material for novels, which explains why she was eager to gather new ideas. She had to strain to create the sort of believable details that enrich *Jane and Prudence* and *Less than Angels*. In "Finding a Voice," the radio talk Pym gave in 1978, she reported that the first three of her novels had been "comparatively easy to dig out." *Less than Angels*, her fourth, combined all the worlds she had ever inhabited, a factor which encouraged inspiration. By the time she came to *A Glass of Blessings*, excavation became more difficult. To amplify her plots, as well as to avoid brooding, Pym continued to take notes on her fascinating neighbors until they finally moved away from Barnes on May 7, 1959.[33]

By the time Pym started *No Fond Return of Love* a note of depression had begun to penetrate her writing. Her books were not selling well. *A Glass of Blessings* had sold even fewer copies than *Less than Angels*, partly as a result of negative early reviews. April 29, 1958, when Pym wrote in her literary notebook that the three reviewers in question were women, she wondered sadly if they were all younger than she (*VPE*, 199). As a result, *No Fond Return of Love* depicts a darker vision of the world than does *A Glass of Blessings*. In her view, the hazards for single older women were increasing dramatically. For example, the sensitive Dulcie of *No Fond Return of Love* is troubled by "a new and particularly upsetting beggar selling matches" (*NFR*, 39). Although Dulcie believes that the Welfare State ought to eliminate sights like that, nonetheless she feels some odd kinship with him, based on a sense of their mutual deprivation. She thinks, "Such a way of earning one's living seemed even more degrading than making indexes for other people's books or doing bits of hack research in the British Museum and the Public Record Office" (*NFR*, 40). An early manuscript had been grimmer still. Pym had imagined her heroine to be a cranky older woman, who worries in a paranoid fashion about the infringement of one's civil rights, rather like an older character in her favorite novel by Louise Field Cooper. Unfortunately, circumstances would often prove the woman to be right.[34]

To make matters worse, suburbia is no longer the place of family love as it was in *Less than Angels*. Instead misfits and eccentric loners inhabit it, all of whom have found slightly strange substitutes for more normal kinds of human affection. Next to Dulcie lives Mrs. Beltane, who makes a child out of her obnoxious dog Felix, just as Squirrel fussed over his dog. Secret eating and spying, which offers a kind of vicarious existence, are all that is left to many of the characters.[35]

In Dulcie's world men clearly have the advantage over women. Early in the novel, Dulcie asks Viola if the conference she attends could possibly be composed entirely of people who, like herself, "correct proofs, make bibliographies and indexes, and do all the rather humdrum thankless tasks for people more brilliant than ourselves?" (NFR, 13).[36] Very quickly, she learns that there is a privileged inner circle. Aylwin Forbes, who gives a speech about "some problems of an editor" (NFR, 25), cannot be classified in such a dreary fashion. He sits in the place of honor at the speaker's table, and when he faints in the course of giving his speech, he is immediately surrounded by a band of admiring women (NFR, 28).

To a large degree, the problems that women face in the novel are those of their creator. Pym uses a minor character, a librarian named Jessica Foy, to voice some personal complaints. Miss Foy protests to herself that Forbes is hardly the best person to discuss the problems of an editor. He "is fortunate in having an exceptionally able assistant editor," no doubt someone very like Barbara Pym herself (NFR, 27). Throughout the novel, professional women serve men while the men blithely accept their privileges. The only woman to resist this role is Miss Faith Randall, an indexer and fellow lecturer, who finds Aylwin's smugness hard to bear. She tells Dulcie that he is "a rather good-looking man who has made a mess of his marriage, by all accounts—I shouldn't have thought that was rare at all" (NFR, 228).

The novel is divided into two uneven parts, based on different literary models. The first is realistic but grim. It describes the heroine's deprived world and inferior status. The second is based on fantasy and fairy tale and provides an unconvincing story book ending for the heroine. Its positive conclusion allows it to be classified as a rather weak example of what Margaret Gullette has called "midlife progress narratives."[37] Both sections were connected to Pym's life in some way: the first to her daily life, the second to her fantasies. The disjunction between the two genres suggests that real life offered Pym very few realistic models for happiness; retreating to fantasy was her only option.

Dulcie as a character has both the weaknesses and the strengths of her creator. On the one hand, she seems to accept the low esteem of women as inevitable; on the other, she has the energy to seek different solutions. She uses her imagination and her detective abilities, Pym's two strong points, to achieve her goal. For example, Dulcie has a deprecating way of describing her work as a kind of service to those who are more intellectual than she (*NFR*, 13). That seems the kind of thing Pym might have said about her job in one of her low moments. Yet Dulcie is more socially isolated than her author or indeed than any of the heroines of Pym's early novels. An orphan, she lives alone in suburban Barnes without any close friends. She has been recently jilted by her fiancé, Maurice Clive, a younger man like Pym's neighbor Squirrel, who works in an art gallery.[38]

Not only does Pym describe women's inferior roles, but she also depicts the changing status of old and young in society. In Pym's youth, rich elders could order the young around with impunity. By the late 1950s, the young, far from fearing their elders, tend to patronize them. For example, upon learning that Dulcie's love affair "had 'gone wrong,'" her niece, Laurel, condescends to her (*NFR*, 45). For a time, it seems that Laurel, and young women of her generation, have usurped the powerful position once occupied by imperious old women, like Miss Doggett, Miss Moberley, and others in Pym's early fiction. Laurel appears to be a barrier to her middle-aged aunt's happiness, by temporarily encouraging the attention of Aylwin Forbes, who is much older than the young girl.[39]

To make matters worse, in the novel family cohesion seems to have disappeared as well. Dulcie gets little support from her sister. Laurel's mother is trapped in an unhappy marriage in which her husband behaves like others who "were so preoccupied with their harmless hobbies that they would hardly have noticed if their wives had been there or not" (*NFR*, 115–16). She has no energy to help her daughter or her sister.

Yet, Pym concludes that life is not really easy for any of the characters. The shortage of eligible men is so acute that it affects even the attractive Laurel. True, she gains the attention of both Aylwin Forbes and Dulcie's neighbor Paul Beltane, but both are inadequate. Aylwin is much too old for Laurel, a fact that he overlooks entirely, but Laurel does not. Paul seems more promising, but eventually his gentleness baffles the young girl, who has stereotyped notions of masculinity. Pym based his character on Bear's friend Paul. The two men worked at a florist's shop, like Paul Beltane, and one Christmas they made two hundred holly wreathes, a detail that Pym borrows for her character.[40] Given Paul Beltane's original source, it is not surprising that he fails to make a satisfactory lover for Laurel.

Robert Long credits Dulcie with being "the spunkiest of Pym's heroines." Yet she is notable, as she tells acquaintances at a conference, chiefly for her fascination with doing "research into the lives of ordinary people." It provides "a sort of compensation for the dreariness of everyday life" (*NFR*, 18). In time her hobby comes in handy. When Dulcie meets the narcissistic Aylwin, as Rossen points out, she knows exactly how to go about tracking him down.[41] In a series of comic scenes, she looks him up in *Who's Who* where she finds his "recreations . . . [are] 'conversation and wine' " (*NFR*, 53). She gathers information about his clergyman brother, Neville, of whom she learns by chance.

After Dulcie discovers the connection between Aylwin and Neville, the novel changes direction entirely. It becomes a fairy tale in which Pym gives full reign to her fantasies. Dulcie travels to Taviscombe to find out more about Aylwin's family, just as Pym went to Minehead in 1957, to investigate the origins of her friends Squirrel and Bear. The high point of that expedition occurred when Pym managed to walk unobserved into the Carlton Private Hotel, run by Squirrel's family. In a notebook she described the hotel living room in exact detail, expressing her joy at being able to gather information successfully.[42] Pym's account of the episode is nearly as breathless with girlish excitement as some of the scenes of Chelsea in her first completed novel, *Young Men in Fancy Dress*. An accurate description of the hotel lounge appears in *No Fond Return of Love* (*NFR*, 179).

Pym's visit to Minehead gave her much personal pleasure but radically altered the direction of her novel. As a result of her trip, she struck up friendships with Squirrel's and Bear's mothers, an event which suggests that her affection for the two young men was genuine. At the same time, the excitement stirred up Pym's yearnings for romance, temporarily overpowering her ironic, detached view of life and altering her artistic perceptions. Writing about Dulcie offered Pym an opportunity to improve upon her own life story. In real life Pym had to substitute friendship with unmarriageable men, like Bear and Squirrel, for romance. Toward the end of the novel Maurice offers Dulcie a sexless relationship as his confidante, a role she staunchly refuses (*NFR*, 239–40). It gave the author great pleasure in awarding Dulcie what life had not given her—a man.

Working like a magician Pym alters the landscape of the book. The novel ceases to be ironic and reverses the strategy of her earlier fiction, in which she withheld the expected romantic ending. As a result the contrived plot satisfies few readers. Benet has sagely observed that Pym, the "generous creator" allows all of her characters to have their hearts' desires, but to do so, she converts her novel from a comedy into a romance. Still, by the end, Aylwin is so thoroughly discredited that he hardly seems a prize worth having. (In a 1958 literary notebook, Pym contemplated having him be a distant relative of the landed aristocracy but later changed his pedigree.)[43] Pym had not lost her habit of paying backhanded compliments to the disdainful but handsome men she admired. Her description of Aylwin sounds like the young clerk in "Midland Bank" or Henry Harvey's entrancing but "repulsive sneering smile," recorded in her Oxford diary on January 25, 1933 (VPE, 19).

Most critics agree that No Fond Return of Love fails to meet the standards of Pym's earlier work. Pym badly needed some new experiences to revitalize her fiction. Lacking any such welcome change, she substituted the attenuated material from her tracking diaries. Curiously, the plot has another personal subtext of which Pym was only partly aware. Benet has noted how many of the characters play roles and that all of them are seen by the others from vastly different angles. In early notes for the novel, Viola is almost Dulcie's equal in importance; in the novel her role is slightly diminished.[44] Both characters represent facets of Pym's own character. The untidy Viola, who applies lipstick "almost savagely, as if she were determined to make herself look as unlike somebody who worked on the dustier fringes of the academic world as possible," is an older and drabber version of Sandra, Pym's chosen persona at Oxford (NFR, 13). In her late twenties, Viola still has Sandra-like mood swings and is often troubled by her emotions. She dismisses Dulcie as "half way to being a dim English spinster" because the older woman accepts her minor role in life without any complaint (NFR, 12). Dulcie, on the other hand, is an attractive version of the Stevie Smith, English spinster role that Pym claimed for herself early in 1938, in her lengthy letter to the Harveys and Liddell (VPE, 69).

Pym took the opportunity to justify her choice of that role: initial appearances turn out to belie the true worth of her characters. Viola turns out to be an invented name; her real name is Violet. She is a deeply conventional woman, easily satisfied by the attentions of Bill Sedge, a Viennese refugee. Benet comments that when Bill Sedge tells her that violet is her color, Viola is "astounded into acknowledging the hitherto rejected name."[45] In contrast, Dulcie looks conventional, but she is not. She expresses disappointment when she learns that Viola just wants to be loved: "In a sense, Dulcie felt as if she had created her and that she had not come up to expectations, like a character in a book who had failed to come alive . . ." (*NFR*, 167). Moreover, Dulcie has the courage to pursue the beautiful Aylwin until she finally wins him. For all her self-effacing qualities, which she shares with her creator, Dulcie refuses to abandon her ideals. Still, in the effort to justify her own fantasies, Pym forsook her own high standards of behavior. Dulcie behaves more like one of Catherine Oliphant's pulp fiction heroines than like the delightfully independent Catherine herself.

Pym was no feminist ahead of her time. Kate Heberlein has treated the subject with some tact, acknowledging that Pym did not consider herself to be one. Nonetheless, Heberlein asserts that in one respect Pym "might even be classified as a radical feminist . . . because she portrays women as not only fundamentally different from men but also as superior."[46] Pym's convictions, however, were more traditional than Heberlein realizes. After all, feminism means more than being aware that women are often exploited by men. For generations traditional women have believed that women are morally superior to men. In most cases, superiority was all that they could claim as compensation for the absence of meaningful power. Such views were common in the days before feminism and are still held by traditional women. In reality, Pym was a middle-aged romantic, who justifiably often felt discouraged by her lot in life. Her career as a novelist was obviously deteriorating. As late as 1963, *No Fond Return of Love* had sold fewer copies than any of Pym's early novels. To make matters worse, her love life was nonexistent. She had to invent feelings for Squirrel to be able to maintain her ability to love. As a result, her novel shows signs of an incompletely repressed female masochism, suppressed anger, and the kind of self-deprecating humor that marked the tradition of female writing in prefeminist days, and which has survived into the postfeminist era as well.

Nevertheless, when one looks at her work from a slightly different angle, Pym's resilience seems quite remarkable. Regardless of the stress and emotional impoverishment of her daily life, she took pride in her ability to lead a normal life and keep a cheerful countenance. Her novel hints at her frustrations, but for the most part she resisted any temptation to share her private feelings with her audience or anyone else, except her sister. Of course, hiding her feelings increased the novel's muted quality and its dull atmosphere.

Even the blurb Pym wrote for the book jacket sounds dreary. She wrote Bob Smith on October 21, 1960, that rereading the book made her feel sad (*VPE*, 200–201).

Not every reader would agree with Pym's judgment, of course. Shortly after publication she received an admiring fan letter from Rachel Cecil, Lord David's wife, in which she expressed her appreciation for the novel's moments of insight and wistfulness. Pym's friend Honor Wyatt liked it enough to promote it for a reading on the "Woman's Hour," although she feared it might be too sophisticated for that audience.[47] Four years later in 1965, *No Fond Return of Love* was recorded and broadcast on that radio program, but sales still did not rise. Changes, however, were in the offing in Pym's personal life, which eventually led to the revitalization of her career.

5

The Expansion of Empathy

Pym began her next novel, *An Unsuitable Attachment*, in a somewhat unsettled frame of mind. The two sisters had moved from Barnes to North London in early 1960. The location offered the writer a new and exciting area to explore, but her literary diaries also reveal occasional moments of melancholy. The last few months in Barnes had been a difficult transition. Her surveillance of her young neighbors ended abruptly in May 1959, when Squirrel and his friend were unexpectedly evicted from their flat. About the same time, the sisters themselves faced a large increase in rent. Finding the amount too much for their salaries, they decided to buy a house in North London, a changing district offering affordable housing.[1]

In retrospect, it is apparent that leaving Barnes marked the close of an era in the author's life. At forty-seven, Pym had not achieved popular success, and she had no reason to expect that the rest of her life would bring any dramatic improvement in her situation. The new neighborhood was considered to be less desirable than the previous one. She could no longer divert herself by taking field notes. But Pym's reaction to that series of losses illustrates her resilience. Within a month, Bear and Paul had become real friends, more than replacing her fantasy relationship with Squirrel. Indeed the sisters saw them so frequently that by June 1959 Pym had declared that further notetaking was unnecessary.[2]

For a while, Pym was distracted by the necessity of furnishing a new house. According to the 1960 literary notebook, trips to Gamage's to buy curtain rods absorbed her time. Yet she quickly returned to writing. The few notes that she made during that period indicate that she was beginning to generate a new plot. In one entry Pym described the unexpected sight of tomatoes in a window, which later became the love apples that catch Sophia's eye (*UA*, 16).[3] At the end of January 1960, Pym reported observing a discomforted young man at Solemn Evensong and Benediction. That image led to a fantasy about a man who might revisit a church to recapture childhood or to relive a nostalgic recollection of "a beautiful server or acolyte," an imagined scene that ultimately became part of the background of Rupert Stonebird (*VPE*, 200).

Pym could not altogether escape the sense of futility that marked *No Fond Return of Love*. She clung to her old subjects even though she had already exhausted many of her best ideas. She was well aware that the management at Cape had changed drastically. Her friends were already expressing concern about the possible fate of this book. On October 13, 1962, she wrote Bob Smith that Daniel George was still at Cape, despite Robert Liddell's report (*VPE*, 207). Apparently Liddell feared that George's departure would spell doom for Pym's manuscript. On the whole, Pym avoided such unpleasant reflections. As long as she could keep busy, she was able to ward off depressing speculations about her future.

Most serious writers alter their style considerably as they grow older. Of course, some stop creating altogether. Others, according to the psychoanalyst Elliott Jaques, survive the difficult transition, face their fear of death, and develop new artistic approaches in late life, based upon their recognition of an important paradox. The mature person realizes that human beings are capable of cruelty, stupidity, and evil actions, but they also possess the capacity to "repair," "mitigate," and "heal" the damage. Serenity comes, Jaques argues in language with religious overtones, when one accepts and integrates both extremes of the human condition.[4]

In 1965 he studied the careers of about three hundred male painters, composers, poets, writers, and sculptors. Of those who continue to work, he found that many experience "a decisive change in the quality and content of creativeness" in their late thirties, developing a more "sculpted" style. Unfortunately, Jaques, as was typical at that time, simply assumes that the lives of western male artists represents human behavior in its entirety, completely ignoring the role that race, ethnicity, class, and gender have in shaping our lives. He recognizes the importance of biological differences, remarking, "The transition [between youth and maturity] is often obscured in women by the proximity of the onset of changes connected with the menopause." In a later version of the same study, published 1980–1981, Jaques emphasizes the importance of developing a stage-theory analysis of life patterns, claiming "The significance of such stages is that they give a systematic picture of a general order to be found in the psychological development of everyone." Not only do other cultures express different attitudes toward aging, which may challenge the universality of Jaques's findings, but even within the confines of western culture, women's creative lives do not necessarily replicate male patterns. Carolyn Heilbrun, for example, argues persuasively that women experience this midlife transformation much later than men.[5] Yet despite the limitations of Jaques's database, his analysis of creativity in later life illuminates certain important aspects of Pym's experience.

One of Jaques's key points is that artists who face their fear of death find new avenues of expression. Retrospective analysis of the past is one way in which many older writers enrich their later fiction. For example, at approximately the same time Pym was drafting *An Unsuitable Attachment*, the older novelist Elizabeth Bowen was struggling to compose *The Little Girls* (1963). In that novel for the first time she recreated in her fiction long-repressed traumatic experiences from her girlhood.[6] Pym, regrettably, postponed such a journey into the past until a series of grave illnesses in her early sixties forced her to alter the literary persona she had constructed at such cost in her early thirties.

Therefore the atmosphere of *An Unsuitable Attachment* is attenuated and restricted. Pym was convinced that people of her sort were being pushed to the periphery. She felt that her genteel world was fast disappearing. She had little confidence that its replacement would have much use for middle-aged spinsters. Nostalgia and anxiety about the future dominate the novel—two qualities that did not endear it to the energetic Cape management.[7] Their refusal to publish was understandable; nonetheless, the novel is worth examining in some detail. Not only does it reveal Pym's state of mind at that time, but it contains some intriguing glimpses of social history that might otherwise be lost.

Although Pym was fascinated by the sights and sounds of her new habitat, the setting for her novel, she never developed the same passion for her characters. Ianthe, the librarian, seems a pale substitute for her lively forerunners. Pym tried to work up enthusiasm for her heroine, and has her identify with Emmeline Summers, the elegant, sophisticated, but scatty heroine of Elizabeth Bowen's *To the North*. Still, Emmeline is the more vital of the two, and Bowen's plot, the more dramatic.[8] Pym gives her protagonist a few positive characteristics, but most of Ianthe's reactions merely reflect the narrowness of her experience. On one occasion, Rupert observes that "Ianthe seemed to be very much the canon's daughter this afternoon" (*UA*, 217). Remaining static in character, she never learns to interpret events accurately or to judge human nature.

To make matters worse, John Challow, the unsuitable man she desires, lacks charm, nor are his limitations convincingly described. At the time, except for Squirrel, Bear, and Robert Smith, Pym had few men friends. Each contributed something to John's character and appearance. For instance, John's slightly tacky clothing came from her careful observations of the sometimes unconventional attire favored by Bear, Squirrel, and their friends.[9] These models, however, were totally inadequate for John as an object of love. Pym toyed with the idea of making him a sinister figure, but he remains a bland but unlikely choice for the fastidious Ianthe.

On the other hand, the vicar and his wife, Mark and Sophia Ainger, are portrayed with more success. Mark is what we now call a 1960s idealist, but Pym created him before that stance had become fashionable. His shyness, Pym recorded in her notes, resembles her diffident friend Bear.[10] Mark, aloof like all of Pym's favorite men, has "that remote expression sometimes found in the eyes of sailors or explorers . . . [and] the air of seeming not to be particularly interested in human beings—a somewhat doubtful quality in a parish priest, though it had its advantages" (*UA*, 17). Mark has deliberately chosen to work in a challenging parish, for reasons that are not entirely clear to his sometimes long-suffering wife. They struggle against the odds to provide a sanctuary for their genteel parishioners while continuing to minister to the needs of the West Indians.

Pym emphasizes that the life of a vicar has deteriorated dramatically since the days of Jane and Nicholas Cleveland in *Jane and Prudence*. In fact, as Jane Nardin points out, the vicarage world has lost its sense of community and purpose. Loyalty to family and church sustain many characters in Pym's early novels, some of whom specialize in keeping an eye on their neighbors. But London life in the 1960s, unlike the village or suburb of the 1950s, made it hard to know, let alone take care of one's neighbor. True, the members of St. Basil's continue to abide by older customs, but Pym does not suggest that their values can sustain them for long. Even the church has become marginal in daily life. St. Basil's is placed in a far corner of the district, "in the better section" of a transitional neighborhood.[11]

Critics have been quick to note the weaknesses of this novel. Its strengths have been largely overlooked, partly because some crucial passages were cut from the published version. Pym's acute portrayal of Mark Ainger, the reformer who ignores his own wife, was a harbinger of things to come. Pym saw his limitations but admired his racial tolerance. In the manuscripts, Pym included a West Indian family among Mark's active parishioners, Granville Jameson and his pushy mother. Granville, who is a server at St. Basil's, is inveigled by an archdeacon into being a server at an Anglo-Catholic church, but at the end he returns to St. Basil's, much to Mark's delight.[12] The whole episode proves that Mark is progressive on the race question, although human enough to be irritated when his black parishioners take advantage of his gentle nature. Cutting these passages eliminated many of Pym's observations about the complexities of life in a newly integrated parish.

Pym had a remarkable grasp of the complexity of people's behavior and feelings. In the early drafts the same character may make a bigoted remark one moment, and then transcend mere prejudice the next. For example, Daisy Pettigrew, the veterinarian's sister, startles guests at a vicarage dinner party by announcing that an African serves at the altar. Mark, needless to say, is momentarily confused. Granville Jameson, the server in question, is West Indian. When Mark rather cautiously comments that Granville is doing a very good job, Daisy replies that the Ethiopians were among the earliest converts to Christianity, the sort of non sequitur that never failed to delight Barbara Pym.[13]

Some of the older characters are less open-minded than Mark, but it would be a mistake to equate Pym's views with their social pronouncements. Entries in her notebooks indicate that she enjoyed racial diversity, although she understood why others might not. For example, she realized that Sophia's anxiety and depression, not mere class bias, make her dislike John Challow so passionately. Sophia needs a confidante but is too tactless and inept to be able to make one of Ianthe. Thus, Sophia distrusts John out of frustration and jealousy; he monopolizes a woman who might otherwise break Sophia's sense of isolation.

In general, Pym emphasizes the limitations and short-sightedness of all her characters in several different ways. She describes them as being in a state of siege. The very language that marks them as members of the upper middle class also provides a clue to their social insecurity. Characters find it difficult to behave appropriately without undue concentration, and are preoccupied with outward appearances and the correct choice of words, lest they appear ridiculous or condescending. Even so trivial a matter as ordering fish and chips in a working-class neighborhood shop becomes an embarrassing ordeal for Mark. Feeling like a foreigner, he fears he might "make a fool of himself by stumbling over the words, not using the correct terminology or not knowing what fish he wanted" (*UA*, 15). Pym's careful ear registered little linguistic signs of social uneasiness and charted the decline in meaning of certain words. In a dispassionate fashion the plot demonstrates the absence of agreement about what constitutes "suitable" behavior or a person. If there had been a consensus about the word's importance, it surely would not have appeared in the text with such monotonous regularity.

Although Pym's analysis of her characters' plight seems very apt, she was one of the few writers of the period who built a plot around the anxieties of abrupt social transformation. An aging spinster herself, she sympathized with marginal people whose timidity made them resist change. When traditional values are threatened, her characters do not feel liberated. Most of them lack self-confidence—except for the nurse, Sister Dew, who is comically self-assured. As a result, they gain surety from Ianthe's outward appearance of cool perfection. Edith Milton has observed that the others regard Ianthe as "a creature who owes it to everyone's high opinion of her to keep herself as inviolate as a rare antique."[14] She must provide the calmness and stability that will counteract their own confusion. No wonder they feel betrayed by her apparent lapse of good judgment when she marries.

For all her sensitive portrayal of the social scene, Pym's plot is vitiated. The women seem to have lost their bearings. Sophia and her sister, Penelope Grandison, are perplexed by the ambiguous and shifting roles for women. Neither is as independent as Mildred or Catherine, the liveliest of Pym's earlier heroines. Nonetheless, their confusions typified women of that generation, who came of age in the late fifties and early sixties, on the cusp of the feminist revolution.

Sophia comes the closest to representing Pym. Yet she exhibits the most puzzling behavior of all of the major characters. She never seems entirely comfortable with her role as a vicar's wife. She supports Mark in his effort to improve the world, but clearly she does not share his missionary feelings. Before she answers the vicarage doorbell, she must compose "her face into the patient sympathetic mask she wore when confronted with one of her husband's black parishioners" (*UA*, 220–21). Left to herself, she would no doubt have lived elsewhere. Even her style of beauty clashes with that seedy environment. She looks "like a figure in a minor Pre-Raphaelite painting" (*UA*, 39). She clearly loves Mark dearly, and they have a "second honeymoon" on the Italian expedition (*UA*, 196). Yet Mark is too remote and diffident to satisfy her need for intimacy. Thus she expends most of her energy on her cat, Faustina, and on her younger sister. Being childless merely adds to Sophia's sense of futility. Doubtless Pym learned about that woe from her colleague, Mrs. Holt, who to her great joy finally became pregnant in 1961.[15]

In general Sophia has two minds about the role of women. She accuses Edwin Pettigrew, Faustina's vet, of implying that clerical work is suitable for women but "slightly degrading" to men (*UA*, 103). Yet on another occasion, Sophia asks Mark plaintively, "what is there for women but love?" (*UA*, 152–53). Indeed, she tries too hard to find her sister a suitable husband. She questions Rupert Stonebird about his marital status so thoroughly that she sounds "almost like a chairman summing up at a meeting." The hapless Penelope is reduced to "listening to Sophia's probings with a kind of fascinated horror" (*UA*, 42).

Unfortunately, Penny, Sophia's "Pre-Raphaelite beatnik" sister, is no clearer about her desires than Sophia (*UA*, 39). In fact Penny merely parodies her sister's refined beauty. Although she dresses in her own inimitable style, she looks like a paler copy of Sophia. The nostalgic quality of the sisters' beauty represents their personal inadequacies, their inability to identify and ask for what they want in life. Penny is also the first of Pym's comic, sexually desperate heroines, the others being Phoebe in *The Sweet Dove Died* and Cressida in *An Academic Question*. At two points, Pym calls her a female Lucky Jim.[16] Unlike Jim Dixon, however, Penelope is surprisingly old-fashioned in many ways. She regards her publishing job as a temporary expedient, her real interest being husbandhunting. Like Sophia, she believes that life without marriage would be meaningless and frequently bemoans the shortage of appropriate suitors.

Nonetheless, Penny's pursuit of Rupert Stonebird is half-hearted, her reasons for marrying, unconvincing. Love seems beside the point. Whenever the two meet, the barriers of age and intellectual interest create traps of misunderstanding. Yet Rupert finds Penelope's childishness somewhat appealing. At twenty-five she looks and acts like a fledgling. The false eyelashes she wears to Ianthe's wedding give her eyes "a curious blundering, half-blind look, as if she could scarcely open them" (*UA*, 250). She resembles a newborn animal and has the disconcerting habit of appearing in ill-fitting finery. The dress she wears to Rupert's dinner party reminds him of "some kind of armour remembered from childhood play-acting" (*UA*, 122–23). By such imagery Pym implies that Rupert is on the verge of falling in love with Penelope. At Oxford after a dream about Henry Harvey, Pym had written in her diary that he felt pity for her, a feeling which she believed was close to love.[17]

Although Penny is representative of many women in the early 1960s, Pym's lack of irony is still striking. Other novels of the period, like Penelope Mortimer's *The Pumpkin Eater* (1962), refute the belief in salvation through marriage. By failing to challenge Penny's facile convictions, Pym endorsed the conventions of popular romance rather than those of sophisticated marriage comedy. Janice Radway has pointed out that romances "are experienced as a reversal of the oppression and emotional abandonment suffered by women in real life."[18] In Pym's case, the writer, not the reader, was clinging to romance conventions to compensate for emotional abandonment. In many ways dependent Penny is a throwback to Pym's earliest heroine, Princess Rosebud, suggesting some regression on Pym's part.

Pym's disappointing appraisal of Penny's predicament owes a great deal to the writer's personal circumstances at the time. Her views of sexual relations were influenced by the kind of self-absorbed man to whom she was habitually attracted. Most of them were decidedly uninterested in women, being either preoccupied literary scholars, anthropologists, or young men of ambiguous sexuality. Like her friends, Rupert Stonebird seems unsure about the benefits of matrimony. He is more comfortable with women who are ineligible. For instance, he saves his best understanding and empathy for Sophia, who by virtue of her marriage is perfectly safe. He feels puzzled by her strong feelings, telling Ianthe that Sophia's mildly depressed behavior reminds him of "the pessimistic Victorians" (*UA*, 216). He senses that she suffers from an unhappy passivity that colors her view of the world. In contrast, he shows little understanding of Ianthe. He waits to court her until after she has fallen in love with John. Rupert, furthermore, recovers quickly when Ianthe declines his attentions. After she marries John, he promptly turns to Penelope. She is the only suitable woman left. Like the men Pym knew best, he saves his deepest feelings for his work. Indeed, the anxiety he experiences when he, ever the anthropologist, sights Penny from afar at the conclusion of the novel, does not bode well for their future.

Despite the absence of male sexuality, this novel marks a breakthrough in Pym's general understanding of the lives of men. With the exception of Alaric Lydgate in *Less than Angels*, whose failed career also aroused Pym's sympathy, Mark Ainger and Rupert Stonebird are unusual in her fiction. Unlike most of her male characters, they are capable of the kind of understanding and diffidence that until then had been the hallmark of her women. Jane Nardin noted that Rupert shares some characteristics that Pym had always treated as being largely feminine.[19] In this novel Pym extends to her male characters the same empathic understanding that she does to her female. As a result, the depressed and hopeless complaints that marred *No Fond Return of Love* are missing from *An Unsuitable Attachment*.

Tracking her neighbors, and later becoming part of their lives, had modified Pym's belief that men had all the advantages. After the move to north London, Bear began to describe his Minehead upbringing and recounted some of the horrors of Squirrel's early life. The more Pym learned, the greater her sympathy became. Perhaps pity is not the way to a man's heart, but it was to hers. Her affection for her friends helped her understand why a proper young woman like Ianthe might fall in love with a man unlike "all the ranks of clergymen and schoolmasters stretching back into the past like pale imitations of men" (*UA*, 198).

Increasing involvement in the parish life of St. Laurence's Brondesbury taught Pym how vulnerable institutions could be in times of abrupt social change. The sisters had discovered the church when tracking the organist Bear to his lair. After they moved into the district, they became part of the church's inner circle and fought hard to keep it going despite its declining numbers. A copy of the church budget of December 31, 1963, is filed among her papers.[20] Over the years, as the congregation dwindled, everyone undertook unaccustomed roles. Many a time Pym described a "cosy" time around the vicarage table, moments that compensated for a sometimes lonely existence. Fighting hard for the church taught her that women were not the only vulnerable members of society. This discovery did not depress her. Instead, buoyed by the excitement of having made the move successfully and proud of her new friendships, she included men and faltering institutions in her boundary of concern.

A remark in Pym's notebook indicates that she was totally unprepared for a negative report from Cape: "To make *my* (literary) soup I don't need cream and eggs and rare shell fish, but just this old cod's head, the discarded outer leaves of a cabbage, water and seasoning." Unfortunately for the immediate success of her novel, few adult readers in the early 1960s longed for another novel about churches, cats, or "cosiness." As Robert Graham pointed out, trips to Rome and tea in the library seemed out of place in the political and social turmoil of the time.[21] Yet Pym had little choice about her subject matter. Her life was neither revolutionary or pathbreaking: domestic occurrences were all that was left.

Few writers of that period led such quiet lives. According to an April entry in Pym's literary notebook, the popular works of 1963 were William Burroughs's *The Naked Lunch,* the Bishop of Woolwich's startling book, *Honest to God,* in which he declared that God is dead, and the first legal publication of Henry Miller's *Tropic of Cancer* (*VPE,* 215). Not only was Pym's literary soup not spicy enough for public taste, but *No Fond Return of Love* had sold fewer copies than any of her other novels. As a result, when the nearly fifty-year-old Pym submitted *An Unsuitable Attachment,* she suddenly found herself without a publisher. In a letter of rejection, G. Wren Howard, Cape's surviving partner, cited financial reasons for the decision.[22]

Cape's decision precipitated the biggest crisis in Pym's career. For a time she seemed paralyzed and unable to adjust to the new circumstances. Very promptly she discovered how dispensable an aging, single woman was to literary circles. For example, she learned only indirectly that Daniel George, her old editor, was distressed by her fate. Shortly thereafter, he had a stroke. Later, when colleagues and friends tried to raise money in his behalf, no one asked Pym to contribute. Moved by the thought of George's plight, she went to considerable trouble to find out the correct place to send her donation.[23] To make matters worse, for a number of years Pym could not find another publisher. Still she revised *An Unsuitable Attachment* and sent it unsuccessfully on the rounds.

As a result of Pym's unhappiness, she had trouble finding the right focus for her next effort, the Rose manuscripts, which eventually became *The Sweet Dove Died.* In its earliest version the novel originated from a clerical scandal that Pym wrote Robert Liddell about in 1954. The incumbent of her church was imprisoned and lost his parish as the result of sexual misconduct. Throughout the 1950s until 1963, when she began writing what he called *The Tariff of Malpractice,* Liddell urged her to include the event in a high church novel.[24] These early manuscripts are autobiographical and often sound depressed. Pym wrote to vent her misery, just as she had in her twenties, with the same unsatisfactory results. In time Pym removed most of the personal material from the novel, but reading her drafts and notes can give much insight into her feelings at the time.

Early entries in her literary notebooks suggest that Pym began *The Sweet Dove Died* before Cape's letter. Bob Smith inadvertently started her thinking about its plot. In September 1961, Pym and her sister Hilary visited a furniture repository in Hendon to collect some furniture Smith had on August 1 offered to lend them for a year. To their surprise, they discovered that many pieces had already been carried off by Joan Wales, a new friend of Smith. On September 22, as soon as Pym had recovered from the immediate shock, she recorded in her literary notebook that the situation had similarities to Henry James's *The Spoils of Poynton*. Two years later, December 8, 1963, Pym wrote Smith that Wales had asked for the rest of the furniture. She added airily that the situation would fit nicely in a novel.[25] From this insight Pym developed the central rivalries of *The Sweet Dove Died*, the dispute of Leonora and Phoebe over the possession of James's furniture, as well as the even fiercer battle between Leonora and Ned for possession of James himself.

Pym was not able to apply this insight at once. An undated entry in the Rose notes reveals that Smith's casual treatment of women made her angry for a short time. Yet rather than complain to him, Pym began recording ideas for her next novel in her literary notebook, sometime between October 1962 and February 1963, before the Cape decision. The incident contributed to the theme of male betrayal in the novel, a motif which culminates in Rose Culver's startling pronouncement that "the odd thing about men is that one never really knows. . . . Just when you think they're close they suddenly go off" (*SDD*, 118). Not surprisingly, the manuscripts feature the deteriorating relationship between Rose and Oliver, a greatly transformed version of Pym's friendship with Smith. Besides using Smith, Pym added one of his friends, an antique dealer who eventually developed into James in *The Sweet Dove Died*.[26]

To complicate matters, on August 30, 1962, Pym met Richard Roberts, a young Bahamian antique dealer, who became the last love of her life. Unfortunately, that love was as one-sided as the others. Roberts had no romantic interest in the much-older woman, although he clearly enjoyed her company and admired her talent. But growing older had not made Pym wiser. She persisted in nursing her tender feelings for Roberts long after she grew aware of his indifference. At the same time, her professional instincts were aroused. His life was far less sheltered than hers and provided potential material for her novels. In a letter of March 1, 1965, she complained to Robert Smith that she regretted that most of Roberts's stories were "beyond my range" (*VPE*, 235). Throughout their friendship, Pym wrote Robert Smith about her misery over the deteriorating situation with Roberts. On one occasion, however, she reversed the situation by confiding in Roberts about Smith.[27]

In some ways the triangle was a tamer version of the tangled encounters of her youth with Henry Harvey and Gordon Glover. Pym felt as outnumbered in this situation as she had with Harvey and Liddell. Smith and Roberts, she assumed, talked about her behind her back.[28] Just as in the past, once Pym finally gave up all hope of a reconciliation with Roberts, she discovered that defeat had enriched her writing in surprising ways. Although the idea did not come to her immediately, she began to write about the often pitiable entanglements between aging women and younger men. Many of the insights into the relationships of her characters in *The Sweet Dove Died* originated with Smith, Roberts, and their circle of friends. Although Pym herself was a member of that group, she could not help observing the ironies of everyone's behavior.

In the early versions, the heroine, Rose Culver, is a woman in her fifties who leads a quiet, domestic life. The main theme is about abandonment, a problem that Pym first mentioned in the manuscript of *Less than Angels*. She referred to the theme in about twenty subsequent drafts and notebooks.[29] Rose has two important relationships that mirror Pym's. The first involves an older man named Oliver and the second a younger woman named Phoebe.

Oliver dominates the beginning. In the past Rose and he had been lovers, but he steadfastly refused to leave his wife. Now, they have learned to satisfy their impulses all too easily with a yearly lunch at his club, the sort of ritual that Pym and Bob Smith enjoyed when he returned briefly to England. Of course, Pym embellished her feelings about Smith considerably. For one thing, she was never in love with him. Yet lacking other men in her life, she almost regretted the absence of strong feeling between them. Creating an unsympathetic character like Oliver served several purposes. It allowed the writer some sense of control over her situation, some measure of revenge. Moreover, making Oliver far less appealing than Smith helped to reconcile her to her old friend. Pym had no wish to hurt Smith's feelings. Indeed when he read the manuscript, he did not recognize any trace of himself in Oliver. In 1978, he wrote how much he had enjoyed the village episodes that she had excised from *The Sweet Dove Died*.[30]

A crisis occurs in the manuscript when Oliver's wife dies, an event similar to the death of Henry Grainger's wife in *The Lumber Room*. Like Beatrice Wyatt, Rose no longer wants to marry the widower but feels hurt when Oliver promptly finds a replacement. The unexpected news of his engagement forces her to confide in Phoebe, a village friend. Phoebe, however, is too young to understand. Rose's relationships with Oliver and Phoebe paralleled Pym's real life situation. During the 1960s, Hazel Holt, Pym's younger colleague at *Africa*, became a close friend, to some extent displacing Robert Smith. Pym, however, obviously did not tell the younger woman everything. After Pym's death Mrs. Holt was shocked to learn of the many unhappy love affairs about which she had been told little (*VPE*, xiv). Differences in age and outlook had been a barrier. Comments in the Rose notes suggest that in midlife Pym took great pride in her ability to keep her own counsel.[31]

At that point, Pym could not resolve her plot. On April 7, 1964, about a year after the Cape decision, she wrote Philip Larkin that she had drafted ten chapters of the novel but felt discouraged (*VPE*, 226). Pym had reason enough to feel disheartened. Her friendship with Richard Roberts was foundering along with the novel, even though he still corresponded erratically. As the situation deteriorated, Pym searched for yet another way of expressing her feelings. She began sketching notes for a novel called "The Outcasts." It begins with a fifty-year-old woman being left at the altar by her husband-to-be, but Pym soon abandoned the effort.[32]

Writing compensated Pym for her misery with Roberts. The unpredictable nature of their relationship was enough to confuse anyone. In June 1965, he asked her to bid on some pictures at Christie's for him. Luckily, the experience provided a new beginning for *The Sweet Dove Died*, the scene where Leonora meets Humphrey and James at the auction. Nonetheless, Pym's happiness was short-lived. By October 20, 1966, she had informed Robert Smith that Roberts had dropped out of her life, and from then on she steadfastly attempted to put him out of her mind. She admitted in a letter to Smith, December 12, 1966, that possibly her sharpness had forced Roberts to flee (*VPE*, 240), but it was December 31, 1970, before she could admit how angry she had been. Her frustration gave her the idea about a young man jilting an older woman. By the time the novel was finally published in 1978, she had written Robert Smith that Roberts was unlikely to recognize himself.[33]

In 1968, Pym submitted copies of one of the drafts to Cape and to Chatto & Windus. They both promptly rejected it. At that point Pym asked Philip Larkin, who had been corresponding with her since 1963, to read the manuscript. On October 17, 1968, he advised her to cut out everything that diverted attention from Leonora's story. Three days later, Pym welcomed his editorial guidance (*VPE*, 247). Despite feeling inadequate to the task, Pym quickly and skillfully followed Larkin's advice. After she removed the village scenes, she expanded and enriched her portrayal of Leonora, her most extreme case of a sexually repressed heroine. As Jane Nardin has pointed out, Leonora's "narcissism" diminishes "even Prudence's vanity." Leonora is one of Pym's most complex characters, a thoroughly human mixture of strengths and weaknesses. She is the only spinster in Pym's fiction to use men as ruthlessly as the men in Pym's novels use women. (The sexually casual Iris Horniblow, a minor character in *An Academic Question*, is divorced.) From the beginning, however, Leonora insists that no one must make any sexual demands on her. James is really looking for a mother and is content to idealize Leonora. This makes him an ideal admirer and worth fighting for. Leonora fends off Phoebe's weak efforts to attract James, but the American Ned, the next lover, is too formidable to be defeated at all.[34]

To describe this conflict, Pym drew on some memories of her own. On one occasion, Leonora visits Keats's house in Hampstead with Ned and James and then briefly stops in Ned's apartment with the two young men. She feels excluded from their lives although the young men are solicitous of her. In fact Ned treats her like a fragile old woman (*SDD*, 154–58). Leonora's feelings were only too familiar to Pym. In 1966, she described an unpleasant dinner during which her male companions had flirted with each other.[35] Not only did that event inspire this scene, but Leonora's misery at Hampstead is recollected later in "Across a Crowded Room," a story Pym wrote in 1978.

Besides expanding Leonora's role, Pym developed two more pathetic friends, Meg and Liz. Pym discovered a sense of kinship with them as well. Liz, a bitter divorcée, dotes on cats, much as the Pym sisters did. Moreover, Meg, who adores her homosexual lover, Colin, tolerates his excesses much as Pym tried to endure Roberts's. On May 24, 1965, near the end of one extended period of estrangement, Pym rejoiced that she had hidden signs of her "fury and bitterness" from him (*VPE*, 235). In the same spirit of conciliation Meg bravely invites the latest male lover of her beloved Colin to her dinner party. Yet Roberts was not the only man to influence this novel. While Pym was rewriting the manuscript, she wrote to Bob Smith that her old friends Bear and Paul had just reappeared in her life.[36]

Despite Pym's massive revision, the next group of publishers turned the manuscript down as well. By April 13, 1973, she had offered *The Sweet Dove Died* to twenty-one publishers with no success (*VPE*, 273). One reader from Peter Davies wrote an extensive critique. He commented upon the beautiful construction of *The Sweet Dove Died* but felt the unpleasant world Pym described lacked interest. Like many other Pym critics, he disliked her attention to detail. He felt that she had little to say, and that the novel could not capture the reader's attention.[37] Although on November 6, 1970, Pym wrote Bob Smith about the rejection quite cheerfully, the point about minutiae must have hurt. Editors and reviewers often disliked the trivial details in Pym's work. This publisher's reader, however, missed the point. Leonora is the kind of neurotic character for whom claustrophobic trivialities have taken the place of larger human feelings.

In fact, Pym's portrait of Leonora is psychologically accurate in this respect. Leonora even has something in common with Flaubert's Madame Bovary, who also causes herself and others enormous pain when her romantic ideals make it difficult for her to adjust to an imperfect world. Flaubert, however, creates some early scenes that guarantee a degree of sympathy for his character, whereas Pym makes little effort to mitigate Leonora's coldness. She leaves it to the reader to develop compassion for her protagonist.[38] Yet, on May 27, 1969, she wrote Philip Larkin that she wondered what sort of reader could possibly see herself in Leonora (*VPE*, 250).

Pym's essentially fatalistic view of life made it hard for her to defend Leonora. In general, she avoided making any psychoanalytic explorations into her characters' pasts, preferring to give credence to their rationalizations. Pym's indifference to psychology can be traced partly to her upbringing. Her family as a whole did not indulge in much self-examination. In their effort to cover-up Frederic Pym's illegitimacy, her parents taught the girls to turn their curiosity outward. The Pym family played detective, investigating the lives of those around them, thereby exploring the secrets of others rather than those of their own. As a result of this systematic habit of projection, the temperamentally introspective Pym learned to distrust her brooding.

Erving Goffman has described what often happens to individuals who attempt to suppress detrimental information about themselves. They try hard to "pass"—to appear to be normal. At the same time, they also internalize the negative attitudes that society has toward people with their kind of affliction or problem. Sometimes, all the advice that an individual receives about behaving unobtrusively "stimulates the stigmatized individual into becoming a critic of the social scene, an observer of human relations." For some reason, Pym, not her father, became "situation conscious," detached rather than absorbed by action. It was she who developed an abiding interest in detective work and an obsession with characters who hide guilty secrets. Yet prying also made her uncomfortable. For most of her life she resisted the impulse to explore the fictional pasts of her characters. In 1969, she even wrote a wry little poem about how most of us try too hard to delve into our pasts.[39]

Luckily Pym had also developed a saving sense of humor; her family had been tolerant rather than judgmental about human foibles. Believing that neurotic behavior was unalterable, she readily accepted her own peculiarities and those of her characters. At this point in her career, however, Pym's prohibition against self-scrutiny had a cost. She overemphasized surface details, including her characters' love of food and clothing, in place of analyzing their psychic life. Thus, like Pym herself, Leonora is an expert at distracting herself from misery and often bravely disguises the signs of pain. An outsider might think that the hurt was minor, but the author knew otherwise. She understood intuitively that her heroine cannot alter her principles or free herself by force of will. The strength of Pym's novel lies in its clarity of presentation. Some may find the inability of the characters to take charge of their lives unappealing, but at that time Pym could not overcome her psychological limitations in life or in fiction.

Thus, Pym's immediate reaction to the rebuff of *The Sweet Dove Died* was to try external methods to make her work marketable. She tried to revive her dormant career by incorporating fresh subject matter into her next effort, *An Academic Question*. As a result, she included a series of controversial topics: abortion, quickie affairs, women living with younger men, the frustrations of graduate wives, riots at universities, and death in an old people's home. The strategy failed miserably.

In retrospect, Pym's attempt to borrow characters and situations from Margaret Drabble's novels was doomed to failure. Lacking first-hand knowledge of marriage, motherhood, or academia, Drabble's favorite topics at that time, Pym gathered her main ideas about life in the redbrick university from Philip Larkin's letters. During the radical period of the 1960s, he objected to the loss of social norms at Hull.[40] As it turned out, Pym was unable to flesh out the skeleton of Larkin's complaints. The novel never took on a life of its own. Instead most of the characters seem unpersuasive and flat. Further, the tone of the first person narration sounds depressed.

In Caro Grimstone, Pym carried her principle that the heroine should embody emotional deprivation to an extreme. Caro, manages to be dissatisfied with her life in a most uninteresting way. Relative affluence has relieved her from the burden of child care, but nothing else occupies her time. She pays little attention to her daughter Kate's welfare and development. In contrast, Margaret Drabble's protagonists are involved in the upbringing of their children, even though they are also preoccupied by their romantic entanglements. Of course Caro's marriage to Alan is a disaster. Like Sophia in *An Unsuitable Attachment*, Caro has married beneath herself socially, on the rebound from a failed love affair with a rising young MP, "a Byronic-looking cad with political ambitions" (*AQ*, 4). The cad is of course a 1970s version of Julian Amery, the young war hero who preoccupied Pym back in 1938.

Although this novel is clearly a failure, the interplay between romance and aging is important. Romance gets short shrift. Most of the men are viewed negatively. For example, Alan Grimstone, like Adam in *Civil to Strangers*, is smug. He treats his wife like a social possession. Like Adam in *Civil to Strangers*, he would rather type than make love (*AQ*, 13).[41] Caro unfortunately lacks the spunk of Adam's wife Cassandra, who departs for Hungary when she can no longer abide Adam's selfishness. Caro does not admire Alan, but she abets him in his efforts to steal a manuscript belonging to a retired missionary, even though she worries about the ethics of doing so. She says feebly, "it would be nice if I could do something to please Alan" (*AQ*, 25).

The family of Bahamian expatriates to whom Caro turns for relief from boredom is not much better. They consist of an unlikely sociologist named Coco, and his mother, Kitty. She is engaged in an act of historic preservation, the rescue of her eternal youth. In a letter to Bob Smith, October 31, 1971, Pym volunteered that Coco and Kitty were something like Richard Roberts and his mother (*VPE*, 264), but certain aspects of Coco are more like Smith himself. In particular the picnic scene, in which Caro complains about Alan's infidelity is reminiscent of an outing Pym took with Smith.

In sheer misery on July 7, 1967, Pym "let fly about Richard" (*VPE*, 243). Burkhart has astutely noted that Coco and his mother are caricatured in this novel, Pym being both too far away and too close to her topics.[42]

In contrast to the weak younger men, aging characters provide some genuine interest in the novel. Pym's portrayals of older characters, beginning with Edith Liversidge in *Some Tame Gazelle*, suggest that she had long been instinctively aware of the psychological alterations of late life, recently described by the psychologist David Gutmann. According to Gutmann, in later life both sexes "can reclaim the sexual bimodality that was hitherto repressed and parceled out between men and women." Older women "repossess the aggressive 'masculinity' that they once lived out vicariously through their husbands." In contrast, older men find it possible to become more gentle and childish than they were before.[43]

Thus, Kitty's aging sister, Dolly, in *An Academic Question*, has given up men for hedgehogs.[44] Worry about their welfare makes Dolly decline to leave town at any time. Once a previous neighbor refused to feed the animals in her absence (*AQ*, 15). Yet Dolly relishes her independence and speaks forthrightly and honestly to Caro at all times. She smokes excessively and runs a junk shop to benefit needy animals. Her scenes enliven an often uninspired text, which explains why much later, Pym transferred some of her eccentricities to Miss Lickerish, a marvelous minor character in *A Few Green Leaves*.

The novel contains other aging characters as well. For example, Caro volunteers to read to an old man, Mr. Stillingfleet, who dies in the course of the novel. Stillingfleet is never described, and he says very little. Yet years before he had written a book, the manuscript of which Alan Grimstone covets. When he dies, Caro attempts to stave off grief by thinking rude thoughts about an old resident who complains about the amount of explicit sex in plays—"you pathetic old creature with your too-bright lipstick and your raddled old face. Nothing's meant for you now" (*AQ*, 53).

Another older character, Alan's department head, Crispin Maynard, is treated like a figure in a genre painting. He often appears in domestic scenes, surrounded by grandchildren. When Caro sees him walking with his dog in the hills surrounding the town, he reminds her of one of Wordsworth's sturdy old men, yet Pym rarely describes Crispin's thoughts and feelings. When his retirement portrait is unveiled, Caro thinks that it discloses a "vulnerable side that all human beings have, the inner doubts, the cry for help—things one didn't associate with Crispin at all." Moments later she decides that she has "been stupidly over-imaginative to read anything disturbing into it" (*AQ*, 165).

Ironically the episode exposes Caro's vulnerability, not Crispin's. What he thinks about his new status is never mentioned. Instead, when he hangs about the department, Caro compares him to an actor who cannot leave the stage gracefully (*AQ*, 160). In actual fact, Crispin's difficulties were based on Professor Daryll Forde, Pym's editor at *Africa*. Newly retired from his university post, he had begun spending his free time at the journal. In a letter to Philip Larkin on February 1, 1970, Pym reported that Forde was making everyone at the I.A.I. "rather fractious" (*VPE*, 254).

Pym's preoccupation with older characters demonstrates that her interests were beginning to shift. Like most aging writers she was no longer fascinated by her heroine's romantic fate. But while she was beginning to lose interest in that topic, she had not yet found a substitute. Growing old was still a problem for other people, not for herself. Elderly characters do not speak for themselves. They are always being observed and commented upon by the young, who are not always kind or perceptive about what they see. In the course of writing *An Academic Question*, however, Pym had a mastectomy. As usual, she turned to fiction for solace. Abandoning her academic novel, she decided to make retirement, aging, and death the subject of her next one, and began taking notes for what became her masterpiece, *Quartet in Autumn*.

6

The Coming of Age

Pym's struggle with cancer in 1971 made her realize that she was growing older and needed to reassess her prospects for the future. Needless to say, forging a novel out of illness and the threat of approaching death was not easy. To do so involved an emotional as well as a literary effort, and her plot mirrors the painful steps of her journey. The central theme of *Quartet in Autumn* is retirement, which is viewed quite differently by retirees and observers. In the novel, observers would like to believe that stopping work represents a liberation, but retirees, like Letty, experience it as an abandonment.[1] As the novel progresses, however, Letty discovers that the truth lies somewhere in between. Although never fully confident, at the end, she believes that she has a future.

Letty's experiences test three current theories about retirement: abandonment, liberation, and what sociologists call "diachronic solidarity." The last one is based on the idea that each generation in turn will help their predecessors, the underlying principle of social security legislation.[2] Letty, however, has no one to rely on, and developing trust in herself is no easy matter. Along the way, she suffers, and even more important, Marcia, her coworker in the office, dies. Marcia's death represents Pym's recognition of the dangers of aging.

Ultimately, the novel becomes a coherent and controlled elegy to the city and to office life, but before Pym began taking notes for it, her thoughts were sorely troubled. She saw death and decay everywhere she turned, partly because such signs existed to be observed. For example, for some time she had been aware of declining membership in the Anglican church. Although she skirted that problem in *An Academic Question*, as early as September 19, 1969, she wrote Philip Larkin that she would write about these matters in her next novel (*VPE*, 251). In 1970, when Pym's I.A.I. office was rearranged, she wondered if all the attendant unpleasant emotions might contribute to the plot.

But at that point, she had no time to begin anything new. Also she was preoccupied with the possibility of radically altering her characteristic style. Realizing that gothic novels were immensely popular, on August 31, 1970, she considered writing an update of *Jane Eyre*, which might express the protagonist's sense of being an outsider (*VPE*, 258–59). (Four years later, after a second hospitalization for a stroke, Pym started a romantic novel about a young woman recuperating from illness and unrequited love but quickly abandoned the effort.)[3] As it turned out, *Quartet in Autumn* is neither gothic nor romantic. Ironically, all Pym's attempts to alter her style merely led her back to her old habit of vicarious observations of the lives of others, and to her life-long preoccupation with spinsters. When completed, the novel provided a new synthesis of all the ideas and themes that had enthralled her for a long time.

Meanwhile the mastectomy made Pym feel completely alone in the world for the first time in her life. On May 1, 1971, she wrote Robert Smith that even her sister, Hilary, was out of the country when she was hospitalized (*VPE*, 261). Although many friends rallied around, the event forced Pym to accept her inner solitude. Then the plight of lonely spinsters, companions, and governesses ceased to be the subject of anxious fantasy but an important new literary topic.

The bleak observations found in *Quartet in Autumn* are not surprising when one considers the problems that Pym faced. The threat of cancer was the most important. But that discovery was reinforced by signs of aging among her friends and acquaintances. The years brought news of the deaths of many old friends and raised the specter of a lonely demise. Pym was well aware that reading obituary notices of her friends heralded her own mortality, whereas in youth she had assumed that seeing death notices of friends would make the old feel triumphant. November 15, 1970, about six months before the surgery, Robert Smith wrote that his friend Joan Wales, of the furniture depository episode, had been found in a diabetic coma. Although she survived, in a later literary notebook entry on

December 8, 1972, Pym started wondering if a solitary character could die of starvation in her novel (*VPE*, 272). In 1977 Richard Roberts recognized that Marcia was very like Joan Wales. In that letter he wrote that Wales was dying, but later reported her to be alive.[4]

Not only was the health of some of Pym's contemporaries beginning to deteriorate, but London was as well. Between 1970 and 1972, several places that were part of Pym's private landscape closed or were torn down. July 3, 1970, the Kardomah was shut where Hazel Holt and she had shared so many companionable lunches (*VPE*, 256). Pym wrote Philip Larkin on November 7, 1971, that St. Laurence's, her church home, had become a victim of redundancy (*VPE*, 266). The disappearance of personal landmarks aroused mixed feelings. Pym was inclined to mourn their loss, but her sharp eyes also recorded the ensuing conflict, which she felt would make good material for her novel. February 4, 1972, she wrote gloomily in the notebook that Gamage's, a store she patronized, was about to close, and her old haunts near her office were being torn down, "Oh unimaginable horror!" March 6, a month later, she noted "change and decay," while predicting that old buildings would be supplanted by characterless replacements (*VPE*, 266). Even her office building was to be eliminated.

In fact, the period of Pym's discontent was quite short. Although her notebook complaints sound similar to E. M. Forster's in *Howards End*, her grief for lost places did not last long. By March 20, 1972, she had found new places to eat and the impending office move had enriched her ideas for a novel (*VPE*, 267). At the same time she became increasingly preoccupied by a much greater problem, that of her own approaching retirement.

Pym had resisted the idea of retirement for many years. Even before completing *An Unsuitable Attachment*, on February 6, 1961, Robert Smith had urged her to leave her job. After the novel's failure, September 4, 1964, Richard Roberts encouraged her to work part time and devote herself to her novels. On March 8, 1965, Smith reiterated his plea. Pym appreciated the concern of both men, but her job represented independence to her, and she was loath to give it up. After all, it had taken her years to become truly independent. Moreover, like many women, her meager salary made her feel insecure about her earning power. Throughout most of their lives, Hilary Walton's larger salary had provided most of their financial resources. For all these reasons, Pym wanted to continue to work, and never did entirely give up her connection with the I.A.I. She finished her last index for them in October 1979, three months before her death.[5]

Thus in 1971, when breast cancer made retirement an obvious step, she was still fearful. Hilary Walton, who was more independent by nature, decided the time had come to move to the country, an idea the two sisters had long planned. Pym agreed in principle, but when Mrs. Walton sold their London house, she wrote Philip Larkin on May 29, 1972, that she planned to work for another year (*VPE*, 268). Of course, the decision to remain at the I.A.I. meant that she had to find a room to rent in someone else's house, a necessity that aroused the same feelings she had described years before in *Something to Remember.*

The irony did not escape Pym's notice. In the same letter to Larkin, Pym facetiously suggested that she might advertise herself in the *Church Times*, as the ideal renter, nonsmoking, genteel, and quiet (*VPE*, 268). The humor covered up real distress at her unaccustomed situation. Traveling to Finstock on weekends was exhausting for her, even a year after her surgery. On July 6, 1972, she reported feeling very ill and alone.[6] As it happened, things worked out much better than she had feared. By October 24 of that year, Pym had written Larkin that she was lodging comfortably in a house where she had kitchen privileges. She declared that the office move had created "great staff dramas," which she considered to be "fruitful novel material" (*VPE*, 271). Pym's new rental provided another opportunity to collect material for her novel. Her status was that of a paying guest. She paid rent for the room but referred to her landlady as "my hostess" (*VPE*, 270–71). Although her situation was pleasant, Pym was quite aware that such arrangements could be most ambiguous socially. She understood exactly what a woman in Letty's position would feel, having shared Letty's anxiety about finding a room and her social discomfort in adjusting (*QA*, 77).

Charles Burkhart has commented on the prevalence of death in the published version of *Quartet in Autumn*. Death plays an even larger role in the manuscripts. For several years Pym thought of her female characters as victims and imagined that one of them would die. Marcia's death seems to have been planned by the end of 1972, and at two points in the manuscripts Pym contemplated having Letty die. Hints that she desires to give up the struggle appeared in Pym's notebook as early as November 5, 1972 (*VPE*, 272).[7]

Making a decision to move had always been much harder for Pym than for Hilary Walton. At every stage in life, the writer invested a great deal of herself in her immediate environment and often appropriated her surroundings for the landscape of her novels. As a result, she felt more intensely rooted than did her more practical sister. For a time, even the idea of leaving London for the country seemed a kind of death. February 4, 1972, Pym recorded in her notebook that "now that the possibility of being 'buried' in the country looms," she was trying to absorb as many impressions as possible. At the same time she observed regretfully that London no longer provided the necessary stability she craved (*VPE*, 266). Indeed, for a time the divided venue merely gave her two places in which to notice signs of death and decay. When she walked in London, December 8, 1972, Pym worried about the plight of street people (*VPE*, 272). When the previous July she had walked in the country or nearby towns, she had lamented that she alone seemed to find the dead animals (*VPE*, 269–70). Even a pleasant stroll in old haunts of Oxford on November 5, 1972, elicited the observation that Addison's Walk seemed "a good place to lie down waiting for death covered in leaves by the still streams" (*VPE*, 272).

On the whole, however, Pym was aware that her sister's decision was sensible, and she wanted to cooperate as much as possible. Instead of grumbling, she used her notebooks to confront her worries at some remove. Also she could justify the entries to herself on the grounds that they provided material for her novel. Indeed, most of these thoughts were attributed to Letty.[8] They also captured Pym's melancholy mood as she approached her sixtieth birthday. March 13, 1973, she wrote Philip that sixty was "the age." Of course, the feeling of obsolescence that Pym noted was not altogether personal. In the same letter she added that the I.A.I. might have already outlived its function. On the other hand she mused, its decay could make "a rich subject for fiction" provided that one brought to it "a novelist's cruelly dispassionate eye, as I fear I sometimes can" (*VPE*, 273).

Through this period Pym observed that breast cancer had made her feel powerless. In the first draft of *Quartet in Autumn* she commented that when she saw eccentric people, they reminded her of herself or of long-ago friends. She did not attempt to review her own past to discover why she felt so vulnerable. According to Robert Butler, a psychiatrist who specializes in treating older patients, many elders begin reviewing their lives at just such moments. Butler has pointed out that life review is sometimes "related to the extent of actual or psychological isolation" and in some cases leads to "anxiety, guilt, despair, and depression." Instead, Pym avoided such dangers by projecting her distress onto her characters Letty and Marcia. She regarded them as innocent victims and sought to explain why they were so alone in the world. To answer that question, she constructed an elaborate past for one of them, to whom she gave a Virginia Woolf childhood, with a Pymian variation.[9] For a while Letty and Marcia were necessary surrogates for her, just as Rose Culver had been in the early 1960s. Pym found it less threatening to review their past history than her own. Writing helped her keep her equilibrium and to behave in a calm and dignified fashion.

Pym constructed curriculum vitae for Marcia and Letty that describe their impoverished past. Letty's life history has much in common with Pym's and Rose Culver's. Like Pym, Letty became attached to a married man while working in censorship during World War II. Like Rose, who is deserted by Oliver, Letty's civil servant married a much younger woman. Letty also has luncheon at the Royal Commonwealth Society with a cousin, who is a business man in Africa. After eating at the same place with Robert Smith on July 10, 1973, Pym decided to use the spot for Letty. As usual Pym recycled old material. The frugal writer observed with delight that she could use her 1971 hospital notes from her mastectomy to describe Marcia's hospitalization. She even tried to include several scenes from the Rose manuscripts, but except for Marjorie's engagement and subsequent jilting, included nothing else.[10]

Marcia's and Letty's lives contain some grim moments. An incident happened to Marcia once on Clapham Common; afterwards she was deserted by her young man. This sounds more ominous than Cousin Bertha's famous "experience" in *Crampton Hodnet* (*CH*, 151). Moreover, Letty's fate is still undecided. She tries to bury herself in the leaves but hates the thought of inconveniencing others. Although Pym has her reject the idea of lying down to die, no positive ending is yet in sight.[11]

Not only did Pym begin her novel in the notebooks, but her entries allowed her to express the fears and the resentment without making matters worse. For example, Letty's reactions to her old friend Marjorie, a minor character in the novel, might well reflect Pym's submerged feelings about her decisive sister. In an early note Letty and Marjorie are sisters, country-dwellers. Further, the misery Letty feels over Marjorie's engagement to David Lydell is reminiscent of Belinda Bede's fear that her sister Harriet might marry Mr. Mole in *Some Tame Gazelle,* a literary event which also stemmed from Pym's relationship with her sister. (At the same time Pym also borrowed a story from her friend Bear. On May 17, 1959, he told her that someone named Marjorie had once fallen in love with him to no avail.)[12] On the whole, Pym found that being the indecisive member of the pair was not an easy role to play. Over time, however, she became more reconciled to her situation and began to reinterpret her characters' plight.

Pym's drafting of the novel was interrupted by a stroke in late April 1974. The illness altered the direction of her art. David Gutmann has observed that having the last child leave home often completely changes the direction of mothers' lives, freeing them from the bonds of parenthood. Surprisingly, ill-health can provide a similar turning point.[13] Pym suffered for a time from aphasia: her spelling deteriorated dramatically, and she could not read (*VPE*, 276-77). On June 23, 1974, she reported her doctor's order to stop working (*VPE*, 278). Almost a year earlier, July 11, 1973, Pym had written Larkin that circumstances had forced her to postpone her plan to retire at sixty. Daryll Forde, the editor of *Africa*, died unexpectedly in May 1973, causing some chaos at the office (*VPE*, 274-75).

The doctor's decisiveness ended years of anxious stalling. Pym, like many people, worried more about retirement just before it happened than afterwards. Bitter remarks about the perils of retirement suddenly appeared in the manuscript. About two months after her stroke, on June 17, 1974, she added stark details to the retirement party that she had mentioned in a previous notebook. Realizing that Marcia and Letty have unimportant positions, the young employees treat them with contempt. Upon rereading the passage, Pym warned herself to soften the tone of that scene.[14]

Luckily for Pym and for her novel, retirement turned out to be a happy time. Far more than she had imagined, settling down for a peaceful life with her sister compensated her for whatever autonomy she lost. She stopped recording dead animals in her notebooks and replaced them with the record of an active social life.[15] Living in Finstock had a soothing effect, and by December 1, 1974, Pym appeared to be reconciled to the situation. She wrote Larkin that when she visited London, it seemed "completely alien." She expressed no profound regret about her move (*VPE*, 280). Moreover, the office had changed so much, with a new director, a new building, and changes of policy, that she was almost grateful not to have to make all those adjustments (*VPE*, 280). Her retirement party was not the unpleasant occasion she had anticipated six months before. Unlike Letty, who read sociology textbooks in her free mornings but was puzzled by their impenetrable vocabulary, Pym was not bored. On March 23, 1975, Pym wrote Larkin that her writing and indexing kept her busy (*VPE*, 281).

Once she began enjoying Finstock, Pym gradually altered her novel. Her revisions transformed it into a moving elegy to London, a personal farewell to the city. She began to enjoy writing this book for the first time. Little traces of her past suddenly appear. For example the wife of Marcia's surgeon, Mr. Strong, is reputed to be the daughter of a diplomat housed in Belgrave Square. Perhaps she is a fictional offspring of Julian Amery, whose fictional counterparts usually resided nearby in Eaton Square. A new sense of urgency and unease empowered Pym. In 1968, Florida Scott-Maxwell, an eighty-five-year-old Jungian analyst, described herself in *The Measure of My Days* as "passionate" and erupting "with hot conviction." Pym reported that the words of old age are "deprivation" and "repression." For so many years she had assumed that age was a time of "calm of mind, all passion spent," and "emotion recollected in tranquillity." Having made her discovery, Pym wished to share it, not evoke our pity.[16]

In her brilliant rendition of Marcia's bizarre behavior, Pym also exposed the dangers of the gerontological theory of disengagement, which was first espoused in 1961. Sociologists and psychologists claimed that it was perfectly normal for individuals to abandon their routine activities after they ceased to work. Researchers even reported evidence of high morale among disengaged older adults at the beginning and end of the process. Marcia, however, goes to abnormal extremes. She is so eager to avoid human contact that she sits in the dark lest the social worker think she is at home, thereby providing an uncomfortable parody of the curates in Pym's manuscripts, who also turn out the lights to avoid designing females (*QA*, 116).[17]

Pym describes Marcia's later days with clinical detachment and detail. The eccentric woman makes it difficult for others to help her. When her neighbors invite her to Christmas dinner, she appears in a startlingly blue dress and eats almost nothing. She shows acute signs of anorexia. Moreover the brightness of her dress indicates the onset of presbyopia. In late life changes in vision make bright colors seem much duller than they appear to younger eyes. Not surprisingly, the young people lack the professional knowledge that would alert them to Marcia's plight. They wonder idly, "perhaps it would have been easier if Marcia had been that much older, really *ancient*" (*QA*, 86).

Even the doctors whom Marcia trusts fail her in the end. Mr. Strong is far too eminent to see patients in the clinic, and the first houseman (resident) is too young to know whether her thinness is normal or not (*QA*, 49). The middle-aged physician who examines her later "was used to patients going on in this way." Listening with half an ear to her complaints, he decides to let "Strong's boys" manage things when she goes in for her planned hospital checkup (*QA*, 153). His kindly suggestion that Mr. Strong would want her to eat better simply encourages Marcia to take a long bus trip to stare at the surgeon's house. The unaccustomed exertion weakens her still further, making opening a tin too difficult a chore. Later when she is found semicomatose, a half-opened tin is nearby (*QA*, 165).

The stroke had changed some of Pym's sentiments. No longer did she feel like a helpless victim. Three years later on October 9, 1977, she wrote Bob Smith that her illness had given her confidence that "I would somehow be sustained." This belief affected her novel. Pym became more accepting of death as a natural process. Furthermore, as she continued in the same letter, Marcia is better off dying happily, "seeing Mr Strong smile," than living on into a memoryless old age, like one of Pym's old friends (*VPE*, 307).

Of course Pym also felt angry at the thought that demented individuals like Marcia could slip so easily "through the net" (*QA*, 187). Yet Pym also disliked the methods Marcia's social worker uses to intervene. (That point especially impressed some of Pym's older readers. Helen MacGregor, an elderly acquaintance from the Romantic Novelists' Association, praised Pym for treating Marcia with respect. MacGregor resented the assumption that aging spinsters needed special assistance.) Rather than pitying Marcia, Pym accepted her desire to die. After all, Pym had struggled with such feelings herself just before retirement. She also understood why Marcia found hospital life so appealing; it is, as Barbara Waxman points out, the "only place where any man has made Marcia the center of attention." The same could have been said of Pym herself. She wrote Philip Larkin on June 22, 1971, that being in the hospital for a mastectomy had its pleasures, one of which was being "a centre of interest" (*VPE*, 262). As a result, Mr. Strong becomes the center of Marcia's universe. For years she has been stockpiling clean nightgowns for a return to hospital, and his warm smile is all she longed for (*QA*, 181).[18]

In contrast, Letty has a brighter future. Her mind is not clouded with fantasies, and she gradually becomes more decisive. She feels the appeal of an "autumn carpet of beech leaves," but firmly puts the idea of death out of her mind (*QA*, 149–50).[19] Then, when she finally catches a glimpse of Holmhurst, the home for the aged recommended by her friend Marjorie, Letty gets angry. She rejects such an inappropriate spot, deeming it a worse fate than what she had half-contemplated before (*QA*, 149–51).

In fact the imagery of death in the novel is surprisingly positive. Just as the stroke forced Pym to move on to the next stage in her life, so Marcia's death liberates her three coworkers. When she dies, she leaves her house to Norman, who for the first time will have enough money to meet his needs. The remaining trio become real friends for the first time.

One of the remarkable qualities of this novel is the sense of felt life that lies behind the printed page. The notes and early drafts indicate that Pym had imagined many details of her protagonists' early lives. She "knew" more about them than was included in her spare plot. Nonetheless, her desire to depict the essence of their experience gave her a sense of urgency. Each scene has dramatic force. Pym resisted mere stereotypes. Instead, her attitude toward the four combined clinical detachment with warm acceptance. For the first time, Pym probed beneath the surface of behavior. Perhaps reading Freud on Leonardo da Vinci in 1970 contributed to her new sensitivity for her characters' unconscious desires. For example, Pym hinted that Norman's pleasure at the sight of a wrecked car has something to do with repressed sexuality (*QA*, 35–36).[20] Such suggestive details sharpen her analysis and add insight.

Of course, Pym felt more distant from Norman and Edwin than from Letty and Marcia. She had no personal experiences to enrich their portraits. As usual the two men combined qualities of her male friends. Edwin's absorption in the life of the church echoes the preoccupations of Robert Smith and Robert Liddell, while Norman's angry outbursts owe something to the letters Philip Larkin wrote over the years. Like Norman, Larkin was quick to express his anger. He pointed out that single people hate holidays and Christmas and must endure musty single rooms in hotels. His complaints enriched Pym's narrative. For example, Christmas is described from the perspective of each of her characters. Larkin's comments about his mother's old-age home may also have fueled Letty's disdain for making a similar move. Furthermore, Pym's analysis of Norman's and Marcia's charged feelings mirrors her own preoccupation with the exact nature of Larkin's and Smith's romantic feelings. Both were attached for long periods to women whom they never married.[21]

Inevitably the women resonate more. Some of Marcia's compulsions represent exaggerated versions of Pym's own habits. In notes recorded April 28–May 20, 1971, after her mastectomy, Pym commented that admiring one's surgeon is inevitable. No doubt, she continued, a batty spinster might express her feelings in an extreme fashion. Indeed, shortly after Pym got home, she looked up her surgeon in a reference book.[22] Unrequited love of all kinds had always been her specialty, and the years Pym had spent taking notes on her neighbors gave her compassion for Marcia's interest in Mr. Strong. In some respects, Marcia is even like Belinda Bede and Barbara Bird; they too are transported by their emotions to another realm.

Pym also understood Marcia's obstinacy and her unwillingness to cooperate with the social worker, Janice Brabner. Although Pym was a compliant person, on occasion she could be very stubborn. When she felt overwhelmed, she knew how to stall. She managed to defer her own retirement several times, always for good reasons. Forty years before, she had postponed leaving Oswestry, even when she felt guilty for not contributing to the war effort. In an astute review of *Quartet in Autumn* on September 18, 1977, Francis Wyndham suggested that Pym instinctively understood that obstinacy can be a form of self-expression, especially when individuals fear a total loss of control. This kind of behavior, he maintained, operates as a defence against a destructive passivity, an insight which helps explain Pym's character as well.[23]

Of course, not all of Marcia's qualities were shared by the author. Marcia is very like the imperious spinsters of her early manuscripts. She resembles the Miss Moberley character, who had become part of Pym's imaginary life in her mid-twenties. Marcia also has much in common with the novelist, Ivy Compton-Burnett, who had long been a subject of fascination to Pym and her novelist friends. Years before, Pym had collected clippings that described the author's peculiarities. In a 1973–1974 notebook of *Quartet in Autumn*, Marcia rolls her dyed hair at the back in Compton-Burnett style. She carries the imperiously eccentric behavior of the reclusive novelist to extremes.[24]

To a degree unusual in Pym's fiction, Marcia also came from the author's unconscious. On February 16, 1969, Pym recorded a curious dream about a woman who has a fit at Gamage's. In the dream she looks up and sees a cottage. Bodies of two dead cats lie stretched on the ground outside, drained of all their fluid.[25] Details about Marcia's isolated life, including the death of her cat Snowy and her own final semicoma, might well have an origin in the anxieties that led to that dream. Of course, Pym added the last minute detail about the fleas leaving Snowy's body after her cat Tom's death in January

1976. On March 8, she wrote Larkin and told him how surprised she had been by the sight (*VPE*, 286).

In a similar fashion, Letty also was partly like Pym. She represented the culmination of the author's fantasies about dependent women, a subject of fascination since girlhood. Letty sees the signs of death that had troubled Pym. Letty's passivity and her sense that life had passed her by were familiar feelings. According to Pym's own remarks, Letty shared her own tendency to live "very much in the present, holding neatly and firmly on to life, coping as best she could with whatever it had to offer" (*QA*, 25). As early as November 7, 1971, Pym had written Larkin that as she grew older, she generally avoided thinking about the past (*VPE*, 265).

Although Pym identified with Letty and Marcia, by the time she was finishing the novel she saw them from a greater distance than she had initially. This difference explains the changes Pym made in the retirement luncheon scene a few months after the stroke. Originally Pym had imagined that the young would have no idea what to think of the two older women. The retirees, after all, are so unimportant in the larger scheme of things. On September 28, 1974, she had added the beginning of the comic retirement speech that gives the novel its distinctive humor.[26] In the published novel, Pym satirizes the whole occasion from an Olympian height. Her real targets are pompous academics who pontificate about a problem while ignoring the individuals involved.

Pym knew that academic abstractions rarely do justice to real experiences.[27] Thus, against the evidence of their eyes, younger workers assume that Letty and Marcia will have a pleasant and fulfilling future. The management, she reports, has devoted a seminar to the issue, "though the conclusions drawn and the recommendations drawn up had no real bearing on the retirement of Letty and Marcia, which seemed as inevitable as the falling of the leaves in autumn, for which no kind of preparation needed to be made" (*QA*, 100–101). Very conveniently everyone declines to worry about them. Yet Letty has too little money, and Marcia, too little sanity. The final version of the speech given by "the (acting) deputy assistant director" is a masterpiece of absurdity. Being unsure what exactly, if anything, the two women have been doing, "under the influence of a quick swig of sherry" he declares that they have been "doing good by stealth" (*QA*, 102), a remark that harkens back to *Excellent Women* (*EW*, 15). In this marvelously comic scene, Pym manages to subvert solemn sociological research. Every detail good-humoredly punctures hypocrisy. Clearly Pym no longer felt personally involved in the situation. The pleasures of life in Finstock allowed her to look back peacefully on her prior employment, without undue resentment.

The treatment that *Quartet in Autumn* received, before the *Times Literary Supplement* brought her name back to public attention, does not reflect well on the publishers to whom Pym sent it. One problem was that publishing in Britain had expanded. The days were gone when the head of the firm read unsolicited novels. Neither Thomas Maschler of Cape nor Hamish Hamilton, head of his firm, read *Quartet in Autumn* personally. Further, the version that Pym sent to Cape and Hamish Hamilton was thirty pages shorter than the one Macmillan published. Cape rejected the manuscript July 1, 1976. Jean Mossop, who had worked for Cape since the 1950s and admired Pym's work, regretfully wrote that despite its excellences, Pym's new novel did not fit their greatly altered list. November 4, 1976, Hamish Hamilton also rejected it. In trying his firm Pym was following the advice of Pamela Hansford Johnson, a well-known novelist herself and the wife of the novelist C. P. Snow. Hamilton, however, thought that *Four Point Turn* was too short and sent a copy of a negative reader's report to Pym. The reader found the plot boring although he admitted to being impressed by Marcia. He declared that Pym's themes of retirement and loneliness were important but not interesting enough for publication. In a fancy of his own making, he suggested that the writer was a social worker who sought to alleviate her distress by writing about her elderly clients.[28]

Fortunately, other readers disagreed. Pym had also sent the manuscript to friends, who were impressed. Larkin, on September 27, 1976, and Smith, on July 29, 1976, both suggested that she lengthen the manuscript, with Smith specifically requesting more information about Norman. Pym promptly added thirty pages of text, including Marcia's last visit to Mr. Strong's house.[29] As a result of all the good advice and much hard work, Pym had a nearly completed manuscript in hand by January 1977, when the miracle occurred.

tion. She was well aware that such admiring publicity at an earlier point would have radically changed her life. At the same time, she thoroughly enjoyed the fuss. Playful asides in the notebooks—such as, perhaps it was not wise to have added an aged cat to a recipe—indicate how pleased she was to be a published author again. Even her handwriting for a time improved dramatically. Yet Pym did not change her habits or her outlook. As late as March 28, 1978, when negotiating rights to *Excellent Women* and subsequent novels with Dutton, she wrote Jean Mossop of Cape that she could not imagine that Dutton would ever considering publishing *Less than Angels*. After all, she recollected with some pain, Vanguard had lost money on their American edition of that novel. Not until *The Sweet Dove Died* became a best seller did she gain any confidence in her fiction's appeal.[3]

This time, however, Pym was extremely lucky in her editors—Alan Maclean and James Wright. The two men handled with ease all the difficult negotiations with Tom Maschler of Cape—who had the rights to her first six novels—and with her American publishers. Dealing with Maschler was not always easy. As late as September 12, 1977, he admitted to Jill Neville of the Sunday *Times* that he had not yet read any of Pym's fiction. Although Maschler promptly reprinted two of her novels, he was cautious about the rest. Maclean made every effort to obtain a commitment from him, but Maschler preferred to wait until sales figures guaranteed that the books would sell well. He did agree to bring out *Less than Angels* and *Some Tame Gazelle* in the fall of 1978. To his chagrin by February 6, 1978, the BBC had asked for radio rights to broadcast *Jane and Prudence,* one of the two novels Maschler had not yet agreed to reprint. He decided to complete the series, but the firm promptly discovered that no one at Cape had a copy of the four remaining novels. Valerie Kettley, Maschler's secretary, wrote Pym February 6 to ask for assistance. When Pym refused to give up her old editions, Kettley advertised for the two copies necessary for each reprint. The advertisements were not completely successful; Kettley had to beg Pym for a Portway reprint of *Some Tame Gazelle.* On March 2 James Wright volunteered to sacrifice the two copies Pym had given him, providing that Cape gave him reprints in return.[4] In triumph on October 28, 1979, Pym sent Philip Larkin the final two reprints (*VPE*, 332).

Pym really was never comfortable with Maschler. He tried to establish friendly relations by using his first name in a letter as early as March 7, 1977, but she continued to address him as Mr. Maschler. Not until January 9, 1978, did she call him Tom. In contrast, Pym developed a warm and friendly relationship with James Wright at Macmillan. He was far younger than she, married with young children. In return Wright became genuinely fond of the self-deprecating older woman. His letters reveal a wit much like her own. His manner of praising her work pleased her. From that perspective, her final days were happy indeed. Pym never met Paul de Angelis, her Dutton editor, and no doubt found his more effusive style less congenial. Still, the New York editor did a masterful job of marketing her books. He solicited blurbs from writers with whom the American audience was familiar. As a result *Excellent Women* became an alternate Book-of-the-Month-Club selection.[5] Thanks to the expertise of all these editors, in her last years Pym achieved genuine popular success, both in England and the United States.

Pym reacted to this change of fortune by starting another novel, *A Few Green Leaves*. Clearly, the vagaries of fate were very much on her mind during that period. These thoughts color the novel, as well as two stories that she completed in 1978, "The Christmas Visit" and "Across a Crowded Room." It appears as if Pym wrote "Across a Crowded Room" first. The *New Yorker* asked Pym to submit a story, March 31, 1978. She sent them "Across a Crowded Room" on March 8, 1979. March 19, they accepted it, almost by return mail. According to Pym's transmittal letter, she had written the story during the summer of 1978. Pym composed "The Christmas Visit" the following autumn. She informed Philip Larkin, October 20, 1978, that the *Church Times* had requested it as well. It was accepted by the editor, November 28, 1978.[6] Both stories address the question of status and reputation from different angles, using very different tones. The twists of their plots illustrate the transience of fame and the deceptiveness of appearances. Although they were completed before Pym knew that her cancer had spread, repeated illnesses had already altered her view of life.

Of the two, "The Christmas Visit" is lighter in tone. Its major theme is the uncertainty of status. It features Sophia and Mark Ainger and their aging cat Faustina. They were all unknown to Pym's public, *An Unsuitable Attachment* having not yet been published. The Aingers have recently moved to the country, to a parish suspiciously like Finstock. They are about to receive a Christmas visit from Sophia's cousin Daisy, who is extremely high church, and Mark's college friend Edmund and his wife.

Edmund, a career diplomat like so many Julian Amery surrogates, is most unpleasant. He is eager to use Mark's parish register to track down his ancestors, all of whom he assumes will be worthy of him. Mark acknowledges his own undistinguished life but has few regrets. He longs to write a sermon about careers that diverge in later life while giving the topic "a pay-off ending."[7] He cannot do so, but Pym provides one for him. Indeed one is tempted to read the story as Pym's final, if unconscious, revenge against Julian Amery. Successful Edmund is mortified to discover that his ancestors were gardeners and agricultural laborers, not lords of the manor. In confusion, he and his wife quickly leave the vicarage, the scene of his embarrassment, taking Daisy with them. Pym handles the whole issue of class with good humor and detachment, but two touches indicate her preoccupation with eschatology. Daisy is horrified by the sight of Faustina among the gravestones. Sophia, however, has purposefully chosen that vicarage to give Faustina a safe spot to play under her watchful eye. She tells Daisy that it is an appropriate place to prepare the sixteen-year-old cat "for her own end."[8] Pym agrees with Sophia. One of her life-long pleasures involved walking among gravestones and imagining the lives of the departed.

The story's ending also ironically foreshadows later developments in Pym's life. As part of a yearly ritual, Sophia puts an old decoration of Father Christmas on a cake. Once again she has forgotten to buy a new decoration. The ornament is so ancient that the fanciful Sophia is reminded of a deserted King Lear. When the guests leave, the Aingers try to slice the cake. So much has been eaten that Father Christmas is perched "on the edge of a precipice." In hindsight the words have an ominous ring. Sophia, however, is unperturbed by any imminence of disaster. She promises Mark to get "new decorations for the cake *next* year."[9] Her promise reveals Pym's pleasure in the sort of endless repetitions that life gives us. That very joy sustained the writer when she discovered that her death was near.

The second story, "Across a Crowded Room," is marked by a sense of regret. Indeed Pym explores varieties of failure, ending with the failure of memory. Aging, the narrator discovers, like the lumber room of Pym's youth, has been a great leveler. All the older characters have become equally preoccupied with their own past lives. Unfortunately, they pay little attention to present company. The narrator, like Pym, is an older woman. She has been invited to an Oxford feast, very like the Rawlinson dinner, which Pym attended on April 19, 1978.

Pym's account of the actual dinner sounds cheerful enough, although she did comment on the preponderance of men. Still the narrator's depressed tone might have some connection with Pym's poor health at the time. Ten days before the dinner she had fainted and been taken to the hospital; ten days after it she was fitted with a pacemaker (*VPE*, 317–18). More important, writing the story provided Pym an opportunity to explore her fears and anger at some remove. Around 1965, she had once written a Firbankian revel about Richard Roberts and Bob Smith when she resented their sometimes highhanded treatment of her. She never completed that story, but sketching it defused her anger and worry about the future. This time not only could she express, albeit indirectly, her anger over years of professional neglect, but she earned $2,410 from the *New Yorker* as well.[10]

From the start, the nameless narrator feels disadvantaged and somewhat bitter. Rather than buy an elegant new dress for the occasion, she feels obliged to blend into the background. She has been invited, she decides, partly out of pity, but also in recognition that with better luck she might have made her mark. Thus she reacts with surprise when Ned, the young American academic who sits next to her at dinner, attempts to flatter her. Subsequently both discover they each have uncomfortably intense memories of a visit to Keats's house in Hampstead. By this time astute readers will of course identify Ned as Leonora's nemesis in *The Sweet Dove Died* and recall the events to which he refers. This narrator, however, is not Leonora.

The conversation with Ned sets the tone for all the subsequent encounters. The older people with whom she makes polite conversation are equally preoccupied with past history. Suddenly in the distance she spots Gervase Harding, presumably someone whom she once loved in Oxford days. (Gervase was one of Pym's literary names for Henry Harvey.) She cannot recall any romantic fervor; therefore she assumes that he will not remember her. She braces herself for his indifference, the necessity of receiving "a blank look . . . men were expert at that."[11] The narrator's hostility was not fully shared by the writer. Pym's last few years were brightened by the reappearance of her old friend Henry Harvey.

Then, to her surprise, the narrator discovers her memory has played her a trick. She has a vague recollection of a wife, whose name she cannot recall. But Gervase denies any marriage. At this point Pym takes up a theme she had touched on before in "Goodbye Balkan Capital," a story she wrote in 1941, when she was still mourning the loss of Julian Amery. This early story provides a contrast to the bitterness of "Across a Crowded Room." In it, Laura Arling, the spinster heroine, has been imagining a glamorous career for Crispin, an Amery figure, for some years. To her surprise in

1941, she discovers that he had retired early and subsequently died. Reflecting on her fantasies about his adventures makes her feel "foolish and a little desolate." At that point she stops revising her picture of Crispin, concluding happily that "in life or in death people are very much what we like to think them." As Anthony Kaufman points out, the story demonstrates Pym's faith in "the permanence of memory" and the triumph of transforming imagination over the sometimes banal reality of the person loved.[12]

In the later story, however, the narrator makes her mistake in public. Gervase himself points out her error. When her gaffe brings their conversation to a premature close, she knows that she will be troubled in the middle of the night by the identity of the mysterious wife whom she has invented for him. Moreover, no one senses her desolation. Her host has missed the interplay. In his innocence he will go home, Pym predicts, and tell his wife that not only did his guest enjoy meeting Ned, but she seemed to have met someone from her past, perhaps an old lover, "he wasn't quite sure what."[13] The story ends on that desolate note; no genuine reunion is possible in later life. Everyone's inner life is barred. Worst of all, the narrator must now revise her dim memory of Gervase, thus losing the solace of memory.

In contrast, *A Few Green Leaves*, the novel that Pym was composing at the same time, is not so grim. Success and James Wright encouraged her to embark on a new project rather than spend precious time trying to resuscitate any of her old manuscripts. As early as November 18, 1976, Pym had toyed with the idea of writing about village life (*VPE*, 288). The novel is both what Constance Rooke calls a "*Vollendungsroman*, the novel of 'completion' or 'winding up,'" and what Margaret Gullette identifies as a midlife progress novel, an unexpected choice for a dying writer. The extent to which Pym managed to breathe new life into old fantasies is nothing short of extraordinary. Penelope Lively comments that "the old flavour is there." Pym's career, she says, was not like that of other writers, the usual process of trial and error. Instead *A Few Green Leaves* represents a revision and continuation of "an already mastered formula." Pym's novel may look effortless, but as Elliott Jaques has pointed out, late life novels often are deceptive. Their ideas represent "reworkings" of old themes, in some cases ideas that the writer has spent a lifetime mulling over.[14] Manuscript evidence demonstrates that Pym wrote the novel as if she were engaged in the process of clearing out her own lumber room, the place where for so long she had stored her uncomfortable memories.

In the novel, Pym reported the news of the death of two characters from early works, borrowed or revised scenes from the unpublished *An Academic Question*, and reworked old obsessions and themes that had intrigued her since she had first begun to write. Furthermore, Pym made more good use of the notes about hospital life she took while recovering from the mastectomy. Fascinated by the hospital hierarchy, she had learned exactly where individuals were placed in the pecking order. She invented stories about her surgeon's home life and began imagining what his wife might be like. As Pym told the Romantic Novelists' Association March 8, 1978, when she first began using the hospital material, she started with a young heroine. Eventually she decided to write *Quartet in Autumn*, which has four aging characters.[15]

Pym spent some time deciding on her heroine's career. She kept debating whether Emma should be the writer of romantic or historical novels or an anthropologist. Making this choice had symbolic meaning to Pym. On July 19, 1976, she had written in an off moment, "Better if I had followed an academic career rather than a novelist's—but it's certainly too late now!" (*VPE*, 287). Emma's final decision to abandon anthropology in order to write novels in the village represents Pym's enthusiastic endorsement of her own choice, but only public recognition could prove that her enforced retirement had really been a liberation. When Pym finally was ready to recognize that fact, however, in some strange but wonderful way Emma, her last heroine, became the heir that she never produced in real life.[16]

Once the decision was made, Pym was free to incorporate many ideas from her literary notebooks. Emma's professional training leads her to write clinically about the village and its inhabitants, using the insights that Pym had recorded about Finstock. For example, November 18, 1976, she had noted that her village got Ramsden's rejected jumble (*VPE*, 288). Further, Emma makes many lists in which she ranks inhabitants in order of their importance. She is aware that the social order in her village, as in Finstock, has declined from the old days when the de Tankerville family controlled the social life. They built the mausoleum that dominates the churchyard, just like the one in Finstock, which was kept up by the du Cros family. As early as October 4, 1975, the Finstock mausoleum had caught Pym's eye (*VPE*, 284). In the novel, however, the family have sold their estate, leaving the battle for command to the clergy and the doctors. March 18, 1972, Pym noted that their rivalry dominates the plot (*VPE*, 298).[17]

Despite Pym's new fascination with doctors, she still maintained that the church provides the center of the village social world. With a self-consciously outmoded sense of loyalty, Emma also ranks the rector, Tom Dagnall, first. His depressed sister Daphne, however, does not share his high status. Daphne is an even more bedraggled version of Julian's sister, Winifred, in *Excellent Women*. The doctors Gellibrand and Shrubsole and their families are next in importance. After them comes Miss Vereker, who for years had been the governess at the big house. The last in a long train of governesses in Pym's fiction, Miss Vereker has a significance beyond her physical presence. Although she does not appear on the scene until very late, her memory is kept alive by the many stories Miss Lee and Miss Grundy, two excellent women of the parish, tell about her. Pym had the idea of finding her wandering in the woods quite early but also contemplated keeping her at the great house.[18]

Despite many echoes from previous work, it is apparent that some of Pym's interpretations of human experience had changed. Her insights into tangled human relationships are much sharper than they were in her early fiction. Couples in this novel struggle for dominance and sometimes hurt each other inadvertently. The clerical pair, Tom and Daphne, is a case in point. Their relationship harkens back to other brother-sister pairs in *So Very Secret, Excellent Women, No Fond Return of Love*, as well as an unpublished short story, "Poor Mildred." In these early examples, Pym tended to take sides. In *Excellent Women* she feels sorry for Winifred, whereas in "Poor Mildred," the sister is a comic villain. By the time Pym wrote *A Few Green Leaves*, however, she had learned to regard both parties from a critical but empathic perspective. (Sometime in 1977, she actually transcribed a definition of empathy from a 1912 psychology book in her literary notebook.) True, Daphne landed on her brother's doorstep shortly after his wife's death and kept Tom from looking for a wife. But Daphne is no household tyrant; she is as trapped as her brother. She hates having to take care of Tom and longs for freedom.[19] At the same time, the situation hurts Tom as well, and Pym achieves some complexity by showing how his development has been retarded. Rather than looking for a new wife, he has channeled his passion into searching for the Deserted Medieval Village, part of the lore of local history. His obsession bores the other villagers who have to endure his long expositions.

Experience had taught Pym how hard it is for older people to alter their behavior. Daphne tries to escape from Tom but has just enough energy to transfer from one jailor to another. When she leaves him for Heather, her librarian friend bosses her unmercifully. Unlike the unobservant Tom who is oblivious to her melancholy, Heather combats Daphne's depression with briskness (*FGL*, 233). Tom's future is brighter, of course. He is somewhat younger than Daphne, quite attractive, and most important, a man. Although he has never sought a replacement for his dead wife, in the course of the novel he finds Emma a congenial companion. At the end, it looks as if the two might well marry and be happy.

Aging, however, did not change all of Pym's ingrained attitudes about feminine psychology. In most of her novels, she tended to describe a world that was unfair to women. The only protagonist for whom Pym lacked enthusiasm was Caro in *An Unsuitable Attachment*. After failing to write with authority about the much younger Caro, it is surprising that Pym once again created a heroine far younger than herself.

Part of the explanation is that Pym had read Sylvia Plath's letters by January 12, 1977. Pym at first assumed that she had little in common with the successful but suicidal young poet. To her surprise, Plath was also preoccupied by men, clothing, and hair styles. Pym's sympathy was further aroused by the thought of the final miserable winter after Ted Hughes had deserted Plath (*VPE*, 288). Plath's letters taught Pym that women in their thirties had their troubles as well. This discovery made it far easier for the aging novelist to write sympathetically about a younger woman, provided that the individual in question is relatively helpless. Indeed, Emma is less able to fight for her rights than most of Pym's earlier heroines.

Emma's passivity and self-defeating nature is not typical for a heroine of the postfeminist period in the late 1970s. Her behavior is, however, vintage Pym. Instead of recognizing Tom's appeal when she arrives in the village, Emma revives a long dead relationship with Graham Pettifer. His wife has left him, fed up with his selfishness, no doubt. He is quite typical of Pym's narcissistic males and is based on her memories of Richard Roberts and her old lover Gordon Glover, who died in 1976. Graham even sends Emma the same Corot card that Roberts had once sent Pym for her birthday, June 7, 1967 (*FGL*, 32; *VPE*, 242). Not surprisingly, Graham uses Emma shamelessly, but for food not sex. Penelope Lively has pointed out that sex comes "a long way down the servicing-priorities of Pym men." Like Oliver in the Rose manuscripts, Graham relishes Emma's good cooking but does not confide in her about the breakup of his marriage.[20]

Luckily for the plot, not all the characters are as passive as Emma.

Graham deserts her as soon as it is convenient. Like the pompous young Simon Beddoes in *Crampton Hodnet*, Graham mixes opportunistic behavior with language that Pym regarded as imprecise and jargonistic (*FGL*, 173).[21] In *Crampton Hodnet*, however, Mrs. Cleveland is unable to assist her daughter. This time a powerful mother comes to Emma's rescue, much as the King and the Queen save Rosebud and George in Pym's opera, *The Magic Diamond*.

Emma's mother, Beatrix, decides to act. She feels responsible for her daughter's future, which may be bleak. Beatrix complains that the professionally unproductive Emma could not "justify such high-minded dowdiness" (*FGL*, 98). Although Beatrix is quite content with widowhood for herself, she wanted Emma to marry and have children, or even have children without a husband (*FGL*, 126). Throughout the novel, Beatrix attempts to monitor Emma's situation, mostly by making statements rather than asking questions, "her usual way of extracting information" (*FGL*, 96). In the end, she intervenes directly. She and her friend Isobel stop Daphne from returning to the village in order to enhance Emma's chances with Tom.

Beatrix's rescue operation was an important fantasy to the novelist, whose own mother had died so long ago. Although the novelist no longer had the naive faith of her girlhood, creating a strong and generous mother in fiction helped her manage her sense of dismay at the signs of her deteriorating health. The idea that Beatrix might intervene to help Emma first appears in the manuscripts about January 1979, roughly the time when Pym's symptoms of malignancy became serious.[22]

Although it has many traces of nostalgia and a valedictory air, *A Few Green Leaves* is not bleak. Pym obviously felt consoled by her sense of belonging to institutions, the church and the village, each with its own corporate life. After she adjusted to being retired, she found residence in Finstock much to her liking. She revelled in the sense of belonging. The village accepted two elderly sisters, whereas the more anonymous city might not. She even had another novelist, Gilbert Phelps, as a neighbor and good friend. Moreover, the village operated by immutable and familiar laws of social distinctiveness, like the unspoken rules that governed Oswestry's social life. It did not take her long to discover where individuals fit in the social chain. All this gave her a sense that she had come home.

Pym learned quickly that country attitudes toward life and death are more ritualized than city ways. Many of the villagers attended funerals, and the births of children and animals were celebrated.

Therefore, when the Pyms' tabby cat produced kittens on April 11, 1979, she wrote Larkin on May 1, that villagers, including many children, came to see the litter (*VPE*, 327). Like old Dr. Gellibrand, who delights in pregnant mothers and signs of burgeoning life, the dying woman rejoiced over such evidence of continuity. In a very real sense, Pym felt that moving to Finstock represented a return home, not to Oswestry precisely, but to the mythical village that first captivated her imagination in her youth.[23]

Artistic work produced by individuals who know they are dying is inevitably assumed to be a swansong. After all, it represents the writer's final message to the world, and while Victorian deathbed scenes are not popular today, we still hope for some reassurance or guidance. John Drury says that at its best, "writing in the face of death . . . gives critically refined value to the tiny details of life by its care and affection and clarity." *A Few Green Leaves*, like all of Pym's work, sounds a remarkably honest note. Throughout her life, writing had provided Pym the only place where she could confront things that were troubling her without the risk of upsetting herself, or her sister and friends. Elliott Jaques comments that when an artist reflects seriously upon death, once again "the quality and content of creativity change to the tragic, reflective, and philosophical." Obviously Pym was able to develop what Jaques calls "constructive resignation," a feeling "that then imparts serenity to life and work."[24] Jaques's insights illuminate Pym's achievement. Thanks to the successful outcome of her reflections upon death, she found it possible to emphasize the comfort of ritual and village ties. She celebrates a paradox. Although one's faith can be shaken, at least for a time, by the challenge of facing death, in the long run the comfort of familiar liturgies and acts of service is sustaining.

Pym handles the question delicately, in an understated and humorous series of scenes. First Tom feels shaken by an encounter with a florist whose faith has evaporated as a result of watching a television show. Tom then ponders if Miss Lee, one of the excellent women of the parish, ever had religious doubts (*FGL*, 201). But distracted by the sight of an oak lectern, which he had always assumed to be brass, he asks her a question. To his surprise he asks whether she has ever wished that the church had a brass rather than a wooden lectern. Miss Lee's sturdy rejoinder that she finds the wood "rewarding" to polish comforts him. He feels reassured by the evidence of her faith. After all, he muses, if she ever did question her faith, she was "too well-bred" to bother him with such worries (*FGL*, 201–2). A few minutes later, Tom sees her companion Miss

Grundy, who tells him that the altar flowers can be kept going by adding "a few green leaves." They "can make such a difference." Although Tom recognizes the truth of that phrase, he feels depressed by the thought that "these elderly women kept giving him ideas for sermons. He determined not to use them" (*FGL*, 202). As it happened Pym acquired Miss Grundy's statement by overhearing the conversation of one of the "flower ladies" in church.[25] Though Pym borrowed the phrase for her book's title, nonetheless she sympathized with Tom's rebellious reaction.

Pym began *A Few Green Leaves* before she knew she was dying and finished it shortly before her death. Her health deteriorated while she was writing. January 13, 1979, Pym learned that she had another malignancy (*VPE*, 322). She finished the first draft February 14, 1979, nine days after her doctor asked her what plans she wished to make for nursing care in her final days (*VPE*, 323). Thus the manuscripts reflect her changing attitudes toward death and her writing. Pym did not change the novel's basic plot. Instead she continued to incorporate new material from her own life, even the sometimes unpleasant details connected with her impending death. Pym's detached tone, however, withholds from the uninformed reader any inkling of personal involvement.

One example occurs when young Dr. Shrubsole, the geriatrics specialist, is thrown off balance by an unpleasant encounter with a dying patient. When he tells her bluntly that she is dying, she comes "back at him by asking" if he believes in an afterlife. He is "stunned" by the question but grateful for the thought that such questions are "the rector's business." He quickly dismisses "the fact that death came to all of us" as "irrelevant" (*FGL*, 209). Pym's objective stance is astonishing. She jotted down the scene just a few weeks after February 5, 1979, when her own "kind and practical" doctor asked where she wished her "end" to be (*VPE*, 323).[26]

Of course, references to death had dominated Pym's manuscripts from the beginning of her career, increasing dramatically after the rejection of *An Unsuitable Attachment*. References to death appear in 66 manuscripts out of a possible 116, making it by far the most important topic of interest in her work. Yet death was never the core of a plot until *Quartet in Autumn*. Visiting graveyards with attractive men had been a lifelong pleasure to the author, one which she also attributes to several heroines, including the elegant Beatrice Wyatt.[27] But youthful romantic speculations about death are quite different from having to face the certainty of one's own demise. Pym learned that death was not romantic. What she feared about dying was the possibility that the process would be unduly protracted. In the middle of January 1979, she reported that rarely was the struggle to hold on to the last vestiges of dignity in the hospital worth it (*VPE,* 323). August 5, she expressed the hope that death itself would not be as fearsome as the preliminary discomfort, her "swollen body" and lack of "interest in food or drink" (*VPE,* 331). She wrote Philip Larkin on October 28 that she was grateful for small mercies, being "quite cheerful" and mentally alert, "even if physically weaker. (Better that way round)" (*VPE,* 332). Reports on her health are interspersed with literary gossip and news of the progress of her novel.

Pym's attitudes have much in common with those of aging protagonists in elder tales, so movingly described by Allan Chinen. He points out that dying at peace necessitates some sense of success in life: "Only after developing a self is self-transcendence possible, and only after experiencing material satisfactions can the individual truly give them up." Thanks to Pym's unexpected literary resurrection, she was able to see herself as part of a larger process. Then she, like the elders in the folk tales, felt prepared to accept personal death as "a simple fact . . . part of the natural life cycle."[28]

This attitude helps to explain some of Pym's decisions about the novel. Even though the aura of dying pervades *A Few Green Leaves,* its heroine is quite young, and none of the main characters dies. The young are not obsessed with the subject at all but attend to other things. In one scene, very like another in the Rose manuscripts, Emma treats the news of death with frivolity.[29] Mrs. Dyer, a villager who cleans the rectory, attempts to make a dramatic story out of the unexpected death of an old man on a pensioner's outing, but Emma and Adam Prince cannot resist spoiling the suspense of her account (*FGL,* 109–10). By emphasizing Emma's and Adam's reactions, Pym humorously shows that healthy, youngish people find it difficult to imagine that they will be old someday.

In this novel, death is a fact of life, not something to be bemoaned. For example, when Miss Lickerish dies, her funeral provides an important moment for village ritual, as well as an opportunity for Pym to anticipate her own funeral at some remove and with considerable humor. Of course, Miss Lickerish bears little resemblance to her creator. She is a hardy old eccentric, who lives in a cottage with flea-infested hedgehogs and a cat. Her death does not arouse excessive regret. After all, she was over eighty and had lived and died according to her own wishes. Still, her final moments have a sculpted sense of dignity. Pym describes the scene with restraint and economy. It begins simply with Miss Lickerish's evening meal. The old woman makes her tea and sits in the dark with "a cat on her knees." At some point during the night, "the cat left her and sought the warmth of his basket, Miss Lickerish's lap having become strangely chilled" (*FGL*, 227).

Miss Lickerish's death, however, is not the central focus of the ending. It appears as part of a larger story, a heroic saga, one which was dear to the novelist's heart. Miss Vereker, the old governess who used to work at the manor, takes a long journey back to the village to revisit the scenes of her vigorous midlife. Walking through the woods, she gets lost and stops to rest on a pile of stones. She is discovered there asleep. Pym contemplates the tired old gentle-woman with respect and affection. She describes carefully Miss Vereker's ancient but good quality clothes, her coat of "ancient fur," her "good Liberty silk scarf," and leather pocketbook (*FGL*, 221). By chance, it turns out that the aging Sleeping Beauty is lying on the very stones that mark the remains of the Deserted Medieval Village, the place which Tom has been seeking ever since his wife died. Without consciously trying, the old woman has rescued him from his dreary archeological obsession. He is now free—and possibly eager—to marry once again.

Like the elders in fairy tales, this old woman leaves the middle-aged Tom an important legacy. She demonstrates, as Sally Gadow contends, that frailty can be a source of strength. Miss Vereker also shares the reactions of some elderly individuals described by Ronald Blythe in *The View in Winter,* particularly their pleasure in "knowing how short a distance one can go—and then going it. The knowing that one need not do more because it is impossible to do more. Ever again." By her act of endurance, this elderly governess converts a novel about worn-out middle-aged characters into a story of hope, a midlife progress novel.[30] Simultaneously, Pym's last governess brought to a close the writer's own personal narrative cycle, begun when she was a child. All by herself Miss Vereker successfully completes a journey to find a magic substance, in contrast to the youthful Rosebud and George in *The Magic Diamond*, who are un-able to take the first step.

The threat of death did not stop Pym from working. Not only was she hurrying to finish *A Few Green Leaves*—indeed both Macmillan and Dutton accepted the manuscript shortly before she died—but ideas for a new novel began to percolate in March, 1979. Of course, she was never well enough to expand on these initial thoughts.[31] Instead, she finished the editorial work on *A Few Green Leaves* and continued to keep active as long as possible, going out for meals with her old friends Henry Harvey and Robert Smith. Harvey was one of her last visitors. He came to see her at the hospice January 8, 1980, three days before she died (*VPE*, 292).

When the time finally came to enter the hospice where she was nursed at the end, Pym took her notebook with her. The last notebook in the Bodleian, however, ends earlier in November 1979, before she left home. Its next-to-last entry includes two lines from a Donne poem, "Difference of sex no more we know / than our guardian angels do" (*VPE*, 333). In the manuscript version, however, Pym misspelled *angels* by reversing the *e* and *l*. Yet the preceding August, she had recorded the same lines quite accurately. Illness had taken its toll. When she first had her stroke she could not read or write, and in her weakened state her ability to spell deserted her again.[32] After she died, her sister Hilary had the phrase "Barbara Pym, Writer" inscribed on her tombstone. It is an epitaph of which the novelist would have been most proud.

Notes

Preface

1. "Reputations Revisited," *Times Literary Supplement,* Jan. 21, 1977.
2. Pym to Jean Mossop, Aug. 14, 1978, PYM MS. 166, fol. 130, comments upon the appearance of the first American edition of *QA.*
3. Anne M. Wyatt-Brown, "*Howards End:* Celibacy and Stalemate," and "A Buried Life: E. M. Forster's Struggle with Creativity."
4. Barbara Brothers, "Women Victimised by Fiction: Living and Loving in the Novels by Barbara Pym," 76–77.
5. Barbara Everett, "The Pleasures of Poverty," 11. Everett says that the early journals are not effectively written. The style is imprecise, and the entries reveal a romantic perspective (13–15).

Rachel Blau DuPlessis, *Writing Beyond the Ending: Narrative Strategies of Twentieth-Century Women Writers,* 66–67, would say that Pym suffered from "romantic thralldom," which is "one version of conventional heterosexual narrative scripts." This polarized, dependent love "is socially learned, and is central and recurrent in our culture." In her novels, however, Pym fought against those bonds.

Peter Ackroyd, "Manufacturing Miss Pym," 861. In contrast, Wendy Smith, "Brief Review," 41, regards some of the novels as somewhat superficial in feeling. In *VPE,* however, Pym is surprisingly capable of expressing deeply felt emotions with real honesty. Victoria Glendinning, "Spontaneous Obsessions, Imposed Restraint," 3, notes the paradox that Pym, whose novels are emotionally constricted, had been "emotionally unrestrained" in her life. Pym's sexual experiments surprise her.

6. Anthony Storr, *The Dynamics of Creation* and *Churchill's Black Dog, Kafka's Mice, and Other Phenomena of the Human Mind;* Silvano Arieti, *Creativity: The Magic Synthesis,* 4.
7. Jay Martin, *Who Am I This Time? Uncovering the Fictive Personality,* 12.
8. Victoria Glendinning, *Elizabeth Bowen: Portrait of a Writer;* Anne M. Wyatt-Brown, "The Liberation of Mourning in Elizabeth Bowen's *The Little Girls* and *Eva Trout*"; Jean Strouse, *Alice James: A Biography;* Linda Wagner-Martin,

Sylvia Plath: A Biography; Diane Middlebrook, *Anne Sexton*. Quotation from Richard Ellman in Phyllis Rose, *Woman of Letters: A Life of Virginia Woolf,* viii. Rose was one of the first biographers to suggest that "A life is as much a work of fiction—of guiding narrative structures—as novels and poems, and that the task of literary biography is to explore this fiction."

9. E. M. Forster, *Howards End*, 32.

10. Roy Schafer, *The Analytic Attitude*, 52. Barbara Johnson and Marjorie Garber, "Secret Sharing: Reading Conrad Psychoanalytically," make good use of their countertransference reactions.

11. Elliott Jaques, "Death and the Mid-Life Crisis." Jaques in "The Midlife Crisis," 4, adds that some artists become creative for the first time at midlife. David L. Gutmann, "Psychoanalysis and Aging: A Developmental View," 489–90. Studies of late style include Kathleen M. Woodward, *At Last, the Real Distinguished Thing: The Late Poems of Eliot, Pound, Stevens, and Williams*; Woodward, "May Sarton and Fictions of Old Age"; Woodward, "Simone de Beauvoir: Aging and Its Discontents"; Janice Sokoloff, *The Margin that Remains: A Study of Aging in Literature*; Margaret Morganroth Gullette, *Safe at Last in the Middle Years: The Invention of the Midlife Progress Novel: Saul Bellow, Margaret Drabble, Anne Tyler, and John Updike*; Anne M. Wyatt-Brown, "Late Style in the Novels of Barbara Pym and Penelope Mortimer."

12. James Britton, *Language and Learning*, ch. 6, analyzes a handful of essays by Clare, written from early childhood to the age of twenty. Such studies are very rare.

Introduction: Creativity and the Life Cycle

1. A. S. Byatt, "Marginal Lives," 862. On the other hand, Patricia Meyer Spacks, *Gossip,* 15, attempts to rehabilitate gossip as a genre worth studying. Clearly Pym's narrative, like gossip's, derives from trivia.

2. Barbara Stevens Heusel, Review of *The World of Barbara Pym*, 162–64. Heusel concludes regretfully that Pym's social milieu may not have given her the freedom to express herself as Yeats did.

3. Hilary Spurling, *Ivy: The Life of I. Compton-Burnett*, 285.

4. Carolyn G. Heilbrun, *Writing a Woman's Life*, 13. Laura L. Doan, "Text and the Single Man: The Bachelor in Pym's Dual-Voiced Narrative," and Barbara Bowman, "Barbara Pym's Subversive Subtext: Private Irony and Shared Detachment"; both describe Pym's construction of a subversive subtext. Doan, "Text," 80, insists that Pym's subtext subverts "the patriarchy." Doan, however, ignores the evidence of division within Pym herself.

5. Park Honan, "Theory of Biography," 112, has pointed out that the bulk of biographical information in most lives comes from the later not the earlier years. As a result, gerontological theory could greatly increase our understanding of that critical period. Georges Gusdorf, "Conditions and Limits of Autobiography," 46; Norman N. Holland, "Unity Identity Text Self," 815.

6. Philippe Lejeune, "The Genetic Study of Autobiographical Texts," 10, n. 1, borrows the term *pre-text* (*avant-texte*) from "French genetic studies to signify all that has been *before* the final text and was written or collected *for* it." Pre-texts include early drafts, plans, and notes of any sort.

Hazel Holt, *A Lot to Ask: A Life of Barbara Pym*, appeared in November 1990, after my book was in press. Janice Rossen, *The World of Barbara Pym*, is the most comprehensive study and is based on extensive primary research. Charles Burkhart, *The Pleasure of Miss Pym,* offers the best guide to Pym's humor.

7. Erving Goffman, *Frame Analysis: An Essay on the Organization of Experience,* 15. Judith Summerfield and Geoffrey Summerfield, *Texts and Contexts: A Contribution to the Theory and Practice of Teaching Composition,* 224, suggest that this kind of story encourages useful role-playing.

Pym kept clippings on eccentric behavior or referred to similar collections in fifteen manuscripts.

8. Judith Fetterley, Introduction to *Provisions: A Reader from 19th-Century American Women,* 9, argues that social comedy comes naturally to women writers. Even in nineteenth-century America, which supposedly had no "fiction of manners," women quite naturally gravitated to a form that emphasized "the connection between manners, morals, social class, and social value."

9. Robert Liddell to Pym, April 25, 1935, PYM MS. 153, fol. 61 verso, reported that Honor Tracy had asked the publishers for whom she worked to read Liddell's first novel. He suggested that perhaps they might look at *STG* if Chatto & Windus turned it down. The brother of one of Pym's Oxford friends had asked his uncle at Chatto to read an early draft of the manuscript.

10. PYM MS. 14, fol. 1 verso, quoted by Michael Cotsell, *Barbara Pym,* 47.

11. Barbara Brothers, "Women Victimized by Fiction: Living and Loving in the Novels by Barbara Pym," 79. Quotation, Janice Rossen, "On Not Being Jane Eyre: The Romantic Heroine in Barbara Pym's Novels," 153. Catherine in *LTA* is an exception.

12. Robert J. Graham, "Cumbered with Much Serving: Barbara Pym's 'Excellent Women,'" 154. On a trip to Cambridge, Pym was surprised to see few homosexuals, Sandra Diary 2, May 13, 1934, PYM MS. 102, fol. 80–80 verso. Literary Notebooks, 1955–1960, PYM MSS. 47–52, tracking notes.

13. *STG* reviews, [n.d.], 1950, PYM MS. 163, fols. 119–22, 205, 209, and 212. Pym's champions, like A. N. Wilson, "St. Barbara-in-the-Precinct," and Philip Larkin, "The World of Barbara Pym," admire the conservative aspects of her writing. Professional writers like Penelope Lively, "Stories and Echoes, Recent Fiction," 76–78, respected Pym's style and wit. Anne Tyler, Eudora Welty, and Mary Gordon gave her novels high praise, "Symposium: Books That Gave Me Pleasure," *New York Times Book Review,* Dec. 5, 1982.

In contrast, Paul Abelman, "Genteelism," 26, declares that Pym shared the social values of Leonora (*SDD*). He angrily insists "that a devout tour of middle-class shrines does not a novel make." Marilyn Butler, "Keeping Up with Jane Austen," 16–17, suggests that *UA* represents Pym's effort to write "a functionalist novel, even if the experiment is leavened with irony." Pym's outsider stance, according to Butler, depletes her characters' inner life.

14. Literary Notebook, July 19, 1955, PYM MS. 46, fol. 28 verso, overheard conversations; Literary Notebook, Jan. 2 and Mar. 14, 1957, PYM MS. 49, fols. 1, 3. Fact-gathering techniques like Pym's were later highly recommended to would-be writers by two composition specialists, Summerfield and Summerfield, *Texts,* 24.

15. Holt, *Lot,* 263.

16. William Shakespeare, *Twelfth Night,* 2.5.117–18. Pym used this quotation frequently, to indicate her respect for emotional restraint.

1. Constructing the Lumber Room

1. James Britton et al., *The Development of Writing Abilities (11–18),* 16; Nancy Martin, *Mostly about Writing: Selected Essays,* 20. Jean Wyatt, *Reconstructing Desire: The Role of the Unconscious in Women's Reading and Writing,* 55–56, using Heinz Kohut's notion of healthy narcissism, declares that such familial support is crucial in the development of a child's creativity.

2. *MD,* PYM MS. 98, fol. 1 b. Like all Pym's writing, it has its comic touches. A program note begs the audience not to overstrain the cast by requesting too many encores. Gilbert and Sullivan, Hilary Pym, "Early Life," 3.

3. Constance Malloy, "The Quest for a Career," 195, n. 3, suggests that Pym "reversed the fairytale in which the man comes to the woman's rescue." Malloy misses the ironies in the situation. *MD,* PYM MS. 98, fols. 2 and 4, photographs of the cast show that Barbara had a crush on her tall cousin, Neville Selway (Prince George). Yet when Prince George asks for Rosebud's help, she is unable to act. Rachel Blau DuPlessis, *Writing beyond the Ending,* 67, declares that romantic thralldom "has the high price of obliteration and paralysis."

Bruno Bettelheim, *The Uses of Enchantment: The Meaning and Importance of Fairy Tales,* 11; *MD,* PYM MS. 98, fols. 7 verso–12 verso.

4. Bettelheim, *Uses,* 11.

5. Pym's emphasis reflects a traditional feminine viewpoint. Carol Gilligan, *In a Different Voice: Psychological Theory and Women's Development,* 9, 19, argues that boys value legal debates and quickly learn to compete. Girls develop "a mode of thinking that is contextual and narrative," rather than agonistic. Walter J. Ong, *Orality and Literacy: The Technologizing of the Word,* 112, points out that the novel only emerged when women began to write. They expressed a more practical and less confrontational view of society than did men.

6. Pym to Robert Liddell, April 24, 1936, PYM MS. 153, fol. 176.

7. Hilary Pym, "Early Life," 2, 4; Holt, *Lot,* 4. Liddell, *An Object for a Walk,* 5, later created a character, Flora, based partly on Pym, whose father manufactures toilet paper.

LR, PYM MS. 6, fol. 4, Mrs Wyatt. The Pym papers add little to our knowledge of Pym's early life. Sandra Diary 1, Aug. 25, 1933, *VPE,* 25, refers to adolescent diaries, but they are not in her papers.

8. Holt, *Lot,* 1–3, tells the story of Mrs. Walton's discoveries.

9. Hilary Pym Walton, interviews with author, May 9, 1985, May 15, 1986. Hilary Pym, "Early Life," 4; Holt, *Lot,* 4–5, speculates that Frederic Pym told her mother, Irena, his first wife, about his illegitimacy. She is completely confident that he told his second wife, Alice.

Toby Boulton to Pym, Nov. 8, 1977, PYM MS. 169, fols. 53–54, reported that Morda Lodge, the Pym's home before World War II, was being haunted by the ghost of an illegitimate child. The coincidence is startling.

10. Hilary Pym, "Early Life," 2; Hilary Pym Walton, interview with author, May 15, 1986, regarding how Pym was like their father. Holt, *Lot,* 3–4, father's early life. Pym did not develop a strong sense of self. D. W. Winnicott, "The Capacity to Be Alone," 34, suggests that being alone in the presence of the mother allows the infant to "discover his own personal life." Anthony Storr, *Solitude: A Return to the Self,* 20, refers to Winnicott's belief that without this interaction individuals can develop a "false self." Some, like Pym, become so

compliant in childhood that they later feel inauthentic. Alice Miller, *The Drama of the Gifted Child: The Search for the True Self,* vii-viii, describes gifted children as being specially influenced by the unconscious messages of their often emotionally needy parents.

11. Karen Horney, *Neurosis and Human Growth: The Struggle toward Self-Realization,* 19.

12. Frederic Pym to Pym, May 3, 1950, PYM MS. 167, fol. 56–56 verso, wrote Pym that he had unexpectedly enjoyed her first novel, *STG.* His taste ran more to thrillers. Hilary Pym, "Early Life," 2–4.

Pym called her golf-loving mother Links and her father Dor; her favorite maiden aunt was called Ack. Walton, interview with author, May 15, 1986, did not know what special meaning the names may have had. She suggested that Dor might have been a corruption of Daddy. My guess is that besides golf, Links could be associated with the ties that bind. Dor sounds like adorable, or perhaps dormouse.

Quotation, Walter Clemons, "An Unnoticed World," 96.

13. Hilary Pym Walton, interview with author, May 15, 1986, story about mother. Photograph is in Holt, *Lot.*

14. Hilary Pym, "Early Life," 3. Hilary Pym Walton, interview with author, May 9, 1985, reported that Pym had little desire to have children. Like Chaucer's Prioress, her characters often express more interest in tiny animals than in babies.

Daybook, Oct. 10, 1939, PYM MS. 105, fol. 154, too much housework. Alan Davis to Pym, July 2, 1945, PYM MS. 148, fol. 33 verso.

15. "Midland Bank: A poem dedicated to JTLI with the Author's Fondest Love (But without his Permission)," PYM MS. 97, fols. 11–12, illustrates Pym's taste in men. Henry Harvey often treated her with disdain.

16. Pym expressed ambivalence toward women as well. In later life, her manuscripts refer to "Too Many Women," Rossen, *World,* 58. LR, PYM MS. 6, fol. 121, designing curates.

17. Holt, *Lot,* 10. Most of the spinsters in Pym's early manuscripts who enjoy many aspects of their daily lives also cherish important memories of lovers from long ago. Hilary Pym Walton, interviews with author, May 9, 1985, May 15, 1986, reported that Pym first began describing Miss Moberley on a bus trip around 1936. Mrs. Walton was still amazed to think that Pym had become so fascinated by the elderly eccentric at such a young age.

18. Amorous misadventures were the result of Pym's chronic tendency to overvalue love, a psychological phenomenon described by Karen Horney, *Feminine Psychology,* 185. Miller, *Drama,* 5–6, 9–14.

Pym's interest in the domestic is similar to that of the nineteenth-century writers whom Mary Kelley, *Private Woman, Public Stage: Literary Domesticity in Nineteenth-Century America,* ix, calls *"literary domestics."* Pym always wrote part-time. Nonetheless, her reasons for emphasizing domesticity were more psychologically complicated than the ones Kelley ascribes to her subjects.

19. "Vicar," PYM MS. 99, fol. 26. Pym's unconscious included images of death, such as the vision of a coffin being carried out of a house in Bayswater, a sight that haunted her in the early days of the war, and visions of a funeral train, Daybook, May [n.d.], 1939, *VPE,* 91; PYM MS. 99, fols. 76–76 verso. No doubt the figure in the coffin was inspired by Julian Amery, the young man who left her to go fight in Spain.

20. "Vicar," PYM MS. 99, fols. 41–44.

21. Hilary Pym Walton, letter to author, July 24, 1986. Pym herself described her milieu as encompassing "the worlds of the village and parish," "Finding a Voice: A Radio Talk," 384.

22. Aldous Huxley, *Point Counter Point*. See Anne M. Wyatt-Brown, "Ellipsis, Eccentricity and Evasion in the Diaries of Barbara Pym," 35–37, for more details about Huxley's influence on Pym.

23. Judith Fetterley, *The Resisting Reader: A Feminist Approach to American Fiction*, xx. Although Pym's later manuscripts show the influence of Charlotte Brontë and Charlotte Yonge, she recalled that reading *Crome Yellow* made her long to become a writer. *YMFD* reflected her fascination with Huxley and with writing about "upper-class" characters in their habitat, "Finding a Voice: A Radio Talk," 382.

24. Hilary Pym Walton, interview with author, May 9, 1985; Talk, Romantic Novelists' Association, Mar. 8, 1978; "Ups and Downs of a Writer's Life," Senior Wives Fellowship, Headington, Oxfordshire, May 15, 1978, PYM MS. 98, fols. 74 and 79. Pym compared *YMFD* to Daisy Ashford's *Young Visitors* (1919) because of its naïveté and distance from adult feelings.

25. *YMFD*, PYM MS. 1, fols. 135–47, 211.

26. *YMFD*, PYM MS. 1, fols. 136, 147. Summerfield and Summerfield, *Texts*, 64, states that often we feel as if we have a "reader-inside-the-head (primarily a *listener* and a *respondent*)." In some cases "this interior interlocutor, felt to be both self and not-self" appears in childhood. Joanne S. Frye, *Living Stories, Telling Lives: Women and the Novel in Contemporary Experience*, 89, suggests that transforming personal experiences into stories allows the writer "to claim experience and to gain a distance on it . . . to see the self as including those experiences without being defined by them."

27. *YMFD*, PYM MS. 1, fols. 253–57, 267. DuPlessis, *Writing beyond the Ending*, and Frye, *Living Stories*, 8–9, point out that contemporary women novelists have struggled to invent endings for women characters that avoid the straightjacket of marriage or death. Some eccentric male writers, like E. M. Forster and Aldous Huxley, also resisted the typical heterosexual plot.

28. "The Sad Story of Alphonse," PYM MS. 97, fols. 3–4.

29. "Henry Shakespeare," PYM MS. 97, fols. 8–9.

30. Holt, *Lot*, 14; "Midland Bank," PYM MS. 97, fols. 10–13; "Satire," PYM MS. 97, fol. 14.

31. "Tame Donkey: Sequel to Midland Bank," PYM MS. 97, fols. 17–21.

32. "Death of a Young Man," PYM MS. 97, fols. 40–58. See especially, Aldous Huxley, "Farcical History of Richard Greenow." In this early story, Huxley carries the distancing narrator to absurd limits. Robyn R. Warhol, "Toward a Theory of the Engaging Narrator: Earnest Interventions in Gaskell, Stowe, and Eliot," 811.

33. Carolyn G. Heilbrun, *Reinventing Womanhood*, 73.

34. "Adolphe," PYM MS. 97, fols. 22–39.

35. Helene Deutsch, *Neuroses and Character Types: Clinical Psychoanalytic Studies*, 263–66. See also Miller, *Drama*, 12.

Jay Martin, *Who Am I This Time? Uncovering the Fictive Personality*, 12, has emphasized that each individual uses this invention in vastly different ways. Some of the people he described are psychotic or emotionally impaired. Pym clearly was not. Whatever her reasons for constructing a literary identity, she had a firm grasp of reality, and at no point lost touch with it. Victoria Glendinning, "Spontaneous Obsessions, Imposed Restraint," 3, traces the origin of Pym's literary style and "presentation of herself" to the "the tragicomic sensibilities" of writers like Stevie Smith, Ivy Compton-Burnett, and Virginia Woolf. Peter Ackroyd, "Manufacturing Miss Pym," 861, argues that Pym recreated herself in her late twenties as a " 'drearily splendid' spinster." Rossen, *World,* 27, discusses the split in Pym's personality between her impulsive and her analytical sides.

36. Sandra Diary 1, July 1, 1933, PYM MS. 101, fol. 74 verso. Quotation, Holt, *Lot,* 2.

37. Thomas Mallon, *A Book of One's Own: People and Their Diaries,* xvi–xvii, 37, comments that most diarists write for an audience, no matter how unconsciously. Writers like Pym observe others rather than analyze themselves. Mary Crawford and Roger Chaffin, "The Reader's Construction of Meaning: Cognitive Research on Gender and Comprehension," 22, suggest that diary and letter writing allow women to express "their own experience."

Commonplace Notebook, [n.d.] c. 1942, PYM MS. 83, fol. 36. "Social Success," Logan Pearsall Smith, *All Trivia: Trivia, More Trivia, Afterthoughts, Last Words,* 48.

38. Writing is an isolated act, which also serves a social purpose. To guarantee that their readers will understand their texts, experienced writers try to imagine themselves as the reader. Vera John-Steiner, *Notebooks of the Mind: Explorations of Thinking,* 136–39, describes the complicated process of converting thoughts into words.

Sandra Diary 1, Jan. 2, 1932, PYM MS. 101, fol. 2, typically daring remark from a young man.

The writing theorist Linda Flower, "Writer-Based Prose: A Cognitive Basis for Problems in Writing," 19–20, categorizes texts as "writer-based" (participant) or "reader-based" (observer) depending on whether authors choose to please an audience or themselves. Summerfield and Summerfield, *Texts,* 5–6, 28, 140, encourage students to role-play so that they can alternate writing "participant" and "spectator" texts. At this point Pym produced the former. Lev Vygotsky, *Thought and Language,* 30, says that children regress to egocentric speech when they need to solve demanding problems. Flower, "Writer-Based," 26, expanding his point about emotional regression, suggests that writers will revert to "writer-based" prose when under intellectual stress.

39. Pym described the sometimes extreme way that she dressed. She attributed such habits to some of her early characters, Beatrice Wyatt, *LR,* and Flora Palfrey, *HFN.* She even fondly recalled the bright nail polish she had worn in youth when describing the past of one of her characters in *FGL,* 99.

Glendinning, "Spontaneous," 3, flatly asserts that Pym's sexual experience exceeds the norm for her class and time. Missing pages in the diaries make her statement difficult to prove.

40. Sandra Diary 1, Jan. 18, 1932, PYM MS. 101, fol. 7, typical tracking entry. Sandra Diary 2, Dec. 5, 1933, PYM MS. 102, fol. 22, Sharp's dream about Robert Liddell.

41. Rossen, *World,* 23–25. Saul Bellow, "The Civilized Barbarian Reader," 38, claims that university training failed to meet his goals as a writer. In contrast, Pym sometimes blamed herself.

42. Hazel Holt, interview with author, May 22, 1985.

43. Sandra Diary 1, May 1–24, 1932, PYM MS. 101, fols. 23–24 verso, Pym idealized Geoffrey, the theology student. She referred to him at least twenty-seven times in this diary. Literary Notebook, July 19, 1977, PYM MS. 77, fol. 20, Pym recorded his death on July 16.

Sandra Diary 1, Jan. [n.d.]–Feb. [n.d.], 1932, PYM MS. 101, fols. 5, 7, 9–10, 12, 13, 16 *passim*, three other men Pym admired from a distance. Rupert Gleadow to Pym, Oct. 20, 1932, Dec. 29, 1932, April 8, 1933, PYM MS. 150, fols. 18 verso, 60 verso, 83, complained that his sexual activities were restricted.

44. Holt, *Lot*, 34. Pym placed great emphasis on food in her recollection of the seduction. In later life food sometimes substituted for sex; her novels are notable for their characters' appreciation of good food and drink. Of course, some of the emphasis on food reflected the behavior of her friends. Her Oxford confidant, Robert Liddell, who settled in Cairo during the postwar period, used to send her descriptions of gourmet meals he was busy preparing in Cairo, knowing full well that England was still being severely rationed. On the other hand, he sometimes sent her food, Robert Liddell to Pym, PYM MS. 155, Mar. 5 [?], 1946, April 17, June 13, 1947, fols. 100, 106–8 verso.

Sandra Diary 1, Oct. 20, 1932, PYM MS. 101, fol. 46, Pym's record keeping. See Wyatt-Brown, "Ellipsis," 42–44, for more details about the seduction and its aftermath.

45. Pym referred to relics in twenty-eight manuscripts. According to Anna Freud, adults console themselves for the loss of a loved one by cherishing such mementos, cited by Kathleen Woodward, *Aging and Its Discontents: Freud and Other Fictions*, 218, n. 18. Pym, however, was self-conscious and humorous about her mourning and made good use of her melancholy in her stories.

46. Gleadow to Pym, Oct. 17, 1932, PYM MS. 150, fols. 13–16. He regretted the fiasco, but still cared for her even though she obviously did not reciprocate his feelings. See Wyatt-Brown, "Ellipsis," 44.

47. Hilary Pym Walton, interview with author, May 9, 1985, mentioned the affair with Gleadow. See Wyatt-Brown, "Ellipsis," 44–45.

48. *LR*, PYM MS. 6, fol. 149. Wyatt-Brown, "Ellipsis," 45, identifies the "lumber room" theme and provides the exact quotation. C. G. Jung, quoted by Storr, "Aspects of Adult Development," 142.

49. Sandra Diary 2, [n.d.] c. Feb. 9, 1934, PYM MS. 102, fols. 42 verso, would try to overcome fear. Gleadow to Pym, Oct. 17, 1932, PYM MS. 150, fol. 14, mentioned "Still She Wished for Company."

50. Sandra Diary 2, Mar. [n.d.] between 2–8, 1934, PYM MS. 102, fol. 48, sex and tea. Ibid., Jan. 26, Feb. 23, 1934, PYM MS. 102, fols. 38, 46, relics and Liddell's look of loathing. Ibid., Feb. 27–Mar. 2, 1934, PYM MS. 102, fols. 47–47 verso; Sandra Diary 3, Nov. 16, 1934, PYM MS. 103, fol. 10 verso, Pym's changing reactions to Liddell were a barometer of her self-esteem.

51. The psychoanalyst Alice Miller, *Drama*, 41, 67, 82–83, claims that most of her patients first became aware of the childish origin of their romantic feelings when they began to rear children. Quotation, Heilbrun, *Writing*, 65.

52. Robert Liddell, "Two Friends: Barbara Pym and Ivy Compton-Burnett," 59.

53. Robert Liddell, *An Object for a Walk*, 28.

54. Sandra Diary 2, Mar. 10 and April 2, 1934, PYM MS. 102, fols. 51, 63.

55. Sandra Diary 3, May [n.d.], 1935, PYM MS. 103, fol. 27. Quotation, Martin, *Who Am I?*, 132. Liddell, "Two Friends," 63.

56. Gleadow to Pym, Oct. 29, 1934, PYM MS. 150, fol. 93, warned her about

Nazis. Sandra Diary 2, Mar. 31, April 6–10, 1934, PYM MS. 102, fols. 57 verso, 66, admired uniforms; swastika pin. Daybook, July 31, 1941, PYM MS. 107, fol. 69 verso, expressed regret about affection for Friedbert.

57. Sandra Diary 2, April 1, 1934, PYM MS. 102, fols. 60–60 verso.

58. Sandra Diary 2, April 18, 1934, PYM MS. 102, fol. 72, Pym's fears of immodesty, cut from *VPE*, 38. Sandra Diary 1, June 9, 1933, PYM MS. 101, fol. 70, told Gleadow about Henry Harvey. Gleadow to Pym, Aug. 3, 1935, PYM MS. 150, fol. 97 verso, could not take Harvey seriously. Honor Wyatt, July 3, 1987, BBC interview, claimed that Pym over dramatized her 1942 affair with Wyatt's estranged husband, Gordon Glover.

59. D. W. Winnicott, "Communicating and Not Communicating Leading to a Study of Certain Opposites," 185.

60. Holt, interview with author, May 22, 1985.

2. Pym's Moratorium

1. Sandra Diary 3, June 19, 1934, PYM MS. 103, fol. 1–1 verso. Throughout her Oxford days, Pym frequently reported mood swings, from mild hysteria to mild depression, often in response to the actions of the men in her life.

2. Sandra Diary 3, June 19, 1934, PYM MS. 103, fols. 1–1 verso, hopes to go to Germany but worries about the future. Pym to Robert Liddell, Jan. 31, Mar. 13, Mar. 30, 1936, PYM MS. 153, fols. 161 verso–162, 170 verso, 175 verso.

Throughout the early days of their correspondence, Robert Liddell encouraged Pym's writing and teased her about Henry Harvey, while at the same time making it clear that Harvey was forming attachments elsewhere, Liddell to Pym, Jan. 19, 1936, PYM MS. 153, fol. 94. Liddell to Pym, Mar. 1, 1936, PYM MS. 153, fol. 102, humorously advised her to forget other men. She should keep to her plan of marrying Henry, a hope which he knew would never be satisfied, while becoming a writer.

3. Hilary Pym Walton, interview with author, May 15, 1986, described Pym's financial reasons for living at home. Sandra Diary 3, Mar. 8, 1935, PYM MS. 103, fol. 19 verso, glad to be with own age group.

4. Rupert Gleadow to Pym, Oct. 10, 1934, PYM MS. 150, fol. 90, surprised about absence of job. Gleadow to Pym, Aug. 3, 1935, PYM MS. 150, fol. 96, noted that being unemployed allowed her to travel whenever she chose.

St. Hilda's College Register, 1893–1972, 91–95. Dorothy Pedley and Hannah Topping, two of her close friends, took further degrees and then began to build their careers.

Pym to Elsie Harvey, July 20, 1938, *VPE*, 84, reported that Mary Sharp, her university confidante, had married shortly after arriving in America. Holt, *Lot*, 90, mentions that Mrs. Walton began her career with the BBC in 1939, two years after receiving her degree.

Heilbrun, *Writing*, 38–39; Elizabeth Abel, Marianne Hirsch, and Elizabeth Langland, Introduction to *The Voyage In: Fictions of Female Development*, 7.

5. Rossen, *World*, 120, calls Helena Napier's (*EW*) return to her mother a "symbolic regression." Erik H. Erikson, *Young Man Luther: A Study in Psychoanalysis and History*, 43, develops the concept of an expanded moratorium. Anne M. Wyatt-Brown, " 'The Lumber Room': Suffering and Creativity in the Novels of Barbara Pym," applies Erikson's concept to Pym.

6. Heilbrun, *Writing*, 49–50. Both Erikson, *Luther*, 98–100, and George Pickering, *Creative Malady: Illness in the Lives and Minds of George Darwin, Florence Nightingale, Mary Baker Eddy, Sigmund Freud, Marcel Proust, Elizabeth Barrett Browning*, 7, have also described the importance of moratorium in the lives of talented young people.

7. A. A. Milne, Introduction to *The Wind in the Willows*, by Kenneth Grahame, pp. vii–x (New York: Limited Editions Club, 1940), quoted by Michael Steig, *Stories of Reading: Subjectivity and Literary Understanding*, 79, defines a household book as a family favorite. It provides "a test of character" for those who seek to become our intimates. Pym had certain books that she regarded as "a touchstone" of the worth of her men friends.

Liddell to Pym, Nov. 17, 1935, PYM MS. 153, fol. 78; Anglo-Catholic Datebook, [n.d.] begun 1935, PYM MS. 89, fols. 9 verso, 27 verso, recorded dates of the college for governesses and Coventry Patmore's conversion.

Howard Gardner, *Artful Scribbles : The Significance of Children's Drawings*, 47, claims that child artists are either *patterners* or *dramatists*. Pym was clearly a dramatist. Throughout her life, she celebrated "the pageantry of interpersonal relations."

8. As early as 1901, Yonge's novels were considered tame according to Edith Sichel, quoted by Elizabeth Segel, " 'As the Twig is Bent . . .': Gender and Childhood Reading," 176.

Sir Paul Harvey, *The Oxford Companion to English Literature*, 867, provides an outline of Keble's life. Yonge was such an ardent disciple of his that local people still believe that she suffered from the pangs of unrequited love.

Quotations, Christabel Coleridge, *Charlotte Mary Yonge: Her Life and Letters*, 183–85. Coleridge declares that readers were inspired by Ethel, who renounces love in favor of doing good works in the parish.

9. Charlotte M. Yonge, *The Daisy Chain or Aspirations: A Family Chronicle*, 179–83. Anglo-Catholic Notebook, PYM MS. 89, fols. 18 verso–19 verso. The author frequently borrowed the names of Yonge's characters: Wilmet, *GB*; Flora, Pym's generic young woman, *HFN* and *JP*; and Robina (Fairfax), a minor figure in *UA*.

10. Charlotte Brontë, *Jane Eyre*. In a manuscript version of *EW*, PYM MSS. 14, fol. 22, Rocky Napier is a painter like Mr. Rochester. Wyatt, *Reconstructing Desire*, 23–40, explores the fantasies aroused by reading *Jane Eyre*. Some readers claim that in childhood the book encouraged their rebellion against the patriarchy. For most, Wyatt concludes, the novel reinforces their oedipal desires. Jan Cohn, *Romance and the Erotics of Property: Mass-Market Fiction for Women*, 51–53, points out that popular romance has adapted Mr. Rochester as its archetypal male hero, but emphasized his sexual appeal.

Jane Eyre was the orphaned daughter of a vicar. Before Mrs. Pym's death most of the vicar's daughters have living parents. After Mrs. Pym's death, the daughters are orphans. Pym also refers to governesses/companions in twenty-seven manuscripts. Dependency worried her.

11. Georges Poulet, "Criticism and the Experience of Interiority," 57–59; Victor Nell, *Lost in a Book: The Psychology of Reading for Pleasure*, 215; Jerome Bruner, *Actual Minds, Possible Worlds*, 26, 35, 37.

12. Joanne S. Frye, *Living Stories, Telling Lives: Women and the Novel in Contemporary Experience*, 5. Quotation, Wolfgang Iser, *The Act of Reading: A Theory*

of Aesthetic Response, 131. Wolfgang Iser, "The Reading Process: A Phenomenological Approach," 297, refers to reader of *Jane Eyre.*

13. Pym to Liddell, July 14, 1937, PYM MS. 153, fol. 185 verso; Russell C. Long, "Writer-Audience Relationships: Analysis or Invention?" 225–26.

14. Liddell to Pym, Sept. 4, 1934, Sept 15, 1936, PYM MS. 153, fols. 40, 125 verso, mentions what a comfort early parts of *STG* were. Robert Liddell, *A Mind at Ease: Barbara Pym and Her Novels,* 14–15, describes the assistance that he gave Pym. Liddell to Pym, Aug. 2, 1945, PYM MS. 155, fols. 87–88, wrote that Jonathan Cape, who had turned the novel down in 1936, had asked to see a revised version. Cape recommended that she make the novel somewhat more spiteful than the earlier version. G. Wren Howard, Cape's partner, wanted her to reduce her copious quotations from English poetry. Liddell to Pym, Aug. 7, Aug. 17, 1937, PYM MS. 155, fols. 91–92 verso, urged her to use the pen name of Crampton Pym, following the tradition of Radcliffe Hall, the famous lesbian writer. He thought that using a man's name would encourage Pym to produce more trenchant prose. Pym, however, preferred to avoid such notoriety. On other matters, Liddell's advice was sound. He encouraged Pym to emphasize Harriet's scheming for her sister and to think of having one of Harriet's suitors propose to Belinda.

Virginia Woolf, "Professions for Women," 238.

15. Norman N. Holland, *The Dynamics of Literary Response,* 30; Madonne M. Miner, "Guaranteed to Please: Twentieth-Century American Women's Bestsellers," 188.

16. Harold Raymond to Pym, Dec. 3, 1935, PYM MS. 163, fols. 43–44.

17. The stories have no dates on them. Liddell to Pym, Nov. 10, 1936, PYM MS. 153, fol. 145, thanks her for sending "Mothers and Fathers." "Trivial Rounds and Common Tasks" refers to the Peace Pledge of March 1938. See reference to Peace Pledge in Daybook, Mar. 3, 1938, *VPE,* 65.

18. Hazel Holt, "The Home Front: Barbara Pym in Oswestry, 1939–1941"; Larkin, quoted by Charles Monteith, "Publishing Larkin," 552.

19. Robyn R. Warhol, "Toward a Theory of the Engaging Narrator: Earnest Interventions in Gaskell, Stowe, and Eliot," 811; "Some Tame Gazelle," [n.d.], 1934, PYM MS. 99, fol. 21.

20. Liddell to Pym, July 30, Sept. 4, Oct. 2, 1934, PYM MS. 153, fols. 39–43 *passim.* Liddell to Pym, Mar. 21, 1934, PYM MS. 153, fol. 27, complained about Alison West-Watson's voracious appetite.

21. Rossen, *World,* 29. *STG* 1, PYM MS. 2, fols. 1, 26, 70; PYM MS. 94, fols. 12 verso, 242, imply intimacy. Pym to Robert Liddell, May 23, 1938, *VPE,* 82–83, discussed a trip to Prague with Friedbert Glück during which he had behaved like a husband.

22. *STG* 1, PYM MS. 2, fols. 36, 174. Sandra Diary 1, May 27, 1933, PYM MS. 101, fol. 67.

23. Laura L. Doan, "Text and the Single Man: The Bachelor in Pym's Dual-Voiced Narrative," 63. *STG* 1, PYM MS. 2, fol. 235a, Belinda complains about Henry.

24. *STG* 1, PYM MS. 2, fols. 278–79, Ricardo's outburst was based in part on a similar episode reported to Pym, Liddell to Pym, Feb. 18, 1935, PYM MS. 153, fol. 56.

Liddell introduced Pym to Compton-Burnett's novels, and both of them were greatly influenced by her work. Charles Burkhart, *The Pleasure of Miss*

Pym, 12–13, discusses Compton-Burnett's effect on Pym's style. Her novels also provided the source of occasional bits of inappropriate violence. Pym to Liddell, Jan. 12, 1940, *VPE,* 100, about Compton-Burnett's influence. She also declared that she loved the details of daily life too much to expunge them as the older novelist habitually did. Pym's imagination was far too tame to grasp some of the radical implications of the older writer's work. "The Novelist's Idea of Everyday Life," Barnes Talk, 1950, PYM MS. 98, fols. 68–71, includes a long passage from a Compton-Burnett novel, in which the speaker describes incestuous feelings. Pym lamely remarked that people probably talked like that then.

STG 1, PYM MS. 2, fols. 411–15, seduction scene. In contrast, Denis Feverel can respond intensely to music without fearing a loss of self-control, *YMFD,* PYM MS. 1, fols. 136, 241–42. *STG* 1, PYM MS. 2, fols. 502–6, 508, Bishop's paranoia.

25. Liddell to Pym, Jan. 19, 1936, PYM MS. 153, fols. 87–89 verso, 94. Pym to Liddell, Jan. 27, 1936, PYM MS. 153, fol. 158. Liddell to Pym, May 4, 1940, PYM MS. 155, fol. 45 verso.

26. Liddell to Pym, Jan. 22, Feb. 5, April 25, 1935, PYM MS. 153, fols. 52, 54, 60, each time addresses her as Cassandra Pym.

27. H. Sagar, literary agent, to Pym, June 15, 1937, PYM MS. 163, fols. 48. He was pleased that Pym had finished *CS,* but reported that *STG* had been rejected ten times, her stories, eight. Sagar to Pym, Aug. 27, 1937, PYM MS. 163, fol. 50, reported Cape's rejection. Harold Raymond, Chatto & Windus, Nov. 1, 1937, PYM MS. 163, fols. 51–52, found *CS* an improvement on *STG,* but too weak to succeed.

CS, PYM MS. 5, fols. 87, 172–73. Holt removed these scenes from the edited version. *STG* 2 and Notes, PYM MS. 3, fol. 3, Pym insinuated that the Archdeacon, a Harvey surrogate, was capable of violent actions. She eventually discarded a Compton-Burnett twist of having Harriet accuse Henry Hoccleve of pushing his wife. "Mothers and Fathers," PYM MS. 94, fols. 7 verso–8, Henry causes his mother-in-law to slip on the ice and then rejects the help of a passing doctor.

28. Liddell to Hilary Pym, Dec. 6, 1937, PYM MS. 154, fol. 68. Holt, *Lot,* 66, quotes the letter in its entirety. Liddell to Pym, June 9, 1937, PYM MS. 154, fol. 24, described Harvey's travel.

29. Liddell to Pym, Dec. 11, 1937, PYM MS. 154, fol. 71, pictures Pym choosing to wear black to a ball, in honor of her widowhood. Refers to the comforts of Compton-Burnett. Sandra Diary 3, Dec. 12, 1937, PYM MS. 103, fols. 65–65 verso. Quotation, Ivy Compton-Burnett, *More Women than Men,* 104.

30. Robert Liddell, "A Success Story," 177. Harvey's wedding may have affected Liddell even more than it did Pym. Liddell to Pym, Dec. 27, 1937, PYM MS. 154, fols. 83–87 verso, described a strange illness that drove him out of Oxford on an unhappy journey. As a result of the attack, he finally gave notice at the Bodleian after years of complaining about his job. Yet he did not actually leave it for the next two and a half years. Liddell to Pym, Feb. 5, 1938, PYM MS. 154, fol. 97, notified Pym that Cape had accepted his novel. Liddell to Pym, July 15, 1940, PYM MS. 155, fol. 55, announced that he was now working in London for the British Council.

31. Amery-like characters appear even more frequently than Harvey-like ones. The Harvey manuscripts include various versions of *STG, CS, GF,*

and these stories: "Back to St. Petersburg," "A Letter From My Love," "Mothers and Fathers," "A Painted Heart," "A Sister's Love," "They Never Write," "Trivial Rounds and Common Tasks," "Unpast Alps," "The Unfinished Flower." Manuscripts inspired by Julian Amery include *GF, LR, HFN, CH, STR,* and *SVS.* Stories and other works include: "The Day the Music Came," "Goodby Balkan Capital," Notes for War Time Novel, Notes for War Time Radio Play, "Something to Remember" and "The White Elephant." Pym wrote one short poem to Harvey, but three to Amery. On the whole, a good source for dating manuscripts is Rossen, "The Pym Papers," 157–60, except for the dating of *GF.* Liddell to Pym, Oct. 11, 1937, PYM MS. 154, fol. 59, refers to *GF*; Pym began *LR* Mar. 10, 1938.

32. Liddell to Pym, Feb. 25, 1937, PYM MS. 154, fol. 10, encouraged Pym to long for middle-age. He urged the twenty-four-year-old Pym to model her behavior on the forty-five-year-old novelist Rose Macaulay, whose talent and commonsense he admired. Only in mid-life, he insisted, was it agreeable to be a woman.

33. Liddell to Pym, Feb. 25, Mar. 14, April 19, May 13, June 9, Oct. 11, 1937, PYM MS. 154, fols. 10–10 verso, 13 verso, 16 verso, 20, 24 verso, and 59.

34. A comment about Ooli's social position was cut from the published version, *GF,* PYM MS. 7, fol. 215.

35. *LR,* PYM MS. 6, fols. 4, 94, 160. Pym later recycled material from *LR* in *JP* and *UA.* Mrs. Cleveland, the vicar's wife in *LR* is like Jane Cleveland in *JP.* Stephen Bone, the curate in *LR,* wears bicycle clips just like Nicholas Cleveland, April 14, 1938, PYM MS. 6, fol. 78 verso. Henry Grainger in *LR,* like Nicholas, smiles benignly over his spectacles, PYM MS. 6, fol. 106.

LR, May 14, 1938, PYM MS. 6, fols. 74–75 and *UA,* 13, two sets of sisters stalk a new man. April 15, 1938, PYM MS. 6, fol. 81 verso and *UA,* 39, Rosamond and Sophia are both Pre-Raphaelite beauties.

36. *LR,* PYM MS. 6, fol. 143. Pym and her heroines regard governesses and companions as an endangered species, but male characters are indifferent. Hughie Otway in *STR* recommends that there be an agency to exterminate them, PYM MS. 11, fol. 59.

Pym never settled on a name for the Amery figure in *LR,* calling him at various points Lawrence/Gerald/Hughie/ Otway/Cleveland. Holt, *Lot,* 78, calls him Gerald Cleveland. Henry Grainger is probably named for an Oswestry youth named Grainger, who nearly died when he ran his motorcycle into Mrs. Pym's car (Pym was a passenger), Pym to Liddell, Jan. 27, 1936, PYM MS. 153, fols. 159–60. The other rider was killed, causing an inquest some months later. Pym described the court scene, which was highly traumatic for both her mother and her, Pym to Liddell, April 24, 1936, PYM MS. 153, fol. 177.

37. *LR,* PYM MS. 6, fols. 149, 189.

38. Holt, *Lot,* 93, describes the early days of the war. Daybook, Oct. 23, Nov. 26, 1939, Feb. 25, 1940, PYM MS. 105, fols. 160 verso, 177 verso, Ack, Pym's Aunt Jane, was operated on and then diagnosed with cancer. Daybook, PYM MS. 106, fol. 19, Ack died.

39. Pym's mood is similar to that of Miss Beatrice Gossage, Notes for a Wartime Novel, PYM MS. 90. Miss Gossage is an early version of Miss Gossett, the governess in Pym's postwar radio play, "Something," PYM MS. 96, fols. 193–229. Miss Gossage falls in love with the oldest son of the family, a Julian Amery surrogate and lives off her memories. She is melancholy. Miss Gossett in "Something" is more stringent.

40. Daybook, June 21, July 12, 13, 1939, PYM MS. 105, fols. 98 verso, 109–109 verso, Pym telephoned Julian Amery. Daybook, Mar. 9 and June 19, 1940, PYM MS. 106, fols. 21, 35 verso; Daybook, July 4, 1941, PYM MS. 107, fol. 63, Pym wrote to Amery.

41. Jill Rubenstein, " 'For the Ovaltine Had Loosened her Tongue': Failures of Speech in Barbara Pym's *Less than Angels*," 579, comments that the few upper-class characters in Pym's novels are both "ineffectual" and inarticulate. Clipping of Mrs. Amery, PYM MS. 97, fol. iii. *HFN*, PYM MS. 9, fols. 6–7, Lyall Wraye's infidelity. Passage was cut from published novel.

42. The Otway/Clevelands of *LR* are transformed and divided into Amery and Pym surrogates. The Wrayes in *HFN* represent another version of the Amerys. The Palfreys of *HFN* are more like the Pyms. Canon and Mrs. Palfrey, with their daughter Flora, first appear as the Wilmots in *CS*, reappear as Jane and Philip Otway/Benjamin Cleveland in *LR*, and later find their apotheosis as the Clevelands in *JP*. Pym recycles minor characters as well, including Connie Aspinall and Agnes Grote, and Beatrice Wyatt and her mother. Agnes is based on Hester Carey, *STG* 1, PYM MS. 2, and later becomes the more interesting Edith Liversidge, *STG*. Mrs. Wyatt in the manuscript version of *HFN* is no longer English. She becomes Gudrun Wyatt, a Swedish tyrant, like Fru Lindblom in *GF*.

43. Connie Aspinall, *STG*, 30; Lady Nollard, *UA*, PYM MS. 20, fol. 15; revision of *HFN*, PYM MS. 87; evacuee smoking in bed, *HFN*, 240; *FGL*, 60.

44. Daybook, June 27, 1941, PYM MS. 107, fol. 61.

45. Vicars' wives include Mrs. Wilmot in *CS*, who is quite bored by her husband's talk of school bills and cricket and Mrs. Cleveland/Otway in *LR*, who attends church on Easter wearing a raincoat, straw hat, and spiked golf shoes, Mar. 28, 1938, PYM MS. 6, fol. 55.

46. Burkhart, *Pleasure*, 12, points out that Mrs. Killigrew talks like an Ivy Compton-Burnett character. Charles Burkhart, "Glamourous Acolytes: Homosexuality in Pym's World," 102, adds that Mrs. Killigrew's desiccated son, a librarian of course, is a spiteful gossip. Margaret Morganroth Gullette, *Safe at Last in the Middle Years: The Invention of the Midlife Progress Novel: Saul Bellow, Margaret Drabble, Anne Tyler, and John Updike*, xvii–xviii, comments on our joy as readers when "dragons," older characters like Miss Doggett, are conquered by the young. Gullette observes that no matter how old we are when we read about the "discomfiture of the dragons . . . we are asked to be psychically adolescent, and accept the given, that our parents' generation represents the wicked world in its conventionality, vice, rigidity, or hypocrisy." In Pym's manuscripts, however, the dragons are members of her grandparents' generation, and they cannot be conquered, merely momentarily subverted.

47. Even Stephen Bone of *LR* shares many typical failings of curates. Only his miserable marriage makes him less complacent.

48. Wyatt-Brown, "Ellipsis," 45, 49, n. 45. Echoes of the Gleadow fiasco abound in this episode. Barbara Bird finds a magazine in the hotel lobby dated 1932, the time of the incident, *CH*, 189. In the manuscript, Barbara prepares a dramatic story to tell her friend Sarah Penrose, as soon as she leaves the hotel. Her evasive replies to Sarah's persistent questioning leave Sarah with the mistaken impression that there has been a sexual encounter. In reality Barbara panicked and fled before anything happened, PYM MS. 10, fols. 263–65. The scene was cut, *CH*, 190.

49. Burkhart, *Pleasure*, 34. Daybooks, 1940–1941, PYM MSS. 106, 107, *passim*, flirting with young soldiers.

50. *CH*, PYM MS. 10, fol. 293; quoted by Rossen, *World*, 31. Hilary Pym Walton, interview with author, May, 9, 1985, said that Pym had discouraged some men from proposing. Holt, *Lot*, 27, 59, Pym formally rejected a few men.

51. Charlotte Brontë, *Villette*. The heroine, Lucy Snowe, is also orphaned early in life. Reacting to the shock of bereavement, she retreats to the country as a companion. After the older woman's death, she begins to take charge of her own destiny. She moves first to London and then to Brussels trying to support herself independently. *STR*, PYM MS. 11, fols. 17, 23, 39–40.

52. *STR*, PYM MS. 11, fols. 52 verso–54, 56, 62–63; Daybook, Oct. 24, 1938, PYM MS. 104, fol. 161, ice cream. Rossen, "On Not Being Jane Eyre," 153, points out that Pym's heroines had to live without the happy ending of *Jane Eyre*. Rossen, "Pym Papers," 159, also suggests that *STR* may have been "an early experiment for *Excellent Women*." The narrator is very like Mildred.

53. *EW*, PYM MS. 13, fol. 1.

54. *STR*, PYM MS. 11, fol. 19. Not only did Pym track men at Oxford, but she walked by Julian's house on occasion, Daybook, Jan. 19, Feb. 5, July 4, July 5, 1939, PYM MS. 105, fols. 22, 30 verso, 105–105 verso.

The Bouldings have something in common with Julian and Winifred Malory, *EW*, and Dulcie's Uncle Bertram and Aunt Hermione, who, though not clergy, are devout celibates and bicker constantly, *NFR*, 100. Lolly's black clothes, *SVS*, PYM MS. 12, fols. 179 verso–80.

55. Daybook, Sept. 14, 1941, PYM MS. 107, fol. 81, began *SVS*. Daybook, Sept. 17, 1943, *VPE*, 157, thinking of revising spy novel.

3. Transitions of War and Deconstructing Comedy

1. Erikson, *Luther*, 103.

2. Holt, *Lot*, 108, describes the break by quoting from Pym's letter to Henry Harvey, [n.d.] c. Jan 1943.

3. Deborah Tannen, *You Just Don't Understand: Women and Men in Conversation*, 49–53, argues that women establish symmetrical or equal relationships by exchanging stories that reveal their common weakness or problems. Men more often form hierarchical or asymmetrical relationships.

4. Gail Godwin, *A Southern Family*, 69; Carolyn G. Heilbrun, *Writing a Woman's Life*, 28; Mervyn Rothstein, "Saul Bellow on Life, Love, Art and 'Heartbreak'," 22.

5. Sandra Diary 3, Nov. 26, 1935, PYM MS. 103, fol. 42, also addressed the reader directly.

Linda Flower, "Writer-Based Prose: A Cognitive Basis for Problems in Writing," 20. Flower would say that Pym had begun to produce "reader-based prose." Quotation, John Bayley, "Snouty," 14.

6. Sandra Diary 1, Mar. or April, 1933, PYM MS. 101, fol. 60.

7. Alan Davis to Pym, July 2, 1945, PYM MS. 148, fol. 31 verso, naval gossip. *A Full Life*, PYM MS. 13, fols. 1, 4, used his story. Davis to Pym, Jan. 11, 1946, PYM MS. 148, fol. 62 verso, mentions "Silence at the End of the Table."

8. Davis to Pym, Aug. 31, 1945, PYM MS. 148, fol. 48, reported that Pym had little idea of the severity of her mother's illness when she left Naples. Holt, *Lot*, 132, says that Pym had been told of her mother's abdominal cancer.

9. Holt, *Lot*, 98, Pym revised *STG* in 1940 and sent it to Curtis Brown, the literary agency, with no success. "Ups and Downs of a Writer's Life," Address to Senior Wives Fellowship, Headington, Oxfordshire, May 15, 1978, PYM MS. 98, fol. 80, discusses circumstances surrounding revision of *STG*.

STG 2 and Notes, PYM MS. 3, fol. 2, Mr. Mold's affair. Liddell to Pym, Oct. 18, 1934, PYM MS. 153, fol. 44, referring to the early short story version, wonders if Mr. Field would make Hilary a suitable mate. Quotation, PYM MS. 3, fol. 2 verso; found in Michael Cotsell, *Barbara Pym*, 21. PYM MS. 3, fol. 12, Pym considered having the Bishop propose to Harriet, but changed her mind. Liddell to Pym, Aug. 17, 1954, PYM MS. 155, fol. 92 verso, suggested that one of Harriet's supposed suitors might propose to Belinda.

10. Holt, *Lot*, 133–34, Mrs. Pym's death. Cotsell, *Pym*, 83, points out that in *GB* when Wilmet's mother-in-law Sybil marries and forces the younger pair to move out, they are liberated by her move. Perhaps Pym in some obscure way realized that her mother's death, sad though it was, had liberated her.

11. Robert L. Rubinstein, "Never Married Elderly as a Social Type: Re-evaluating Some Images," 109.

Jaber F. Gubrium, "Being Single in Old Age," 31, points out that single people endure "the 'crisis' of marriage . . . in early adulthood, when most people marry." Afterwards, however, single people adjust to their solitary life. In old age they are spared the pangs of bereavement of losing a spouse. Harold Raymond to Pym, Dec. 3, 1935, PYM MS. 163, fol. 43.

12. Vera John-Steiner, *Notebooks of the Mind: Explorations of Thinking*, 131.

13. Jonathan Cape to Pym, Mar. 29, 1949, PYM MS. 163, fol. 56. Liddell to Pym, Aug. 17, 1945, PYM MS. 155, fols. 92–92 verso, re-read the novel and offered much good advice. In subsequent letters he urged her to complete the revision. Liddell to Pym, Mar. 11, 1948, Tuesday in Passion Week (April 12), 1949, PYM MS. 155, fols. 116, 130. The first expressed joy that her revisions were finally complete, the second that the book would now be published.

14. Robert Emmet Long, *Barbara Pym*, 34–35; quotation, 38. Bowman, "Pym's Subversive Subtext," 90–91, Belinda's thoughts. See also Anne M. Wyatt-Brown, "E. M. Forster and the Transformation of Comedy," chapter 1, for the role of marriage in comedy.

15. Long, *Pym*, 31, thinks the marriages balance the rejections and restore the social order. Long, 39, also declares that Mr. Mold "is a humors character from Dickens," whose only function is to propose to Harriet. Grote proposes to Belinda merely "to provide a kind of balance to the proposal made to her sister." In fact, Grote's behavior signifies that Pym had finally overcome her despair about losing Henry Harvey.

Diana Benet, *Something to Love: Barbara Pym's Novels*, 16, convincingly argues that *STG* contains "an unmarriage plot," one which emphasizes the importance of love, but devalues marriage.

16. Virginia Woolf, "Professions for Women," 238.

Notes for Wartime Radio Play, PYM MS 99, fol. 8, the governess feels daring when she reads Patmore's poetry.

17. Bowman, "Pym's Subversive Subtext," 84. Philip Larkin to Pym, Sept. 27, 1976, PYM MS. 151, fol. 115.

18. Anne M. Wyatt-Brown, "From Fantasy to Pathology: Images of Aging in the Novels of Barbara Pym," 5, senior scholars. Charles Burkhart, *The Pleasure of Miss Pym*, 31, compares *STG* to Elizabeth Gaskell's *Cranford*.

19. E. M. Forster also experimented with comedy because he was unwilling to celebrate marriage, the traditional comic ending, Wyatt-Brown, "Forster." E. M. Forster, "Nottingham Lace,".identified with his young hero who dislikes suburban life and was judged to be inadequate by his elders. Forster understood the predicament but could not devise a way for his hero to escape.

20. Daybook, Aug. 25 and Oct. 15, 1941, PYM MS. 107, fols. 76, 88 verso.

21. Burkhart, *Pleasure*, 62–63; Rossen, *World*, 103–6.

April 4, 1978, "Finding a Voice: A Radio Talk," 384, mentioned learning from the anthropologists.

22. *STG* I, PYM MS. 2, fol. 2, Hawaii. Long, *Pym*, 35–36, finds the passionless Bishop awkward when dealing with sexuality.

23. Long, *Pym*, 26, and Benet, *Something*, 52, discuss sexual innuendos. Reader to Pym, April 16, 1952, PYM MS. 167, fol. 113, *EW*.

24. Fan to Pym, Oct. 27, 1977, PYM MS. 169, fols. 191–93. Alan Davis to Pym, May 31, 1950, PYM MS. 167, fol. 28.

25. "A Wedge of Misery Tea Time," PYM MS. 99, fols. 46–48.

26. Gordon Glover to Pym, May 1, 1950, PYM MS. 167, fol. 32.

27. Literary Notebook, May [n.d.], Sept. 12, c. Jan., 1950, PYM MS. 40, fols. 12, 16–16 verso, 18–20, 25 verso, ideas for "The Day the Music Came," "Pilgrimage," "The Rich Man in His Castle," "A Few Days Before Winter," "The Funeral." All rejected as too conventional.

Chloris Heaton Ross, *Woman and Beauty*, to Pym, Dec. 7, 1949, PYM MS. 163, fol. 4, accepted "The White Elephant."

Literary Notebook, [n.d.] c. Mar., [n.d.] c. fall 1950, PYM MS. 41, fols. 14, 18, ideas for "So, Some Tempestuous Morn" and "English Ladies." Dorothy Daly, literary agent, to Pym, Nov. 30, 1953, PYM MS. 163, fol. 24, reported that these stories were rejected for being too conventional, whereas "A Few Days Before Winter," was much too daring.

Notebook, July 22, 1945, PYM MS. 84, fol. 1 verso, "Silence at the End of the Table." Notebook, ideas for "Silence at the End of the Table" and material for "Something to Remember," July 22, 1945, PYM MS. 84, fol. 1 verso.

28. Daly to Pym, Nov. 16, 1953, PYM MS. 163, fol. 23.

29. Liddell to Pym, St. James Day (Oct. 23), 1948, PYM MS. 155, fol. 120, told her not to despair about being thirty-five; after all she might marry the vicar of St. Gabriel's, unless he was already married or celibate. Liddell to Pym, Oct. 15, 1950, PYM MS. 156, fol. 16, teased Pym about her possible personal involvement with her Barnes's vicar, his sister, and the children. Mildred's reaction to similar remarks indicates how Pym felt.

30. Rocky's talk provides an example of the linguist Robin Lakoff's third rule of politeness, encouraging friendly or intimate feelings of camaraderie, Robin Lakoff, "The Logic of Politeness: Or Minding Your P's and Q's," in C. Corum, T. C. Smith-Stark, and A. Weiser, eds., *Papers from the Ninth Regional Meeting of the Chicago Linguistic Society*, 292–305 (Chicago: Chicago Linguistics Society, 1973), cited by Georgia M. Green, *Pragmatics and Natural Language Understanding*, 143–44. Pym is well aware that a lonely spinster like Mildred would find Rocky's interest in her personal life irresistible. On the other hand, Rocky is merely treating Mildred like the WRNS officers during the war whom he so effortlessly set at ease, *EW*, 9.

31. [n.d.] c. spring, 1952, PYM MS. 163, fols. 205, 209, 212, 214, reviews *EW*.

quotation, Larkin to Pym, July 14, 1964, PYM MS. 151, fols. 22–23; quoted in Hazel Holt, "Philip Larkin and Barbara Pym: Two Quiet People," 60.

Quotation, Philip Larkin, "The World of Barbara Pym," 260.

32. Notebook, June 7, 1946, PYM MS. 84, fol. 7 verso.

33. Literary Notebook, April 1, 1965, PYM MS. 61, fol. 3, commented upon Richard Roberts's gift of intimacy.

Pym loved birthday cards and valentines; on her birthday June 2, 1964, she recorded her pleasure when Richard Roberts gave her an antique cup, *VPE*, 227.

Everard Bone's first name is typical of those of romance heroes, Jan Cohn, *Romance and the Erotics of Property: Mass-Market Fiction for Women*, 26.

34. "The Novelist's Use of Everyday Life," Barnes talk, 1950, PYM MS. 98, fol. 63. *Full Life*, PYM MS. 13, fol. 8 verso, Everard might propose to Mildred properly. Barbara Evans to Pym, April 15, 1952, PYM MS. 167, fol. 98, complains about *EW*.

35. Burkhart, *Pleasure*, 35; Long, *Pym*, 55; Benet, *Something*, 45. Cf. Rossen, "On Not Being Jane Eyre," 147–48.

36. Cohn, *Romance*, 22, points out that in popular romances, the heroine has hostile feelings toward the hero despite his sexual allure. Everard and Mildred are not sexually dynamic. Cohn, 165, describes the conventions of popular romance, which assign the heroine a new economic status and an exciting sex life. Mildred, however, gains neither one by marrying Everard.

Long, *Pym*, 55. Long, 88, suggests that Mildred "will be cannibalized by Everard Bone's sense of masculine importance."

37. Fan to Pym, June 7, 1952, PYM MS. 167, fols. 103–4 verso. BBC correspondence on radio serial, Mar. 25, May 8, 1952, PYM MS. 163, fols. 157, 173, broadcast started April 28, 1952, and following two weeks. Royalty Statement, June 30, 1952, PYM MS. 163, fol. 184, shows that two months after the serial, *EW* had sold 5,477 copies. Pym to John Guest, Longmans, May 26, 1963, PYM MS. 164, fol. 140, *STG* sold 3,722 copies.

A Full Life, PYM MS. 13, fols. 1–1 verso, was less cheerful than *EW*. Two of the three women, an anthropologist (Mrs. Mogden, later Helena Napier), a vicar's sister (Winifred Malory) and a spinster (Mildred Lathbury) are deserted by the men in their lives. Mogden wants to free himself for his Wren mistress; Malory wants to marry. The women end by living together. Later the spinster is asked to become a companion. From the start, however, Mildred is to suffer from unrequited love for Rocky Napier. Whether or not the widow, Allegra Gray, should try to marry Everard Bone or Julian Napier is less important.

38. PYM MSS. 13, 84, fol. 5 verso; 90, fols. 3–16; 96, fols. 193–229; and 99, fols. 6–10 represent Pym's attempts to interweave her governess fantasy with her war experiences. Notes for a Wartime Novel, PYM MS. 90, fols. 4, 9, Pym contrasted a modern intelligent woman in WW II, whose love affairs lack poetry and intelligent conversation, to a Victorian spinster. The spinster Gossy, however, took over and became the focus of the Radio Play.

Notebook, Mar. 3, 1946, PYM MS. 84, fol. 7, mentions a woman dressed in cast-off clothing, who becomes Winifred Malory in *EW*. *Full Life*, PYM MS. 13, fol. 18, Mildred Lathbury appears, a clergyman's daughter. Instead of being a companion, she works in a missionary society that ministers to the needs of impoverished gentlewomen.

Daniel George to Pym, March 15, 1951, PYM MS. 163, fol. 128.

39. Inconsistencies in the correspondence make it hard to know exactly when *JP* was reprinted. J. C. Parry, Marks and Spencer, to G. Wren Howard, director of Cape [copy sent to Pym], Nov. 10, 1953, Howard to Pym, Dec. 4, 1953; Pym to Cape, April 3, 1955, PYM MS. 163, fols. 245, 248, 251. Pym to John Guest, Longmans, May 26, 1963, MS. 164, fol. 140, *JP* had sold 5,219 copies, making it second only to *EW* with 6,752. Although Cape's letters to Pym are cordial, she never repeated the success of *EW*.

40. Notes for BBC Radio Talk, broadcast April 4, 1978, PYM MS. 98, fol. 32; quoted by Mary Strauss-Noll, "Love and Marriage in the Novels," 80.

41. Helen Phillips, Presentation to Drawing Circle, Belfast, Ireland, Mar. 20, 1978, PYM MS. 98, fol. 117, reported Pym's claim to have based Jane on her mother.

Literary Notebook, [n.d.] 1950, PYM MS. 41, fols. 5, 11.

42. At one point Jane discusses medieval banks, using material from "Henry Shakespeare," a story Pym wrote when she was sixteen, PYM MS. 97, fols. 7–8. Although Long, *Pym*, 78, stresses the borrowing from *CH* in his analysis, he is unaware that Pym recycled material from other early material.

Elizabeth Taylor to Pym, Sept. 27, Oct. 3, 1952, PYM MS. 162–63, fols. 2–4, went with Pym to a P.E.N. meeting (an international association for prominent authors) to hear Angus Wilson. (Pym was a member of P.E.N. and the Society of Authors, PYM MS. 100, fols. 13–22.) George to Pym, Oct. 10, 1952, PYM MS. 148, fol. 86, saw them at meeting. Quotation, Diana Benet, *Something*, 48.

43. Literary Notebook, June 1, 1952, PYM MS. 43, fol. 2. Cf. Benet, *Something*, 49. She declares that "Jane has a conviction of personal uselessness and lives a strangely unfocused existence." Prudence is no better: "The model each woman has assumed dictates self-defeating behavior." Long, *Pym*, 87–88, accuses Nicholas of being childish, and blames Nicholas for depriving Jane "of a spacious adult world in which to live." According to Long, Jane gave up her research when she married. She "is 'devoured' by" Nicholas.

44. Burkhart, *Pleasure*, 33. He is, however, referring to *JP* not "So, Some," but it is true in both cases.

"So, Some Tempestuous Morn," PYM MS. 94, fols. 152, 157–58, Miss Morrow's lapses, clergyman's memory, and cake. PYM MS. 94, fol. 163, is a later version in which Miss Morrow waves to the clergyman from her bedroom window, a clearly provocative act. Dorothy Daly to Pym, Oct. 22, 1954, PYM MS. 163, fol. 28, "So, Some," rejected.

45. Burkhart, *Pleasure*, 36, calls Jane "fey, poetic, and sudden." Anatole Broyard, "Reading and Writing: Overflowing Her Situation," 27, calls Jane "The Woman Who Overflows Her Situation." Like some of E. M. Forster's mother figures, Jane tries "to connect the low and the high, the near and the far, the everyday and the eternal." Pym, however, treats Jane with amusement.

Helen Phillips, Presentation, PYM MS. 98, fol. 118, compared *JP* to E. F. Benson's *Make Way for Lucia*, a saga dear to Pym's heart.

46. Long, *Pym*, 86. Literary Notebook, [n.d.], 1950, PYM MS. 41, fol. 6 verso, friend was drying tobacco leaves. Quotation, Burkhart, *Pleasure*, 38. Most of the critics have noticed Pym's hostility to the males in this novel.

47. Rebecca West, "And They All Lived Unhappily Ever After," *Times Literary Supplement*, 26 July 1974, 779, discusses the negative view of marriage to be found in the novels of Margaret Drabble, Penelope Mortimer, and Doris Lessing among others.

48. Wyatt-Brown, "Forster," chapters 5 and 6, Stephen in *The Longest Journey* and Mrs. Wilcox in *Howards End* both resonate like Ibsen characters. They are identified with the land that they love.

49. Marks and Spencer to Cape, Oct. 30, 1953, PYM MS. 163, fol. 234, treated a statement by Miss Doggett as if Pym had herself insulted their goods. G. Wren Howard to Pym, Dec. 4, 1953, PYM MS. 163, fol. 248, reported that Cape agreed to change all future printings. Nonetheless the 1979 reprint contains the disputed passage, *JP,* 125. Pym to Jonathan Cape, April 3, 1955, PYM MS. 163, fol. 251, novel jinxed. Michael Howard, Director Cape, to Pym, July 1, 1957, PYM MS. 164, fols. 15, asked her to be especially careful about libel. M. M. Bakhtin, "Discourse in the Novel," 320, discusses how author and characters engage in a "novelistic dialogue" within a novel.

4. Playing Detective in Suburbia

1. Royalty report, Dec. 31, 1953, PYM MS. 163, fol. 257, within three months of publication, *JP* had sold 4,657 copies, 820 fewer than *EW.* Pym to John Guest, Longmans, May 26, 1963, PYM MS. 164, fol. 140, eventually *JP* sold 5,219 copies, 1,533 fewer than *EW.* Graham Watson, Curtis Brown, April 2, 1954, PYM MS. 147, fol. 175.

2. Correspondence Watson and Pym, Oct. 13, Nov. 5, and Nov. 8, 1953; April 3, 1954–April 3, 1955, PYM MS. 147, fols. 170–72, 176–88. Dorothy Daly, literary agent, to Pym, Nov. 16, 1953, PYM MS. 163, fol. 23, Watson had asked Daly to place Pym stories. Wyatt-Brown, "Ellipsis," 24–25, also covers the situation.

Michael S. Howard, *Jonathan Cape Publisher: Herbert Jonathan Cape, G. Wren Howard,* 273–74, confirms Watson's analysis of Cape's shortcomings. Howard is the son of G. Wren Howard, Cape's partner.

3. Barbara Everett, "The Pleasures of Poverty," 20, argues that Pym invests this insignificant suburb with considerable feeling and meaning.

4. Jane Nardin, *Barbara Pym,* 98.

5. Jill Rubenstein, " 'For the Ovaltine Had Loosened her Tongue': Failures of Speech in Barbara Pym's *Less than Angels,*" 576–77.

6. Georgia M. Green, *Pragmatics and Natural Language Understanding,* 1. Rubenstein, "Failures of Speech," suggests that many characters in *LTA* fail to communicate. The discourse of some is grounded in fact, whereas others veer unpredictably into fantasies. M. M. Bakhtin, "Discourse in the Novel," 356, declares that dialogue in the novel makes the most of "the mutual nonunderstanding represented by people *who speak in different languages.*"

7. Rossen, "On Not Being Jane Eyre," 148, 155, n. 1. Her comment that Pym converts *Jane Eyre* "into a drawing room mode" also applies to *LTA,* as well as to the novels she discusses.

Literary Notebook, Jan. 1955, PYM MS. 45, fol. 24, scene from *Jane Eyre.*

8. Literary Notebook, [n.d.] c. Jan., 1952, PYM MS. 43, fols. 14 and 15; Literary Notebook, Nov. 17, Dec. 31, 1954, PYM MS. 45, fols. 20–21, 23 verso, Peter Lloyd. Liddell to Pym, Aug. 1, 1936, PYM MS. 153, fol. 119, reported Harvey's churlish behavior about Pym's typing.

Quotation, John Halperin, "Barbara Pym and the War of the Sexes," 93.

9. Critics disagree about which character is central in *LTA.* Diana Benet,

Something to Love: Barbara Pym's Novels, 64, believes that Tom is most important. Robert Emmet Long, *Barbara Pym*, 103, claims that neither dominates. The narrative "reflects the leveling effect of modern society, the reduction of size and effectiveness in individuals." Rossen, *World*, 144–45, 149, regards Catherine as the most important. Rossen notes that Catherine, like Pym herself, uses her craft to write out her fantasies and gain control of them.

LTA, PYM MS. 16, fols. 3, 8, Deborah, Catherine's desire for stability. Literary Notebook, May 5, 1955, PYM MS. 46, fol. 12 verso, Vogue extract.

10. Holt, *Lot*, 162, describes Smith's introduction. Pym to Robert Smith, Oct. 24, 1955, PYM MS. 162/1, fol. 9, defends Catherine.

Jan Cohn, *Romance and the Erotics of Property: Mass-Market Fiction for Women*, 5, points out that in popular romance women are the experts in love, for "men are now busy elsewhere." Quotation from Rossen, *World*, 145. Catherine's story is mentioned in *GB*, 152.

11. Literary Notebook, Dec. 1954, PYM MS. 45, fol. 23, refers to Woolf's diary. *STG*, draft 2 and notes, [n.d.] PYM MS. 3, fol. 5, Pym compared the scene where Harriet prepares the macaroni to Woolf's *To the Lighthouse*. E. M. Forster, *Howards End*, 30–32. Quotation from Nardin, *Pym*, 92.

12. Daniel George to Pym, Mar. 31, 1955, PYM MS. 163, fol. 277, liked *LTA*; Jonathan Cape to Pym, Apr. 14, 1955, PYM MS. 163, fol. 281, liked *LTA*; Jenifer Armour, Advertisement Manager, Cape, Oct. 11, 1955, PYM MS. 163, fol. 299, apology; G. Wren Howard to Pym, Oct. 28 and Dec. 6, 1955, PYM MS. 163, fols. 301, 303, subscription figures and BBC; Jean Mossop, Cape, to Pym, Aug. 2, 1956, PYM MS. 163, fol. 304, Vanguard contract. Pym to John Guest, Longmans, May 26, 1963, PYM MS. 164, fol. 140, sales figures for all six novels.

13. Vanguard brochure, PYM MS. 100, fol. 25 verso. Pym to John Guest, Longmans, May 26, 1963, PYM MS. 164, fol. 140, lists *EW, JP*, and *GB* as Book Society Recommendations. Jean Mossop to Pym, Jan. 12, 1978, PYM MS. 166, fol. 96, Vanguard reverted rights. Royalty reports from Vanguard, Nov. 4, 1957–May 1, 1977, PYM MS. 163, fols. 340–68. Cape to Pym, May 29, 1957, PYM MS. 164, fol. 5, accepted *GB*.

14. Jan Fergus, "*A Glass of Blessings*, Jane Austen's *Emma*, and Barbara Pym's Art of Allusion," 116 *passim*, gives a subtle reading of the similarities and differences between *GB* and *Emma*. Fergus, 117–21, also discusses many differences between the manuscript and *GB*. One other change is important as well. In "Lime Tree Bower," PYM MS. 17, fol. 1, Piers is the brother of Mary Beamish, a churchy woman whom Wilmet sometimes dislikes. In *GB*, his sister is Wilmet's best friend Rowena Talbot. The change gives Piers a slightly more elevated social status, as well as increasing Wilmet's opportunities to see him.

15. *LR*, PYM MS. 6, fol. 191, curate separates from his wife; cf. PYM MS. 17, fol. 1. "Lime Tree Bower," PYM MS. 17, fols. 1–2, 3–3 verso, 6, details from the plot.

16. "Lime Tree Bower," [n.d.] June-July 1955, PYM MS. 17, fols. 10–13. Parallel quotation in manuscript, PYM MS. 17, fol. 33.

17. Literary Notebook, Jan. 2, 1957, PYM MS. 49, fol. 1.

18. Benet, *Something*, 80; Nardin, *Pym*, 105. Nardin, 104, says that Wilmet emphasizes "the altruistic aspects of her desire to get close to him," in order "to have her Christianity and her extramarital attachment, too."

19. Literary Notebook, May 15, 1955, PYM MS. 46, fol. 16, Smith lent novel.

Smith to Pym, June 5 and Nov. 7, 1955, PYM MS. 160, fols. 3, 12, church gossip. Recently, Robert Smith, "Remembering Barbara Pym," 161, has identified the vicar as Father Twisaday of All Saint's Notting Hill, who bears some resemblance to Father Thames.

20. "Lime Tree Bower," PYM MS. 17, fols. 1–2, 34 verso, sideman and server; PYM MS. 91, fols. 1, 8–8 verso, protégé.

Quotation, Charles Burkhart, *The Pleasure of Miss Pym*, 10. Pym to Smith, Sept. 26, 1967, PYM MS. 162/1, fol. 76, said that she felt as if she had invented her neighbors. Literary Notebook, [n.d.] before July 2, 1959, PYM MS. 52, fol. 4 verso and Holt, *Lot*, 179, both reiterate the point.

21. "Midland Bank," "A Fragment Inspired by Pass Moderations," "Another Fragment (To LMF before I knew his name)," and "To Lindley MacNaghten Fraser," PYM MS. 97, fols. 10–13, 61–63. Literary Notebook, June 1, 1956, PYM MS. 48, fol. 29; July 9, 1958, PYM MS. 51, fol. 20, snubbing. Although Holt, *Lot*, 177, correctly differentiates Squirrel from Bear, in "Lime Tree Bower," Pym referred to the former as "little brown bear," PYM MS. 17, fol. 34 verso; also quoted by Fergus, "Art," 119. Literary Notebook, Oct. 3, Dec. 7, 1957, Apr. 19, 1958, PYM MS. 50, fols. 24, 17, 9, diminutives for Squirrel, and Sept. 21, 1957, fol. 24 verso, poem to Little Bear.

22. The problem of male inadequacy bothered Pym. She was five feet, nine inches tall. She described men as being shorter and weaker than women in thirteen manuscripts and notebooks; eight references come after this novel.

23. Smith to Pym, Jan. 27, 1958, PYM MS. 160, fol. 22, and Holt to Pym, Aug. 26, 1959, PYM MS. 168, fol. 16, tracking reports. Literary Notebook, Nov. 12, 1956, PYM MS. 48, fol. 14 verso, asked herself to stop.

The ratio of tracking to nontracking material varies so much from notebook to notebook that it is almost impossible to establish a clear pattern. The purely literary entries, however, do decrease as the lists and the field notes expand, PYM MSS. 48–52.

24. Rossen, *World*, 28, identified *STG* as a *roman à clef.* Holt, *Lot*, 179–82, who was part of Pym's saga, identified some of Pym's characters in *GB*.

Literary Notebook, Aug. 30, 1958, PYM MS. 51, fol. 14 verso, visit to Bear's flat. Bear, like Bill Coleman, *GB*, 86, had two first names. Charles Burkhart, "Glamourous Acolytes: Homosexuality in Pym's World," 101, refers to Bill Coleman but does not connect him to the tracking notes.

"Lime Tree Bower," PYM MS. 17, fol. 34 verso, Squirrel appears.

25. "Lime Tree Bower," PYM MS. 17, fols. 13, 36 verso, Gordon Glover and Starky. Hilary Pym Walton, interview with author, May 9, 1985, Piers and Bear.

26. Fergus, "Art," 112, insists that this passage refers only to Wilmet, but it is impossible to tell.

Quotation, Joyce Carol Oates, Jay Parini, "My Writing Is Full of Lives I Might Have Led," 19.

27. Halperin, "War," 94–95, claims that Pym shows a low regard for men in *GB*. She portrays marriage "as a dead end," and notes that men continue to tyrannize women despite their weaknesses.

28. Elizabeth Bowen, *Death of the Heart*, 250, and David John Moore Cornwall [John le Carré], "The Clandestine Muse," 13, discuss spying.

M. M. Bakhtin, "Forms of Time and of the Chronotope in the Novel: Notes toward a Historical Poetics," 123–27, discusses eavesdropping. Spacks, *Gossip*, 15, 156.

29. Hilary Pym Walton, interview with author, May 9, 1985, detective family. Holt, *Lot*, 175, declared, "It is most rewarding to weave a saga around someone you can actually observe."

30. Princess Rosebud delights in having an important secret to keep, *MD*, PYM MS. 98, fols. 8 verso–11. Elizabeth Taylor, *At Mrs Lippincote's*, 214.

31. Notes for Rose novel, PYM MS. 26, fols. 15, 27, sociologists spy. Pym to Smith, Nov. 3, 1954, PYM MS. 162/1, fol. 4, Denton Welch. Smith, "Remembering Pym," 162, discusses Pym's fascination with Welch.

32. For more details, see Wyatt-Brown, "Ellipsis," 31–32. I.A.I. to Pym, Jan. 24, 1974, PYM MS. 150, fol. 123, 1974 salary. Literary Notebook, PYM MS. 48, fols. 7 verso–8, Frederic Pym's troubles. When Pym looked up her mother's will, she discovered that it had been written before she was born.

33. "Finding a Voice: A Radio Talk," Apr. 4, 1978, 384. Insights from experts on continuity theory would suggest that Pym felt the need for change in her life, Robert C. Atchley, "A Continuity Theory of Normal Aging," 185. Literary Notebook, May 7, 1959, PYM MS. 52, fol. 16 verso, Squirrel's departure.

34. Pym to John Guest, Longmans, May 26, 1963, PYM MS. 164, fol. 140, gives the sales figures for all six novels. Literary Notebook, [n.d.] between May 17 and June 16, 1957, PYM MS. 49, fol. 7 verso, eccentric woman.

35. Literary Notebook, Oct. 6, 1957, PYM MS. 50, fol. 22 verso. Benet, *Something*, 89–90, analyzes the connection between eating and spying.

36. Pym to G. Wren Howard, May 27, 1960, PYM MS. 164, fol. 66, called the novel, *The Thankless Task*. Novel refers four times to indexing and church work as being thankless tasks, *NFR*, 13, 27, 75, 251.

37. Gullette, *Safe at Last*, xv.

38. Several covert references to Squirrel and Bear appear, suggesting that Pym enjoyed references that only she and her friends would recognize. The stone squirrel in the garden *NFR*, 77, refers to Squirrel. Literary Notebook, May 4, 1958, PYM MS. 51, fol. 26, describes some music that Pym heard Bear play in church. Dulcie sees the same piece on the organist's music stool at Neville Forbes's church, *NFR*, 104.

39. Gullette, *Safe at Last*, xviii, when discussing "the plot of progress" in novels of midlife, wonders who will be the "stand in for the dragons" when middle-aged writers no longer regard older people as threats to happiness. Anne M. Wyatt-Brown, "Late Style in the Novels of Barbara Pym and Penelope Mortimer," 838, points out that a reversal takes place in Mortimer's *The Handyman* (1983). Like Pym in *NFR*, Mortimer tells the story from the perspective of an older woman, Phyllis Muspratt, and "describes the antics of Phyllis's grown-up children ironically, dispassionately, and without quarter." For the first time in her career, Mortimer shows no more sympathy for young adults than her young protagonists displayed for their mothers-in-law in Mortimer's early novels.

40. Literary Notebook, Dec. 1, 1957, PYM MS. 50, fol. 17 verso.

41. Long, *Pym*, 129. Rossen, *World*, 39, says that Dulcie knows how to track her prey.

42. The earlier notes that predated the trip had been extremely dull, Literary Notebook, [n.d.] Jan. 1957, PYM MS. 49, fols. 1 verso–2. Notebook, *No Fond Return of Love*, July 10–11, 1957, PYM MS. 91, fols. 6–7 verso, description of hotel.

43. Quotation, Benet, *Something*, 101. Long, *Pym*, 136, thinks that beginning

with Dulcie's trip to Taviscombe the novel "begins to read like a romance." Michael Cotsell, *Barbara Pym*, 93, makes little distinction between the two genres. Literary Notebook, July 11, 1958, PYM MS. 51, fol. 4, hints of Aylwin's aristocratic connection.

44. Burkhart, *Pleasure*, 43, says that the novel is less good than the others. Benet, *Something*, 90-95, describes the multiple roles characters assume.

Notes, *No Fond Return of Love*, PYM MS. 91, fol. 3, Viola is described as a rejected woman of twenty-seven. At one point Pym thought Viola might have an illegitimate child by Aylwin, but later decided the child would be plain not illegitimate, *NFR*, PYM MS. 18/1, fol. 19, PYM MS. 18/2, fol. 2 verso. No child appears in the novel. Long, *Pym*, 232-33, uses Kate Heberlein's description of the manuscript.

45. Benet, *Something*, 91.

46. Kate Browder Heberlein, "Thankless Tasks or Labors of Love: Women's Work in Barbara Pym's Novels," 3.

47. Lady David Cecil to Pym, Oct. 31, 1961; Honor Wyatt to Pym, Feb. 15, 1961, PYM MS. 168, fols. 33-33 verso, 40. Liddell to Pym, Feb. 27, 1961, PYM MS. 157, fol. 7, complained that Dulcie was not a good churchwoman; otherwise she would never have chased after a divorcé.

5. The Expansion of Empathy

1. Literary Notebook, Aug. 28, 1959, PYM MS. 52, fol. 5 verso, Pym attempted to use the dreary details of her life as the beginning of another novel. She imagined the narrator as a widow of sixty, about to retire to the country. Literary Notebook, May 31, 1959, PYM MS. 52, fol. 15, Bear told Pym that Squirrel had been evicted. Hilary Pym Walton, interview with author, May 9, 1985, gave reasons for leaving Barnes.

2. Literary Notebook, June 25, 1959, PYM MS. 52, fol. 12 verso.

3. Literary Notebook, Oct. 18, 1959, PYM MS. 53, fol. 1.

4. Jaques, "Death," 512-13.

5. First and second quotations, Jaques, "Death," 502-3. Third quotation, Jaques, "Midlife Crisis," 2, importance of stage theory. Jaques also suggests that another stage of creative development may begin about eighty, provided the artist does not suffer from dementia. Carolyn G. Heilbrun, *Writing a Woman's Life*, 49.

6. Elizabeth Bowen, *The Little Girls*. Wyatt-Brown, "The Liberation of Mourning."

7. Peter F. Alexander, *William Plomer: A Biography*, 212, reports that Plomer, the second Cape reader, advised the press not to accept *UA*. Pym never had a comfortable relationship with him. Daniel George to Pym, May 18, 1957, PYM MS. 164, fol. 4, Cape's other reader and supporter of Pym, told her that he would have to maneuver a bit to get a contract for *GB*, but that Plomer would not interfere.

8. *UA* I, [n.d.] after Aug., 1960, PYM MS. 19, fol. 16, Bowen heroine. Elizabeth Bowen, *To the North*. Rossen, *World*, 70, comments that compared to Emmeline, Ianthe seems a trifle "faded."

9. Literary Notebook, Mar. 8, 1959, PYM MS. 52, fol. 22.

10. *UA* notes for revision, PYM MS. 20, fol. 2 verso.

11. Jane Nardin, *Barbara Pym*, 52. Quotation, Robert Emmet Long, *Barbara Pym*, 153.

12. *UA* draft 1, PYM MS. 19, fols. 84, 85, 234.

13. *UA* 1, PYM MS. 19, fol. 30 verso. *UA* notes for revision, PYM MS. 20, fol. 12, Pym recorded an acquaintance's non sequitur with glee.

14. Edith Milton, "Worlds in Miniature," 11. She also suggests that the novel "is a celebration of unsuitability."

15. Richard Roberts to Pym, Aug. 6, 1964, PYM MS. 159, fols. 18–21, urged Pym to revise. Roberts disliked Rupert Stonebird, Mark, Sophia, and Penelope, and wanted Pym to focus more on Ianthe's passion for John. On the letter itself, Pym protested that Ianthe is hardly capable of lust and that Sophia is necessary to speak for the author. *UA* notes for revision, PYM MS. 21, fols. 29, 54, 72 and 197–201, attempts to follow his other suggestions. Holt wisely omitted those scenes from the published version.

Rossen, "On Not Being Jane Eyre" 155–56, n. 7, commented upon Roberts's letter and Pym's response.

In retrospect, Pym's reliance on Sophia was unfortunate in one respect. Sophia is too much like Rosamond Bone in *LR*. Philip Larkin to Pym, Oct. 27, 1963, PYM MS. 151, fol. 18, commented that *UA* seemed too much like her earlier work.

Pym to Robert Smith, Mar. 16, 1961, PYM MS. 162/1, fol. 19 verso, informed him of Holt's pregnancy.

16. *UA* draft 1, PYM MS. 19, fols. 27 verso, 90 verso.

17. Sandra Diary 1, Sept. 20, 1933, PYM MS. 101, fol. 90.

18. Janice Radway, *Reading the Romance: Women, Patriarchy, and Popular Literature*, 55.

19. Nardin, *Pym*, 44–45.

20. Dec. 31, 1963, PYM MS. 98, fols. 52–53, St. Laurence's budget.

21. Literary Notebook, Feb. 8, 1962, PYM MS. 56, fols. 3–3 verso, quoted by Rossen, *World*, 20. Graham, "Cumbered with Much Serving," 154.

22. Pym to John Guest, Longmans, May 26, 1963, PYM MS. 164, fol. 140, list the sales figures for her early novels: *STG*, 3,722; *EW*, 6,752; *JP*, 5,219; *LTA*, 3,657; *GB*, 3,310; *NFR*, 3,288. *JP* started the downward slide in sales.

G. Wren Howard, Mar. 19, 1963, PYM MS. 164, fols. 130, rejected *UA*.

23. Pym to Smith, May 24, 1963, PYM MS. 162/1, fol. 29, Daniel George's stroke. Letter to the Editor, Bookseller, Dec. 7, 1963; Pym to Editor, Bookseller, Dec. 11, 1963, asking for copy of previous letter announcing fundraising effort; Editor to Pym, Dec. 13, 1963, sending copy of original letter; John Carswell to Pym, Dec. 17, 1963, PYM MS. 148, fols. 102–5, thanks for generosity.

24. Rose manuscripts, PYM MSS. 26–28. Notes for Rose novel, June 2, 1963, PYM MS. 26, fol. 1 verso, wondered if the Rose manuscript would be the long-awaited *The Tariff of Malpractice*.

Liddell to Pym, Jan. 4, Feb. 9, July 15, 1954, April 23, 1959, PYM MS. 156, fols. 48, 49, 52. Liddell to Pym, June 15, 1959, PYM MS. 156, fols. 84–85, the vicar died; Liddell also declared that Cape would now take a novel as daring as *Tariff.* Liddell to Pym, July 13, 1961, PYM MS. 157, fol. 11, regretted that illness had kept Pym from an unfrocking, a ceremony she could include in *Tariff.* Liddell to Pym, Ascension Day [May 23], 1963, PYM MS. 157, fol. 32, encouraged her to keep on with *Tariff.*

25. Literary Notebook, Sept. 22, 1961, PYM MS. 55, fol. 14, *The Spoils of*

Poynton. Smith to Pym, Aug. 1, 1961, Oct. 1, 1961, PYM MS. 160, fols. 51–51 verso, 53, about furniture. Pym to Smith, Dec. 8, 1963, PYM MS. 162/1, fols. 35–37, topic suitable for a novel. Liddell to Pym, Ascension Day [May 30], 1957, PYM MS. 156, fol. 69, expressed a worry that if Pym left *Tariff* too long, Robert Smith would take his place in the plot, which is what happened.

26. Notes for Rose novel, PYM MS. 26, fols. 8 verso, 12–12 verso, anger with Robert Smith; first reference to rivalry in manuscript.
Literary Notebook, [n.d.] spring 1962, PYM MS. 56, fol. 11 verso, antique dealer. Literary notebook, [n.d.], late 1962 or early 1963, MS. 57, fol. 3, ideas for her novel.

27. Literary Notebook, Aug. 30, 1964, PYM MS. 59, fol. 7 verso, recorded first meeting with Roberts two years before.
Roberts to Pym, July 4, 1964, PYM MS. 159, fols. 15–16, responded to Pym's remarks about Smith.

28. Notes for "The Outcasts," July 8, 1966, PYM MS. 85, fols. 4–4 verso.

29. *LTA*, PYM MS. 16, fol. 15 verso.

30. The situation was similar to when writing about Adam in *CS* helped Pym recover her good humor with Henry Harvey. Smith to Pym, Aug. 23, 1978, PYM MS. 161, fol. 93 verso, admired drafts of *UA* and Rose novel.

31. The pattern of rejected men proposing to someone else originated in *STG*. When Belinda rejects the Bishop, he proposes promptly to Connie Aspinall.
Notes for Rose novel, PYM MS. 26, fol. 36 verso, not confiding.

32. Notes for Rose novel, PYM MS. 26, fol. 16, hopeless love. Literary Notebook, Feb. 23, 1965, PYM MS. 61, fol. 2, "The Outcasts." Pym's attempt to write a Firbankian revel about Bob Smith and Roberts was not very successful either, Bob Smith and Richard Roberts Story, [n.d.], PYM MS. 99, fols. 49–52.

33. Correspondence Roberts and Pym, June 22 and July 1, 1965, PYM MS. 159, fols. 43–43 verso, 52. Pym to Smith, Oct. 20, 1966, PYM MS. 162/1, fol. 69 verso, Roberts gone. Pym to Smith, Dec. 31, 1970, Pym to Smith, PYM MS. 160, fol. 170, Pym's anger. Pym to Smith, Aug. 13, 1978, PYM MS. 162/2, fol. 71, *SDD* and Roberts.

34. Pym to G. Wren Howard, Cape, June 5, 1968, PYM MS. 164, fol. 175, submitted Rose novel. Michael Howard, Cape, to Pym, July 9, 1968, PYM MS. 164, fol. 177, rejected Rose novel. Elizabeth Coates, Chatto & Windus, to Pym, Oct. 11, 1968, PYM MS. 164, fol. 182, rejected Rose novel. Larkin to Pym, Oct. 17, 1968, PYM MS. 151, fols. 52–53.
Quotation, Nardin, *Pym*, 114. Literary Notebook, [n.d.] late Aug., 1971, PYM MS. 69, fol. 4, Iris Horniblow. *SDD* draft, PYM MS. 29, fol. 2, thought of calling *SDD* The Pyrrhic Victory.
Pym considered various endings. In Rose draft, PYM MS. 27, fols. 81–86, Leonora defeats Ned. He moves to Vine Cottage in Rose's village, hoping that Rose will mother him, leaving James free to receive Leonora's chaste attentions. In Literary Notebook, May [n.d.], 1969, PYM MS. 67, fol. 7, Ned asks Leonora to forgive James. Pym contemplated having James unexpectedly marry someone else, but discarded the idea as too similar to Fabian and Jessie Morrow in *JP*.

35. Notes for Rose novel, PYM MS. 26, fol. 36, Keats's house. Notes for "The Outcasts" Mar. 10, 1966, PYM MS. 85, fol. 3 verso, unpleasant dinner.

36. Literary Notebook, Feb. 20, Apr. 1, Apr. 5, May 29, 1965, PYM MS. 61, fols. 1 verso, 3–3 verso, 7, quarrel and reconciliation.

Pym to Smith, Jan. 9, 1969, PYM MS. 162/1, fol. 85.

37. Correspondence with publishers, Jan. 15–March 14, 1968, PYM MS. 164, fols. 163–238; Oct. 7, 1969 to Nov. 12, 1970, PYM MS. 165, fols. 1–10, futile attempts to place *SDD*.

James Wright, Macmillan, to Pym, June 9, 1977, PYM MS. 165, fol. 30, asked for only six minor updates to the novel.

Mark Barty King, Director, Peter Davies, to Pym, Oct. 20, 1970, PYM MS. 165, fols. 3–4, enclosed a reader's report.

38. Literary Notebook, May 17, 1964, PYM MS. 59, fol. 2 verso–3, describes a friend of Liddell, an older woman who fusses in a silly way over younger men. Pym wished to allow Leonora some measure of dignity.

Some critics have hated Leonora. Jeremy Treglown, "Snob Story," 27, insists that Leonora's upper-middle-class life is of no interest to him.

39. Erving Goffman, *Stigma: Notes on the Management of Spoiled Identity*, 111. Literary Notebook, Oct. 3, 1969, PYM MS. 66, fol. 12, poem.

40. Caroline Moorehead, *Times*, Sept. 14, 1977, PYM MS. 98, fol. 24, reported that Pym wanted to imitate Drabble but could not. *AQ* 2, PYM MS. 23, fol. 21, considered imitating Drabble's *The Garrick Year*.

Larkin to Pym, July 1, 1968, PYM MS. 151, fol. 47 verso–48, complained about students.

41. *CS*, PYM MS. 5, fol. 87.

42. Burkhart, *Pleasure*, 51; Burkhart, "Glamourous Acolytes," 98–99.

43. Literary Notebook, Dec. 31, 1954, *VPE*, 193, Pym commented that men became vaguer with age, whereas women became sharper.

Quotation, David L. Gutmann, *Reclaimed Powers: Toward a New Psychology of Men and Women in Later Life*, 203. In middle age Pym was not always happy about the changes she sensed in herself.

44. Literary Notebook, July 19, 1969, PYM MS. 66, fol. 4, hedgehogs. Larkin to Pym, Apr. 27, 1978, PYM MS. 152, fol. 39, mentioned seeing a hedgehog.

6. The Coming of Age

1. Rossen, *World*, 172, points out that in *QA* old age can be liberating for the "forceful and authoritative" like old Mrs. Pope, who uses her age as an excuse to avoid unpleasant tasks.

2. Martha Baum and Rainer C. Baum, *Growing Old: A Societal Perspective*, 1–13.

3. Literary Notebook, June 6, 1970, PYM MS. 66, fol. 17, office rearranged. June 4, 1974, PYM MS. 159, fols. 162–64, romantic novel.

4. *QA* notes 1, c. May 8, 1973, PYM MS. 31, fol. 9 verso, Rose (later Letty) discovers a woman at risk. Transcript "Something to Remember," PYM MS. 96, fol. 205, Miss Lomax reads obituaries out loud to her companion. Lady Nollard, *HFN*, 259, reads them with "gloomy relish." Robert Smith to Pym, Nov. 15, 1970, PYM MS. 160, fol. 166, Joan Wales found in coma. Richard Roberts to Pym, Oct. 14, 1977, Nov. 22, 1977, PYM MS. 159, fols. 92–93, Marcia compared to Joan Wales.

5. Smith to Pym, Feb. 6, 1961, Mar. 8, 1965, PYM MS. 160, fols. 38 verso, 88. Roberts to Smith, Sept. 4, 1964, PYM MS. 159, fols. 22–22 verso. Pym to I.A.I., Oct. 9, 1979, PYM MS. 150, fol. 187, would submit bill for the index after she returned from hospital.

6. Literary Notebook, July 6, 1972, PYM MS. 70, fol. 6 verso.

7. Burkhart, *Pleasure*, 54. Long, *Barbara Pym*, 237, claims that Pym originally planned to write about one woman character until 1973, but the Oct. 2, 1972, entry in her literary notebook mentions two unmarried women, *VPE*, 270.

QA draft 1, [n.d.] entry before Aug. 15, 1973, PYM MS. 33, fol. 81, contemplates having Letty's funeral. Literary Notebook, Jan. 15, 1974, PYM MS. 72, fol. 6 verso, says that both would die despite the welfare state.

8. QA notes 1, c. May 8, 1973, PYM MS. 31, fols. 9 verso–10; [n.d.] after Nov. 7, 1973, QA draft 1, PYM MS. 33, fol. 95; *Four Point Turn*, [QA] [n.d.], c. 1975, PYM MS. 34, fol. 81, Letty's thoughts about death.

9. QA draft 1, [n.d.], PYM MS. 33, fol. 79 verso.

Robert N. Butler, "The Life Review: An Interpretation of Reminiscence in the Aged," 67–68. Jaques, "Death," 513, notes that when the future seems circumscribed, elders turn to events in the past and connect them to the present and to what is left of the future.

Literary Notebook, Jan. 18, 1973, PYM MS. 71, fols. 8–9, Pym's story features a sacrificial mother and selfish father. The father's scholarship brings about the mother's untimely death. When she dies, he buries himself in the page proofs of his latest book, a heartless response, typical of Pym's less appealing male characters. The daughter grows up fearing mental collapse, but becomes self-sufficient. The father dies at eighty-seven, the same age as Pym's father. Daybook, July 26, 1966, PYM MS. 132, fol. 44 verso, records the date of Frederic Pym's funeral.

Barbara Frey Waxman, *From the Hearth to the Open Road: A Feminist Study of Aging in Contemporary Literature*, 2, 107, describes Letty as the heroine of a "*Reifungsroman*," a novel in which growing older involves "ripening" or maturing, not decaying. Letty, Waxman declares, learns to take charge of her future. In the course of the action, she discovers that she needs to "analyze her past." From this analysis, Waxman concludes, Letty eventually "actively construct[s] a meaningful future in retirement." Letty seems more passive to me. She resists change as long as possible, but finally unforeseen circumstances oblige her to reconsider her relationship with her friend Marjorie.

10. QA draft 1, [n.d.] 1973, PYM MS. 33, fols. 88, 95–98, Marcia's and Letty's c.v.s, Letty rejects idea of dying, lunch with cousin. Literary Notebook, July 10, 1973, PYM MS. 71, fol. 20 verso, lunch with Smith. QA draft 1, [n.d.], second entry c. summer 1973, PYM MS. 33, fols. 27, 80, Belgrave Square and hospital notes; Oct. 18, 1973, PYM MS. 33, fol. 82, scandal. This is the clerical scandal that Liddell urged Pym to write about in *Tariff of Malpractice*, Liddell to Pym, July 15, 1954, PYM MS. 156, fol. 52. Rose Novel draft, [n.d.], PYM MS. 27, fols. 51–52, similar scandals. Rose notes, [n.d.], PYM MS. 26, fols. 10–11, engagement and subsequent jilting.

11. QA draft 1, [n.d.] 1973, PYM MS. 33, fol. 88. Marcia's experience also parallels a comic one mentioned in the radio script "Something to Remember," PYM MS. 96, fol. 222. QA draft 1, after Nov. 7, 1973, PYM MS. 33, fols. 95, 98, Letty tries to bury herself in the leaves.

12. Literary Notebook, June 12, 1972, PYM MS. 70, fol. 5 verso, Letty and Marjorie. Literary Notebook, May 17, 1959, PYM MS. 52, fol. 15 verso, Marjorie and Bear.

13. Gutmann, *Reclaimed Powers*, 208.

Anne M. Wyatt-Brown, "Creativity in Midlife: The Novels of Anita Brookner," 176, suggests that the art historian Brookner started to write novels in her fifties out of a desperate need to control her destiny. A key passage occurs at the end of her third novel, *Look at Me*, 190. Frances Hinton suddenly realizes that her old nurse, the last reminder of her parents, may not live forever. "Almost as if for protection, I got up and found my notebook and my pen, and sat down again, determined to write something."

14. Kathryn L. Cooper and David L. Gutmann, "Gender Identity and Ego Mastery Style in Middle-Aged, Pre– and Post–Empty Nest Women," 350, find great anxiety among "pre-nest" women, but a new pride in achievements among "post-nest" ones. Pym's nervous anticipation was understandable.

QA notes 1, Mar. 6, 1974, PYM MS. 31, fol. 34, briefly mentions retirement party. *QA* notes 2, June 17, 1974, PYM MS. 32, fols. 4–7, adds details. fol. 5 verso, modify the tone.

15. Lord David Cecil to Pym, Sept. 28, 1977, PYM MS. 148, fol. 8 verso, thought Letty might come to enjoy life in the country despite the dead animals.

16. Florida Scott-Maxwell, *The Measure of My Days*, 13.

"Calm of mind," is the last line from John Milton's "Samson Agonistes," l. 1,758. "Emotion recollected. . . ." is from William Wordsworth's "Preface to Second Edition of the *Lyrical Ballads*." See also passage *QA* draft 1, Nov. 7, 1973, PYM MS. 33, fol. 86, quoted in Wyatt-Brown, "Late Style," 837.

17. Elaine Cumming and William E. Henry, *Growing Old: The Process of Disengagement*, 136. They claimed that the final stages of disengagement can be quite happy, 227. Elders often spend their last days "preoccupied" with themselves. Under ideal circumstances the older person's "bonds have been all but severed—disengagement is complete, he is free to die, and death is the last logical step in the process of living."

CS, PYM MS. 5, fol. 103; "Henry Shakespeare," PYM MS. 97, fol. 8.

18. Rossen, *World*, 94, comments that Mr. Strong plays the role of "high priestly figure." Yet Pym does not share Marcia's demented fantasy. She points out that Mr. Strong is human; the smell of lavender makes him "a boy of seven again," *QA*, 179.

Helen MacGregor to Pym, [n.d.] summer or fall 1978, PYM MS. 171, fols. 152–52 verso. See also, Martin Geeson to Pym, Aug. 8, 1979, PYM MS. 173, fol. 36, who was delighted that unmarried people were taken seriously in *SDD*.

Waxman, *Hearth*, 115.

19. Pym associates falling leaves with a desire for death. In *SDD*, 149, James has "a sudden impulse to run down and bury himself in those leaves, covering over his head and body in an extravagant gesture of concealment, return to the womb or whatever one called it."

Waxman, *Hearth*, 108, insists that "life-loving Letty has not shown any tendency to court death." She concludes that "Letty Crowe will simply not eat crow any longer." The manuscripts provide incontrovertible evidence that Letty, like many other Pym characters, is death absorbed, but manages to overcome the pull toward despair and death.

20. Literary Notebook, Feb. [n.d.] 1971, PYM MS. 68, fol. 22 verso, Freud on Leonardo.

Janine Chasseguet-Smirgel, *Sexuality and Mind: The Role of the Father and the Mother in the Psyche*, 77–78, reports that one of her patients, like Norman, had an irrational hatred of cars. She connected the obsession with his desire to possess the analyst and through her, his mother. Cars in his view are like the "undesirable contents" of her body. They block his path to her womb.

21. Michael Cotsell, *Barbara Pym*, 122, also agrees that Larkin's letters contributed to Pym's portrait of Norman. Larkin to Pym, Sept. 11, 1968, Feb. 3, 1970, July 18, 1972, July 22, 1975, PYM MS. 151, fols. 51-51 verso, 61 verso, 72-73, 93-94. Literary Notebook, July 22, 1970, PYM MS. 68, fol. 1 verso; Literary Notebook, July 30, 1976, PYM MS. 76, fol. 1 verso, Smith's and Larkin's love life.

22. *QA* miscellaneous notes, [n.d.] between Apr. 28-May 20, 1971, PYM MS. 35/2, fol. 1 verso, recorded a license plate number and speculations on her surgeon's address. Literary Notebook, c. Apr. [n.d.] 1972, PYM MS. 69, fol. 13, lists all three of her doctor's names.

Waxman, *Hearth*, 115, claims that "Pym's irony in writing the desexed old spinster's body and then plunging Marcia into romantic fantasies effectively dismantles the spinsterly stereotype." Waxman underestimates Pym's complex achievement by emphasizing its implications for contemporary feminism. Pym believed Marcia's love to be painfully predictable, quite like her own reactions. Miscellaneous notes *QA*, [n.d.] c. May 1971, PYM MS. 35/2, fol. 1 verso, Pym commented that most women patients would admire their surgeons greatly, but an unbalanced spinster might carry romantic feelings to extremes. Realizing that many readers would not understand or accept Marcia's feelings, Pym raises her aging character above mere stereotypes by presenting her fantasies with unusual particularity and thereby affording the old woman understanding and respect.

23. Francis Wyndham, "The Gentle Power of Barbara Pym," Review of *QA*, Sunday *Times*, Sept. 18, 1977, PYM MS. 165, fol. 124.

24. Clippings, PYM MS. 98, fol. 26a, Ivy Compton-Burnett. Elizabeth Taylor to Pym, Feb. 25, 1951, July 17, c. 1950s, PYM MS. 162/3, fols. 1, 19 verso; Taylor to Pym, [n.d.] c. 1950, PYM MS. 167, fols. 64-64 verso. Compton-Burnett was a cult figure for Robert Liddell, Taylor, and Pym. Literary Notebook, [n.d.] between Nov. 29, 1973-Jan. 15, 1974, PYM MS. 72, fol. 6, Marcia's hair like Compton-Burnett's.

25. Feb. 16, 1969, PYM MS. 86, fols. 1-2.

26. *QA* notes 2, Sept. 28, 1974, fol. 9, speech.

27. As late as 1966, George L. Maddox, "Retirement as a Social Event in the United States," 357-65, ignores the problems of women because there were no studies of their retirement. An early study of women and retirement appeared in 1976, Robert C. Atchley, "Orientation toward the Job and Retirement Adjustment among Women."

28. Tom Maschler, director of Cape, to Pym, Feb. 9, 1977, PYM MS. 166, fol. 67, asked about *Four Point Turn* [*QA*], and said that he wanted to read it himself. Pamela Hansford Johnson to Pym, Dec. 17, 1976, PYM MS. 165, fol. 82, complained that Hamish Hamilton had not received her letter in time. Thus he had not read *QA* himself.

Jean Mossop, Cape, to Pym, July 1, 1976, PYM MS. 165, fol. 72, regretful rejection. Hamish Hamilton to Pym, Nov. 4, 1976, PYM MS. 165, fols. 77-78, with reader's report.

29. Larkin to Pym, Sept. 27, 1976, PYM MS. 151, fol. 115 verso. Smith to Pym, July 29, 1976, PYM MS. 161, fol. 68. *QA* miscellaneous notes, Nov. 13, 1976, MS. 35/2, fols. 5-7.

7. Clearing the Lumber Room

1. "Reputations Revisited," 66–67.

Pamela Hansford Johnson to Pym, Oct. 15, 1976, PYM MS. 165, fol. 74, suggested Pym send *Four Point Turn* to Hamish Hamilton with her recommendation. Hansford Johnson to Pym, Dec. 17, 1976, PYM MS. 165, fol. 82, later suggested Pym send it to Alan Maclean of Macmillan. Pym to Hansford Johnson, Jan. 3, 1977, PYM MS. 165, fol. 83, agreed to do so when she finished adding some scenes. Pym to Alan Maclean, Macmillan, Feb. 2, 1977 PYM MS. 165, fol. 85, sent him *QA*, mentioned *TLS* Jan. 21 article and said the novel was intended to be amusing.

2. James Wright, Macmillan, to Pym, July 19, 1978, PYM MS. 165, fol. 43, *SDD* #5 on *Times* bestseller list. Gayner Johnson (Wright's secretary), Macmillan, to Pym, July 28, 1978, PYM MS. 165, fol. 45. *SDD* #3 on list. Wright to Pym, Aug. 15, 1978, PYM MS. 165, fol. 49, *SDD* had already nearly caught up with *QA*.

3. Literary Notebook, Mar. 7, 1977, PYM MS. 77, fol. 4 verso, cat recipe. Constance Malloy, "The Quest for a Career," 16–17, describes Pym's joyful reactions.

Jean Mossop to Pym, Jan. 6, 1978, PYM MS. 166, fol. 93, Dutton offered to publish *EW*. Pym to Jean Mossop, Jan. 10, Mar. 28, 1978, PYM MS. 166, fols. 95, 111. In the first letter accepts Dutton's offer to publish *EW*, hopes it will do better than *LTA*. In second, agrees to an option for Dutton to publish *LTA* or *STG* rather than *GB*. Still unable to believe that Dutton would ever consider *LTA*.

Robert Liddell to Pym, Nov. 16, 1956, PYM MS. 156, fol. 64, was more realistic about the fate of English novels in America. He told her to appreciate American reviews even if *LTA* did not sell well. Liddell to Pym, Nov. 30, 1957, PYM MS. 156, fol. 75 verso, reported that he had never earned back his American advance.

4. Jill Neville to Pym, Sept. 12, 1977, PYM MS. 169, fol. 194, Maschler's admission.

Maclean to Maschler, Dec. 16, 1977, PYM MS. 166, fol. 87, requested firm date for last two novels. Macmillan willing to take over. Maschler to Maclean, Dec. 21, 1977, PYM MS. 166, fol. 91, second set scheduled for autumn. No date for last pair. Macmillan could take over if Cape did not reprint final two. Maschler to Pym, Dec. 23, 1977, PYM MS. 166, fol. 89, no commitment. Wright to Pym, Dec. 29, 1977, PYM MS. 166, fol. 90, reprints must appear within a two-year period. Pym to Maschler, Jan. 9, 1978, PYM MS. 166, fol. 94, suggested pairing *STG* and *LTA* or *STG* and *JP* for next reprinting. Requested definite date for final two. Macmillan would take over. Maschler to Pym, Jan. 12, 1978, PYM MS. 166, fol. 97, still hedged. Macmillan would substitute if necessary. Planned to read the most recent reprint in proof. Wright to Pym, Jan. 17, 1978, PYM MS. 166, fol. 99, urged her to issue ultimatum to Maschler. Macmillan about to search for offset material. Serena Probert, Cape, to Pym, Feb. 6, 1978, PYM MS. 166, fol. 102, BBC obtained permission to broadcast *JP*. Cape distressed by choice.

Valerie Kettley (secretary to Maschler), to Pym, Feb. 6, 1978, PYM MS. 166, fol. 101, requested copies of each novel to offset. Pym to Kettley, Feb. 12, 1978, PYM MS. 166, fol. 104, refused. Kettley to Pym, Feb. 22, 1978, PYM MS. 166, fol. 105, will advertise. Wright to Pym, Mar. 2, 1978, PYM MS. 165, fol. 131, volunteered his two copies. Kettley to Pym, Mar. 31, 1978, PYM MS. 166, fol. 112, no luck finding *LTA* and *STG*. Received Wright's copy of *LTA*; please send Portway edition of *STG*.

5. Correspondence between Pym and Maschler, Mar. 7 and 9, 1977, Jan. 9, 1978, PYM MS. 166, fols. 72–73, 94.

Wright to Pym, June 7, 1977, PYM MS. 165, fol. 30, urged her to update *SDD*. No more dated than a Jane Austen novel. Wright to Pym, Aug. 17, 1977, PYM MS. 165, fol. 113, asked about new novel (*FGL*). Mentioned young children. Wright to Pym, Aug. 23, 1977, PYM MS. 165, fol. 115, in response to her comment that no one would like Emma in *FGL*, remarked that Jane Austen had said much the same thing about her heroine Emma.

Paul de Angelis, Dutton, to Pym, Feb. 15, 1978, PYM MS. 166, fol. 160, enthusiastic about signing her. Pym to de Angelis, Mar. 31, 1978, PYM MS. 166, fol. 166, said that John Bayley, Beryl Bainbridge, and Jilly Cooper read her fiction. Doubted if Margaret Drabble or Jean Rhys did. Hoped that her old favorite, Louise Field Cooper, would read her novels. De Angelis to Pym, Apr. 17, 1978, PYM MS. 166, fol. 168, requested blurbs from Pamela Hansford Johnson, Drabble, Beryl Bainbridge, Iris Murdoch, and Gail Godwin. De Angelis to Pym, June 7, 1978, PYM MS. 166, fols. 171–72, enclosed blurbs from Cooper, Murdoch, Johnson, and Bayley. The latter compared novels to Larkin's poetry and Austen's novels. De Angelis to PYM, June 26, 1978, PYM MS. 166, fol. 173, *EW* an alternate selection of Book-of-the-Month Club.

6. Frances Kiernan, *New Yorker*, to Pym, Mar. 31, 1978, PYM MS. 158, fol. 171, requested a story. Pym to Frances Kiernan, *New Yorker*, Mar. 8, 1979, PYM MS. 158, fol. 169, sent "Across a Crowded Room." Kiernan to Pym, Mar. 19, 1979, PYM MS. 158, fol. 170, accepted it. Bernard Palmer, *Church Times*, to Pym, Nov. 28, 1978, PYM MS. 171, fol. 193, accepted "The Christmas Visit."

7. "Christmas Visit," 360.

8. Ibid.

9. Ibid., 366.

10. Literary Notebook, Apr. 19, 1978, PYM MS. 79, fols. 11–12 verso, 12 verso. "Bob and Richard Story," [n.d.] c. 1965, PYM MS. 99, fols. 49–52. Check voucher from the *New Yorker*, $2,410 for "Crowded Room," PYM MS. 158, fol. 174.

11. "Crowded Room," 375–76.

12. "Goodbye Balkan Capital," 354–55. Anthony Kaufman, "The Short Fiction of Barbara Pym," 57.

13. "Crowded Room," 380.

Kaufman, "Short Fiction," 66, also compares "Balkan Capital" to "Crowded Room," saying that the latter emphasizes Pym's "sense of resignation, of age, and of time passing inexorably."

14. Constance Rooke, "Hagar's Old Age: *The Stone Angel* as *Vollendungsroman*," 31; Gullette, *Safe at Last*; Penelope Lively, "The World of Barbara Pym," 47. Jaques, "Death," 504.

15. Out of Pym's fourteen major themes, nine dominate *FGL*: love, death, religion, food, dependency, eccentricity, gender, class, and generational differences. Fabian Driver (*JP*) and Esther Clovis (*LTA* and *UA*) die. Esther Clovis's funeral service nearly duplicates material in *AQ*, but it provides a chance for Emma to meet Claudia, the wife of Emma's old lover. Their meeting

is a more comic version of Caro's nonconfrontation with Cressida (*AQ*, 93–94, 128–30).

Talk, Romantic Novelists' Association, Mar. 8, 1978, PYM MS. 98, fol. 77. Literary Notebook, Sept. 19, 1976, PYM MS. 76, fol. 6, beginning of a romantic novel.

FGL notes, [n.d.] c. Apr. 2, 1978, PYM MS. 35/2, fol. 9; June 4, 1974, MS. 159, fol. 162, first mention of Emma, who is recovering from an illness; Apr. 28–May 20, 1971, PYM MS. 35/2, fols. 3–3 verso, describes a surgeon with a clergyman brother, who had once considered taking holy orders himself. In *QA*, the surgeon became Mr. Strong, while the clergyman was Father G., Edwin's friend. *FGL* notes, [n.d.], PYM MS. 35/2, fols. 3, 8, Pym invented another brother for Father G., Dr. Gellibrand in *FGL*. She added a brash young doctor, Martin Shrubsole, thus incorporating fantasies from the notes about the surgeon's wife Jennifer and their new house. When Pym described Avice Shrubsole and her undistinguished house in *FGL*, her sense of irony transformed the original picture. Later Father G.'s younger brother split into two characters, Shrubsole and Dr. G.

16. *FGL* notes, [n.d.] c. Apr. 2, 1977, PYM MS. 35/2, fols. 9 verso–10, Emma writing a Regency novel. Literary Notebook, Oct. 8, 1977, PYM MS. 78, fol. 8 verso, Emma an anthropologist.

Rossen, *World*, 156, calls *FGL* an apologia. Wyatt-Brown, "Late Style," 838, calls Emma Pym's heir.

17. *FGL* notes, MS. 35/2, fol. 8, rivalries.

18. *FGL* notes, [n.d.] c. Apr. 2, 1977, PYM MS. 35/2, fols. 8 verso, 9, 12 verso, Tom Dagnall, the rector, takes advantage of the kindness of women. His sister types for him until her eyes ache. Being unable to drive, he constantly imposes on the women in the local history society for rides. When the depressed older woman of the notes (who later becomes his sister, Daphne), needs help, he gives her typing. Literary Notebook, c. Mar. 18, 1977, PYM MS. 77, fol. 6, Tom's sister, like Dolly in *AQ*, becomes preoccupied with hedgehogs. *QA* and *FGL* Notebook, PYM MS. 35/2, fols. 10 verso, 11 verso, Miss Vereker.

19. *FGL* notes, PYM MS. 35/2, fol. 23; *FGL* draft 3, PYM MS. 38, fol. 27, describe the pecking order in each relationship, Daphne over Tom, Miss Lee over Miss Grundy, and Christabel Gellibrand over her husband, Doctor Gellibrand. Daphne ends by resenting Tom, Miss Grundy resents Miss Lee, but Dr. G. is so absorbed by his work and his affection for the "good old days" that he does not seem to mind his wife's bossiness.

Bickering clergymen and sisters: Julian and Mildred Boulding in *SVS*, Julian and Winifred Malory in *EW*, and an unnamed clergyman and sister whom Aylwin sees on the train, *NFR*, 210.

Literary Notebook, [n.d.] c. Dec. 1977, PYM MS. 78, fol. 25.

Daphne's situation is quite typical of women described by the psychologist Jean Baker Miller, *Toward a New Psychology of Women*, 85–89, who have lived their lives through men. They too suffer from depression and anger.

20. Nardin, *Barbara Pym*, 143–46, argues that Emma is very like her namesake in Jane Austen's novel. Nardin points out many parallels between *FGL* and *Emma*. Yet, Emma Howick's passivity is fundamentally unlike the behavior of Austen's Emma.

Literary Notebook, Sept. 26, 1976, PYM MS. 76, fol. 8 verso, a vivid 1964 memory of Richard Roberts.

Quotation, Lively, "World," 46.

FGL draft 1, PYM MS. 36, fols. 18–20, Graham confides a bit.

21. *FGL* notes, Jan. 17, 1979, PYM MS. 35/2, fol. 27.

22. *FGL* notes, [n.d.] late Jan. or early Feb., 1979, PYM MS. 35/2, fols. 27 verso, 29 verso; *FGL* draft 1, PYM MS. 36, fol. 147, first appearance of Beatrix's rescue mission. Literary Notebook, Dec. 7, 1978, PYM MS. 80, fol. 16 verso, recorded a strange dream that an older friend of hers was pregnant. Perhaps the excess fluid from the growing tumor caused that dream. *VPE*, 322, Jan. 8, 1979, she told her doctor she was retaining fluid.

23. Literary Notebook, c. Apr. 11, 1979, PYM MS. 81, fol. 8 verso.

Pym even managed to work World War II memories into the plot. For a short time, beginning Oct. 26, 1976, she had attempted to revise *HFN*, PYM MS. 87, fols. 1–10.

24. John Drury, "Outward Show and Inward Seeking," 524; Jaques, "Death," 505.

Mariolina Salvatori, "Thomas Hardy and Eugenio Montale: In Mourning and in Celebration," 162, points out that creating elegies can allow individuals to control "their fear" while constructing "a minute though permanent memorial piece which defies their own impermanence" and that of those they love.

25. Gilbert Phelps, "Fellow Writers in a Cotswold Village," 38.

26. Martin's encounter first appears in *FGL* draft 3, MS. 38, fol. 150. Cf. Literary Notebook, [n.d.] c. June, 1968, PYM MS. 65, fol. 12 verso, Kitty (*AQ*) too well mannered to ask clergyman questions about death for which he has no answers.

27. *LR*, PYM MS. 6, fol. 55.

28. Allan B. Chinen, *In the Ever After; Fairy Tales and the Second Half of Life*, 61, 63.

29. Rose draft, [n.d.], PYM MS. 27, fol. 30.

30. *FGL* notes, [n.d.] after Apr. 2, 1977, PYM MS. 35/2, fols. 10 verso, 13, 15, 22 verso, references to Miss Vereker. Idea for walk in woods came early. *FGL* notes, Mar. 26, 1978, PYM MS. 35/3, fol. 13, governess fond of village. *FGL* draft 1, PYM MS. 36, fols. 50, 125, 139, Miss Vereker sits on Deserted Medieval Village.

Sally Gadow, "Frailty and Strength: The Dialectic in Aging," 146; Ronald Blythe, *The View in Winter: Reflections on Old Age*, 18; Gullette, *Safe at Last*.

31. Correspondence from Macmillan and Dutton, Nov. 20, 1979–Jan. 9, 1980, PYM MS. 165, fols. 148–64. Literary Notebook, Mar. 10, 1979, PYM MS. 81, fol. 1, plot of final story quite typical of her initial efforts. Two women from slightly different social backgrounds would meet at college and continue their friendship even after one married. On June 24, 1979, Pym sketched out a few ideas at greater length, this time adding that the single woman might visit her friend. There she would meet the husband (*VPE*, 329).

32. Holt, *Lot*, 279. Literary Notebook, Aug. 9, 1979, PYM MS. 81, fol. 20; Literary Notebook, Nov. 21, 1979, PYM MS. 82, fol. 6, Donne poem. Literary Notebook, Nov. 30, 1979, PYM MS. 82, fol. 7, clipping from the *Church Times*, a notice of the reappearance of *JP* and *NFR*.

Bibliography

Works of Barbara Pym
Juvenilia
The Magic Diamond. PYM MS. 98, fols. 1a–12 verso. 1922.
Young Men in Fancy Dress. PYM MS. 1. August 1929–April 1930.

School Literary Magazine: Short Stories and Poems
"Adolphe." PYM MS. 97, fols. 22–39. July 1931, March 1932.
"Death of a Young Man." PYM MS. 97, fols. 40–58. September 1931.
"Henry Shakespeare." PYM MS. 97, fols. 5–9. January 1931.
"Midland Bank: A poem dedicated to JTLI with the Author's Fondest Love (But without his Permission)." PYM MS. 97, fols. 10–13. January, April 1931.
"The Sad Story of Alphonse." PYM MS. 97, fols. 1–4. February 1930.
"Satire." PYM MS. 97, fols. 14–16. July 1931.
"Tame Donkey: Sequel to Midland Bank." PYM MS. 97, fols. 17–21. August 1931.

Poems Written at Oxford
"A Fragment Inspired by Pass Moderations." PYM MS. 97, fols. 61–63. December 1931.
"Another Fragment (To LMF before I knew his name)." PYM MS. 97, fol. 62. December 1931.
"For H. S. H. [Henry Harvey] (Ch. Ch.) [Christ Church]." PYM MS. 97, fol. 64. February 1933.
"Fragment." PYM MS. 97, fol. 70. October 1938.
"Fragment Inspired by Tennyson." PYM MS. 97, fol. 69. October–November 1938.

187

"Frivolous Lines inspired by looking up at the Randolph Hotel, Oxford with Julian Amery on a fine sunny afternoon, it being early closing day." PYM MS. 97, fols. 65–68. March 3, 1938.

"Lines Written to a Dear Young Friend on his Nineteenth Birthday." PYM MS, fol. 68. March 27, 1938.

"Sonnet, written to Julian, anniversary of meeting." PYM MS. 97, fol. 71. December 3, 1938.

"To Lindley MacNaghten Fraser." PYM MS. 97, fol. 63. March 1932.

Post-Oxford Manuscripts

Civil to Strangers. In *Civil to Strangers and Other Writings.* Edited by Hazel Holt. New York: Dutton, 1988. PYM MS. 5. July 1935–October 1936.

Gervase and Flora. In *Civil to Strangers and Other Writings.* Edited by Hazel Holt. New York: Dutton, 1988. PYM MS. 7. 1937–February 1938.

Home Front Novel. In *Civil to Strangers and Other Writings.* Edited by Hazel Holt. New York: Dutton, 1988. PYM MSS. 8–9. Notes begun, October 1939.

The Lumber Room. PYM MS. 6. Begun March 10, 1938.

Something to Remember. PYM MS. 11. Begun June 14, 1940. PYM MS. 99, fols. 76–76 verso, notes.

So Very Secret. In *Civil to Strangers and Other Writings.* Edited by Hazel Holt. New York: Dutton, 1988. PYM MS. 12. Begun September 1941.

Short Stories

1930s–1940s

"Back to St. Petersburg." PYM MS. 92, fols. 51–70. September 1938 or 1939.

"A Letter from My Love." PYM MS. 92, fols. 262–77. c. 1936.

"Mothers and Fathers." PYM MS. 94, fols. 1–15. November 1936.

"A Painted Heart." PYM MS. 94, fols. 16–30. 1936.

"A Sister's Love." PYM MS. 94, fols. 132–48. c. 1938.

"They Never Write." PYM MS. 94, fols. 218–29. Submitted 1935.

"Trivial Rounds and Common Tasks." PYM MS. 94, fols. 230–46. April 1938.

"The Unfinished Flower." PYM MS. 94, fols. 247–59. 1937.

"Unpast Alps." PYM MS. 94, fols. 260–69. 1935.

"The Vicar Floating By." PYM MS. 99, fols. 24–44 c. 1941.

Postwar
"English Ladies." PYM 92, fols. 129–55. 1950, 2 versions.
"A Few Days Before Winter." PYM MS. 92, fols. 166–82; 184–99; PYM
  MS. 94, fols. 118–20. 1949.
"The Funeral." PYM MS. 92, fol. 200–213. 1950.
"The Pilgrimage." PYM MS. 94, fols. 31–43. 1952.
"Poor Mildred." PYM MS. 94, fols. 56–75. c. 1950s.
"The Rich Man in His Castle." PYM MS. 94, fols. 76–89, 90–117, 121–31.
  Begun 1949, 3 versions, the first submitted to *Housewife* and rejected
  1950.
"A Wedge of Misery Tea Time." PYM MS. 99, fols. 46–48. c. 1948.

Radio Play
"Parrot's Eggs." PYM MS. 96, fols. 105–28. Rejected by BBC, October
  1949.

Miscellaneous Notebooks
Anglo-Catholic Datebook. PYM MS. 89. Begun late 1935.
"Bob Smith and Richard Roberts Story." PYM MS. 99, fols. 49–52, c.
  1965.
Diaries and Daybooks. PYM MSS. 101–145, 1932–1979.
Literary Notebooks. PYM MSS. 40–82, 1948–1979.
Miscellaneous Notes and Dreams. PYM MS. 86, 1969.
Notebook. Ideas for "Silence at End of the Table" and material for
  "Something to Remember." PYM MS. 84. 1945.
Notebook, *No Fond Return of Love.* PYM MS. 91. mid-1950s, 1957 visit to
  Carlton Hotel.
Notes for "The Outcasts." PYM MS. 85, 1964–1966; see also PYM MS.
  61, fols. 2–2 verso.
Notes for a Wartime Novel. (Became radio play, "Something to Remem-
  ber.") PYM MS. 90, 1945.
Notes for Wartime Radio Play "Something to Remember." PYM MS. 99,
  fols. 6–13. c. 1943.
Points from War Time Novel (*Home Front Novel*). PYM MS. 87, October
  1976.

Talks
"The Novelist's Use of Everyday Life." PYM MS. 98, fols. 56–73, Barnes,
  1950.
Romantic Novelists' Association. PYM MS. 98, fols. 74–78. March 8, 1978.

"Ups and Downs of a Writer's Life." Address to Senior Wives Fellow-ship, Headington, Oxfordshire, PYM MS. 98, fols. 79–83, May 15, 1978.

Published Material
Novels
Excellent Women. 1952. Reprint. London: Jonathan Cape, 1977. PYM MS. 13, *A Full Life*, 1948. PYM MS. 14, *Excellent*, 1949.

A Few Green Leaves. New York: Dutton, 1980. PYM MSS. 35/2, fols. 8–38 verso, April 2, 1977–September 19, 1979; PYM MS. 35/3. April 16, 1977–March 26, 1978. Draft 1, PYM MS. 36, [n.d.]. Draft 2, PYM MS. 37, [n.d.]. Draft 3, PYM MS. 38, [n.d.].

A Glass of Blessings. 1958. Reprint. London: Jonathan Cape, 1977. Began as "Lime Tree Bower." PYM MS. 17, 1955.

Jane and Prudence. 1953. Reprint. London: Jonathan Cape, 1979. No MS.

Less than Angels. 1955. Reprint. London: Jonathan Cape, 1978. PYM MS. 16, begun April 26, 1953.

No Fond Return of Love. 1961. Reprint. London: Jonathan Cape, 1979. PYM MS. 18, October 23, 1957–January 7, 1959. Notes, PYM MS. 91, [n.d.] c. June 30–July 11, 1957. First title, *The Thankless Task.*

Quartet in Autumn. 1977. Reprint. New York: Dutton, 1978. PYM MS. 31, notes 1, April 23, 1973–March 6, 1974. PYM MS. 32, notes 2, June 17, 1974–September 28, 1974 [possibly December 1974]. Draft 1, PYM MS. 33, August 15, 1973–November 7, 1973. Draft 2, *Four Point Turn*, PYM MS. 34, finished September 1, 1975. MS. dated 1976. Miscellaneous notes, PYM MS. 35/2, fols. i verso–7, April 28, 1971–November 13, 1976.

Some Tame Gazelle. 1950. Reprint. London: Jonathan Cape, 1978. Short story version, PYM MS. 99, fols. 18–23, 1934. Draft 1, PYM MS. 2, 1935–1936. Draft 2 and notes, PYM MS. 3, 1944–1945.

The Sweet Dove Died. 1978. Reprint. New York: Dutton, 1979. PYM MS. 26, Notes for Rose novel, 1963, 1967–1968. PYM MS. 27–28, Rose novel, c. 1964–1967. PYM MS. 29, *Sweet Dove*, revision following Larkin's instructions. PYM MS. 25, final draft of *Sweet Dove*, sent to Macmillan. PYM MS. 99, fols. 60–74, 1969.

Edited Works
An Academic Question. Edited by Hazel Holt. London: Macmillan, 1986. Notes, PYM MS. 35/1, [n.d.], c. January 26, 1972–September 9, 1972. Draft 1, PYM MS. 22, [n.d.]. Draft 2, PYM MS. 23, [n.d.] c. November 6, 1965. Draft 3, PYM MS. 24, [n.d.].

Crampton Hodnet. Edited by Hazel Holt. New York: Dutton, 1985. PYM MS. 10, 1939–1940.

An Unsuitable Attachment. Edited by Hazel Holt. London: Macmillan, 1982. PYM MS. 19, draft 1, 1960–1962. PYM MS. 20, notes for revision, 1962–1963. PYM MS. 21, draft 2, some written after rejection, 1963–1964. PYM MS. 99, fols. 91–121, notes for revision, 1962–1963, 1972.

A Very Private Eye: An Autobiography in Diaries and Letters. Edited by Hazel Holt and Hilary Pym. New York: Dutton, 1984.

Short Stories

"Across a Crowded Room." In *Civil to Strangers and Other Writings*. Edited by Hazel Holt. New York: Dutton, 1988. PYM MS. 92, fols. 1–29. *New Yorker*, July 16, 1979, 34–39. Notes, "Across the Crowded Room." PYM MS. 88, 1978.

"The Christmas Visit." In *Civil to Strangers and Other Writings*. Edited by Hazel Holt. New York: Dutton, 1988. PYM MS. 92, fols. 71–77. *Church Times*, 1979; requested fall 1978.

"The Day the Music Came." PYM MS. 92, fols. 93–104. 1950. Published as "Dreams à la Carte," *Woman's Own*, February 22, 1986, 14–16.

"Goodbye Balkan Capital." In *Civil to Strangers and Other Writings*. Edited by Hazel Holt. New York: Dutton, 1988. PYM MS. 92, fols. 245–61. Rejected by *Penguin, New Writing*, 1941.

"So, Some Tempestuous Morn." In *Civil to Strangers and Other Writings*. Edited by Hazel Holt. New York: Dutton, 1988. PYM MS. 94, fols. 149–204, 1951, three versions.

"The White Elephant." PYM MS. 94, fols. 292–300. Published in *Women and Beauty*, 1949. Orig. titled "The Jumble Sale." Idea 1941, written 1949.

Postwar Radio Talk

"Finding a Voice: A Radio Talk." In *Civil to Strangers and Other Writings*. Edited by Hazel Holt. New York: Dutton, 1988. PYM MS. 96, fols. 2–15. Broadcast BBC Radio 3, April 4, 1978.

Radio Play

"Something to Remember." PYM MS. 96, fols. 193–229. Accepted by BBC, July 1949; broadcast in 1950.

Secondary

Abel, Elizabeth, Marianne Hirsch, and Elizabeth Langland. "Introduction." In *The Voyage In: Fictions of Female Development*. Hanover, N.H.: University Press of New England, 1983.

Abelman, Paul. "Genteelism." Review of *The Sweet Dove Died. Spectator,* July 8, 1978, 26.

Ackroyd, Peter. "Manufacturing Miss Pym." Review of *A Very Private Eye. Times Literary Supplement.* August 3, 1984, 861.

Alexander, Peter F. *William Plomer: A Biography.* New York: Oxford University Press, 1989.

Arieti, Silvano. *Creativity: The Magic Synthesis.* New York: Basic Books, 1976.

Atchley, Robert C. "A Continuity Theory of Normal Aging." *Gerontologist 29* (April 1989): 183–94.

———. "Orientation Toward the Job and Retirement Adjustment among Women." In *Time, Roles, and Self in Old Age,* 199–208. Edited by Jaber F. Gubrium. New York: Human Science Press, 1976.

Bakhtin, M. M. "Discourse in the Novel" (1934–1935). In *The Dialogic Imagination: Four Essays.* Edited by Michael Holquist. Translated by Caryl Emerson and Michael Holquist. Austin: University of Texas Press, 1981.

———. "Forms of Time and of the Chronotope in the Novel: Notes toward a Historical Poetics" (1937–1938). In *The Dialogic Imagination: Four Essays.* Edited by Michael Holquist. Translated by Caryl Emerson and Michael Holquist. Austin: University of Texas Press, 1981.

Baum, Martha, and Rainer C. Baum. *Growing Old: A Societal Perspective.* Englewood Cliffs, N.J.: Prentice-Hall, 1980.

Bayley, John. "Snouty." Review of *The Faber Book of Diaries* and *A Lasting Relationship: Parents and Children over Three Centuries. London Review of Books,* June 4, 1987, 14.

Bellow, Saul. "The Civilized Barbarian Reader." *New York Times Book Review,* March 8, 1987, 1, 38.

Benet, Diana. *Something to Love: Barbara Pym's Novels.* Columbia: University of Missouri Press, 1986.

Bettelheim, Bruno. *The Uses of Enchantment: The Meaning and Importance of Fairy Tales.* New York: Knopf, 1976.

Blythe, Ronald. *The View in Winter: Reflections on Old Age.* New York: Harcourt Brace Jovanovich, 1979.

Bowen, Elizabeth. *Death of the Heart.* 1938. Reprint. Harmondsworth: Penguin, 1986.

———. *The Little Girls.* 1963. Reprint. Harmondsworth: Penguin, 1982.

———. *To the North.* 1932. Reprint. Harmondsworth: Penguin, 1984.

Bowman, Barbara. "Barbara Pym's Subversive Subtext: Private Irony and Shared Detachment." In *Independent Women: The Function of Gender in the Novels of Barbara Pym.* Edited by Janice Rossen. Sussex: Harvester; New York: St. Martin's, 1988.

Britton, James. *Language and Learning*. London: Penguin Books, 1970.

Britton, James, et al. *The Development of Writing Abilities (11–18)*. Houndmills, Basingstoke: Macmillan, 1975.

Brontë, Charlotte. *Jane Eyre*. Edited by Q. D. Leavis. 1847. Reprint. Harmondsworth: Penguin, 1984.

———. *Villette*. Edited by Mark Lilly. 1853. Reprint. Harmondsworth: Penguin, 1986.

Brookner, Anita. *Look at Me*. London: Jonathan Cape, 1983.

Brothers, Barbara. "Women Victimised by Fiction: Living and Loving in the Novels by Barbara Pym." In *Twentieth-Century Women Novelists*. Edited by Thomas F. Staley. London: Macmillan, 1982.

Broyard, Anatole. "Reading and Writing: Overflowing Her Situation." *New York Times Book Review*, August 15, 1982, 27.

Bruner, Jerome. *Actual Minds, Possible Worlds*. Cambridge: Harvard University Press, 1986.

Burkhart, Charles. "Glamourous Acolytes: Homosexuality in Pym's World." In *Independent Women: The Function of Gender in the Novels of Barbara Pym*. Edited by Janice Rossen. Sussex: Harvester; New York: St. Martin's, 1988.

———. *The Pleasure of Miss Pym*. Austin: University of Texas Press, 1987.

Butler, Marilyn. "Keeping Up with Jane Austen." Review of *An Unsuitable Attachment*. *London Review of Books*, May 16–19, 1982, 16–17.

Butler, Robert N. "The Life Review: An Interpretation of Reminiscence in the Aged." *Psychiatry: Journal for the Study of Interpersonal Processes* 26 (February 1963): 65–76.

Byatt, A. S. "Marginal Lives." Review of *An Academic Question*. *Times Literary Supplement*, August 8, 1986, 862.

Chasseguet-Smirgel, Janine. *Sexuality and Mind: The Role of the Father and the Mother in the Psyche*. New York: New York University Press, 1986.

Chinen, Alan B. *In the Ever After; Fairy Tales and the Second Half of Life*. Wilmette, Ill.: Chiron Publications, 1989.

Clemons, Walter. "An Unnoticed World." Review of *Glass of Blessings*. *Newsweek*, April 14, 1980, 96.

Cohn, Jan. *Romance and the Erotics of Property: Mass-Market Fiction for Women*. Durham: Duke University Press, 1988.

Coleridge, Christabel. *Charlotte Mary Yonge: Her Life and Letters*. London: Macmillan, 1903.

Compton-Burnett, Ivy. *More Women than Men*. 1933. Reprint. London: Allison & Busby Ltd, 1983.

Cooper, Kathryn L., and David L. Gutmann. "Gender Identity and Ego Mastery Style in Middle-Aged, Pre- and Post–Empty Nest Women." *Gerontologist* 27 (June 1987): 347–52.

Cornwall, David John Moore [John le Carré, pseud.]. "The Clandestine Muse." *The Johns Hopkins Magazine,* August 1986, 11–16.

Cotsell, Michael. *Barbara Pym.* Macmillan Modern Novelists. Houndmills, Basingstoke: Macmillan, 1989.

Crawford, Mary, and Roger Chaffin. "The Reader's Construction of Meaning: Cognitive Research on Gender and Comprehension." In Elizabeth A. Flynn and Patrocinio P. Schweickart, eds. *Gender and Reading: Essays on Readers, Texts, and Contexts.* Baltimore: Johns Hopkins Press, 1986.

Cumming, Elaine, and William E. Henry, *Growing Old: The Process of Disengagement.* New York: Basic Books, 1961.

Deutsch, Helene, *Neuroses and Character Types: Clinical Psychoanalytic Studies.* New York: International Universities Press, 1965.

Doan, Laura L. "Text and the Single Man: The Bachelor in Pym's Dual-Voiced Narrative." In *Independent Women: The Function of Gender in the Novels of Barbara Pym.* Edited by Janice Rossen. Sussex: Harvester; New York: St. Martin's, 1988.

Drury, John. "Outward Show and Inward Seeking." Review of Philip Toynbee's *End of a Journey. Times Literary Supplement,* May 13–19, 1988, 524.

DuPlessis, Rachel Blau. *Writing beyond the Ending: Narrative Strategies of Twentieth-Century Women Writers.* Bloomington: Indiana University Press, 1985.

Erikson, Erik H. *Young Man Luther: A Study in Psychoanalysis and History.* 1958. Reprint. New York: Norton Library, 1962.

Everett, Barbara. "The Pleasures of Poverty." In *Independent Women: The Function of Gender in the Novels of Barbara Pym.* Edited by Janice Rossen. Sussex: Harvester Press; New York: St. Martin's, 1988.

Fergus, Jan. "*A Glass of Blessings,* Jane Austen's *Emma,* and Barbara Pym's Art of Allusion." In *Independent Women: The Function of Gender in the Novels of Barbara Pym.* Edited by Janice Rossen. Sussex: Harvester; New York: St. Martin's, 1988.

Fetterley, Judith. Introduction. *Provisions: A Reader from 19th-Century American Women.* Edited by Judith Fetterley. Bloomington: Indiana University Press, 1985.

———. *The Resisting Reader: A Feminist Approach to American Fiction.* Bloomington: Indiana University Press, 1978.

Flower, Linda. "Writer-Based Prose: A Cognitive Basis for Problems in Writing." *College English* 41 (September 1979): 19–37.

Forster, E. M. *Howards End.* Edited by Oliver Stallybrass. Vol. 4. The Abinger Edition of E. M. Forster. 1910. Reprint. London: Edward Arnold, 1973.

———. "Nottingham Lace." In *Arctic Summer and Other Fiction.* Edited by Elizabeth Heine and Oliver Stallybrass. London: Edward Arnold, 1980.

Frye, Joanne S. *Living Stories, Telling Lives: Women and the Novel in Contemporary Experience.* Ann Arbor: University of Michigan Press, 1986.

Gadow, Sally. "Frailty and Strength: The Dialectic in Aging." *Gerontologist* 23 (1983): 144–47.

Gardner, Howard. *Artful Scribbles: The Significance of Children's Drawings.* New York, Basic Books, 1980.

Gilligan, Carol. *In a Different Voice: Psychological Theory and Women's Development.* Cambridge: Harvard University Press, 1982.

Glendinning, Victoria. *Elizabeth Bowen: Portrait of a Writer.* Harmondsworth: Penguin Books, 1985.

———. "Spontaneous Obsessions, Imposed Restraint." Review of *A Very Private Eye. New York Times Book Review,* July 8, 1984, 3.

Godwin, Gail. *A Southern Family.* 1987. Reprint. New York: Avon Books, 1988.

Goffman, Erving. *Frame Analysis: An Essay on the Organization of Experience.* 1974. Reprint. Boston: Northeastern University Press, 1986.

———. *Stigma: Notes on the Management of Spoiled Identity.* 1963. Reprint. New York: Simon & Schuster, 1986.

Graham, Robert J. "Cumbered with Much Serving: Barbara Pym's 'Excellent Women.'" In *"For Better or Worse": Attitudes toward Marriage in Literature.* Edited by Evelyn J. Hinz. 2d ed. Winnipeg: University of Manitoba Press, 1985.

Green, Georgia M. *Pragmatics and Natural Language Understanding.* Hillsdale, N.J.: Lawrence Erlbaum Associates, 1989.

Gubrium, Jaber F. "Being Single in Old Age." *International Journal of Aging and Human Development* 6, 1, 1975: 29–41.

Gullette, Margaret Morganroth. *Safe at Last in the Middle Years: The Invention of the Midlife Progress Novel: Saul Bellow, Margaret Drabble, Anne Tyler, and John Updike.* Berkeley: University of California Press, 1988.

Gusdorf, Georges. "Conditions and Limits of Autobiography." Translated by James Olney. In *Autobiography: Essays Theoretical and Critical.* Edited by James Olney. Princeton: Princeton University Press, 1980.

Gutmann, David L. "Psychoanalysis and Aging: A Developmental View." In *The Course of Life: Psychoanalytic Contributions toward Understanding Personality Development.* Vol. 3, *Adulthood and the Aging Process.* Edited by Stanley I. Greenspan and George H. Pollock. Adelphi Md.: National Institute of Mental Health, Department of Health and Human Services, 1980–1981.

————. *Reclaimed Powers: Toward a New Psychology of Men and Women in Later Life.* New York: Basic Books, 1987.

Halperin, John. "Barbara Pym and the War of the Sexes." In *The Life and Work of Barbara Pym.* Edited by Dale Salwak. Iowa City: University of Iowa Press, 1987.

Harvey, Sir Paul. *The Oxford Companion to English Literature.* 3d ed. 1946. Reprint. Oxford: Clarendon Press, 1950.

Heberlein, Kate Browder. "Thankless Tasks or Labors of Love: Women's Work in Barbara Pym's Novels." *Barbara Pym Newsletter* 2 (June 1987): 1–5.

Heilbrun, Carolyn G. *Reinventing Womanhood.* New York: Norton, 1979.

————. *Writing a Woman's Life.* New York: Norton, 1988.

Heusel, Barbara Stevens. Review of *The World of Barbara Pym* by Janice Rossen. *South Atlantic Review* 54 (January 1989): 162–64.

Holland, Norman N. *The Dynamics of Literary Response.* 1968. Reprint. New York: Norton Library, 1975.

————. "Unity Identity Text Self." *PMLA* 90 (October 1975): 813–22.

Holt, Hazel. *A Lot to Ask: A Life of Barbara Pym.* London: Macmillan, 1990.

————. "The Home Front: Barbara Pym in Oswestry, 1939–1941." In *Independent Women: The Function of Gender in the Novels of Barbara Pym.* Edited by Janice Rossen. Sussex: Harvester; New York: St. Martin's, 1988.

————. "Philip Larkin and Barbara Pym: Two Quiet People." In *Philip Larkin: The Man and His Work.* Edited by Dale Salwak. Iowa City: University of Iowa Press, 1989.

Honan, Park. "Theory of Biography." *Novel: A Forum on Fiction* 13 (Fall 1979): 109–20.

Horney, Karen. *Feminine Psychology.* Edited by Harold Kelman. 1967. Reprint. New York: Norton Library, 1973.

————. *Neurosis and Human Growth: The Struggle toward Self-Realization.* 1950. Reprint. New York: Norton Library, 1970.

Howard, Michael S. *Jonathan Cape Publisher: Herbert Jonathan Cape, G. Wren Howard.* London: Jonathan Cape, 1971.

Huxley, Aldous. "Farcical History of Richard Greenow." In *Limbo.* New York: George H. Doran, n.d.

————. *Point Counter Point.* London: Chatto & Windus, 1928.

Iser, Wolfgang. *The Act of Reading: A Theory of Aesthetic Response.* Translated by David Henry Wilson. Baltimore: Johns Hopkins Press, 1978.

————. "The Reading Process: A Phenomenological Approach." *New Literary History: A Journal of Theory and Interpretation* 3 (1972): 279–99.

Jaques, Elliott. "Death and the Mid-Life Crisis." *International Journal of Psychoanalysis* 46 (1965): 502–14.

————. "The Midlife Crisis." In *The Course of Life: Psychoanalytic Contributions toward Understanding Personality Development.* Vol. 3, *Adulthood and the Aging Process.* Edited by Stanley I. Greenspan and George H. Pollock. Adelphi, Md.: National Institute of Mental Health, Department of Health and Human Services, 1980–1981.

Johnson, Barbara, and Marjorie Garber. "Secret Sharing: Reading Conrad Psychoanalytically." *College English* 49 (October 1987): 628–40.

John-Steiner, Vera. *Notebooks of the Mind: Explorations of Thinking.* 1985. Reprint. New York: Harper & Row, 1987.

Kaufman, Anthony. "The Short Fiction of Barbara Pym." *Twentieth Century Literature* 32 (Spring 1986): 50–77.

Kelley, Mary. *Private Woman, Public Stage: Literary Domesticity in Nineteenth-Century America.* 1984. Reprint. New York: Oxford University Press, 1985.

Larkin, Philip. "The World of Barbara Pym." *Times Literary Supplement* (March 11, 1977): 260.

Lejeune, Philippe. "The Genetic Study of Autobiographical Texts." *Biography: An Interdisciplinary Quarterly* 14 (Winter 1991): 1–11.

Liddell, Robert. *A Mind at Ease: Barbara Pym and Her Novels.* London: Peter Owen, 1989.

————. *An Object for a Walk.* London: Longmans, 1966.

————. "A Success Story." In *The Life and Work of Barbara Pym.* Edited by Dale Salwak. Iowa City: University of Iowa Press, 1987.

————. "Two Friends: Barbara Pym and Ivy Compton-Burnett." *London Magazine* (August/September 1984): 59–69.

Lively, Penelope. "Stories and Echoes, Recent Fiction." *Encounter* 58 (April 1982): 74–81.

————. "The World of Barbara Pym." In *The Life and Work of Barbara Pym.* Edited by Dale Salwak. Iowa City: University of Iowa Press, 1987.

Long, Robert Emmet. *Barbara Pym.* New York: Ungar, 1986.

Long, Russell C. "Writer-Audience Relationships: Analysis or Invention?" *College Composition and Communication* 31 (May 1980): 221–26.

Maddox, George L. "Retirement as a Social Event in the United States." In *Middle Age and Aging: A Reader in Social Psychology.* Edited by Bernice L. Neugarten. Chicago: University of Chicago Press, 1968. Reprinted and abridged from *Aging and Social Policy.* Edited by John C. McKinney and Frank T. de Vyver. New York: Appleton-Century Crofts, 1966.

Mallon, Thomas. *A Book of One's Own: People and Their Diaries.* New York: Penguin Books, 1984.

Malloy, Constance. "The Quest for a Career." In *The Life and Work of Barbara Pym.* Edited by Dale Salwak. Iowa City: University of Iowa Press, 1987.

Martin, Jay. *Who Am I This Time? Uncovering the Fictive Personality.* New York: Norton, 1988.

Martin, Nancy. *Mostly about Writing: Selected Essays.* Upper Montclair, N.J.: Boynton/Cook Publishers, 1983.

Middlebrook, Diane Wood. *Anne Sexton: A Biography.* Boston: Houghton Mifflin, 1991.

Miller, Alice. *The Drama of the Gifted Child: The Search for the True Self.* Translated by Ruth Ward. New York: Basic Books, 1981.

Miller, Jean Baker. *Toward a New Psychology of Women.* 2d ed. Boston: Beacon Press, 1986.

Milton, Edith. "Worlds in Miniature." Review of *An Unsuitable Attachment. New York Times Book Review,* June 20, 1982, 11, 25.

Miner, Madonne M. "Guaranteed to Please: Twentieth-Century American Women's Bestsellers." In Elizabeth A. Flynn and Patrocinio P. Schweickart, eds. *Gender and Reading: Essays on Readers, Texts, and Contexts.* Baltimore: Johns Hopkins Press, 1986.

Monteith, Charles. "Publishing Larkin." *Times Literary Supplement,* May 21, 1982, 551–52.

Mortimer, Penelope. *The Handyman.* London: Allen Lane, 1983.

Nardin, Jane. *Barbara Pym.* Boston: Twayne, 1985.

Nell, Victor. *Lost in a Book: The Psychology of Reading for Pleasure.* New Haven: Yale University Press, 1988.

Ong, Walter J. *Orality and Literacy: The Technologizing of the Word.* 1982. Reprint. London: Routledge, 1989.

Parini, Jay. "My Writing Is Full of Lives I Might Have Led." *The Boston Globe Magazine* (August 2, 1987): 19, 62–67.

Phelps, Gilbert. "Fellow Writers in a Cotswold Village." In *The Life and Work of Barbara Pym.* Edited by Dale Salwak. Iowa City: University of Iowa Press, 1987.

Pickering, George. *Creative Malady: Illness in the Lives and Minds of George Darwin, Florence Nightingale, Mary Baker Eddy, Sigmund Freud, Marcel Proust, Elizabeth Barrett Browning.* 1974. Reprint. New York: Dell Publishing, 1976.

Poulet, Georges. "Criticism and the Experience of Interiority." Translated by Catherine Macksey and Richard Macksey. In *The Structuralist Controversy: The Languages of Criticism and the Sciences of Man.* Edited by Richard Macksey and Eugenio Donato. Baltimore: Johns Hopkins Press, 1972.

Pym, Hilary. "The Early Life." In *A Very Private Eye: An Autobiography in Diaries and Letters.* Edited by Hazel Holt and Hilary Pym. New York: Dutton, 1984.

Radway, Janice. *Reading the Romance: Women, Patriarchy, and Popular Literature.* Chapel Hill: University of North Carolina Press, 1984.

"Reputations Revisited." *Times Literary Supplement,* January 21, 1977, 66–68.

Rooke, Constance. "Hagar's Old Age: *The Stone Angel* as *Vollendungsroman.*" In *Crossing the River: Essays in Honour of Margaret Laurence.* Edited by Kristjana Gunnars. Winnipeg, Manitoba: Turnstone Press, 1988.

Rose, Phyllis. *Woman of Letters: A Life of Virginia Woolf.* New York: Oxford University Press. 1978.

Rossen, Janice. "On Not Being Jane Eyre: The Romantic Heroine in Barbara Pym's Novels." In *Independent Women: The Function of Gender in the Novels of Barbara Pym.* Edited by Janice Rossen. Sussex: Harvester; New York: St. Martin's, 1988.

―――. "The Pym Papers." In *The Life and Work of Barbara Pym.* Edited by Dale Salwak. Iowa City: University of Iowa Press, 1987.

―――. *The World of Barbara Pym.* Houndmills: Macmillan, 1987.

Rossen, Janice, ed. *Independent Women: The Function of Gender in the Novels of Barbara Pym.* Sussex: Harvester; New York: St. Martin's, 1988.

Rothstein, Mervyn. "Saul Bellow on Life, Love, Art and 'Heartbreak'." *New York Times,* Wednesday, June 3, 1987, National edition, 22.

Rubenstein, Jill. "'For the Ovaltine Had Loosened her Tongue': Failures of Speech in Barbara Pym's *Less than Angels.*" *Modern Fiction Studies* 32 (Winter 1986): 573–80.

Rubinstein, Robert L. "Never Married Elderly as a Social Type: Reevaluating Some Images." *Gerontologist* 27 (February 1987): 108–13.

St. Hilda's College Register, 1893–1972. Oxford: Bocardo & Church Army Press, 1977.

Salvatori, Mariolina. "Thomas Hardy and Eugenio Montale: In Mourning and in Celebration." *Journal of Aging Studies* 1 (1987): 161–85.

Salwak, Dale, ed. *The Life and Work of Barbara Pym.* Iowa City: University of Iowa Press, 1987.

Schafer, Roy. *The Analytic Attitude.* New York: Basic Books, 1983.

Scott-Maxwell, Florida. *The Measure of My Days.* 1968. Reprint. New York: Penguin Books, 1979.

Segel, Elizabeth. "'As the Twig is Bent . . .': Gender and Childhood Reading." In Elizabeth A. Flynn and Patrocinio P. Schweickart, eds. *Gender and Reading: Essays on Readers, Texts, and Contexts.* Baltimore: Johns Hopkins Press, 1986.

Smith, Logan Pearsall. *All Trivia: Trivia, More Trivia, Afterthoughts, Last Words.* New York: Harcourt, Brace, 1934.

Smith, Robert. "Remembering Barbara Pym." In *Independent Women:*

The Function of Gender in the Novels of Barbara Pym. Edited by Janice Rossen. Sussex: Harvester; New York: St. Martin's, 1988.

Smith, Wendy. "Brief Review." Review of *A Very Private Eye. New Republic* (July 16 and 23, 1984): 41.

Sokoloff, Janice. *The Margin That Remains: A Study of Aging in Literature.* New York: Peter Lang, 1987.

Spacks, Patricia Meyer. *Gossip.* 1985. Reprint. Chicago: University of Chicago Press, 1986.

Spurling, Hilary. *Ivy: The Life of I. Compton-Burnett.* New York: Knopf, 1984

Steig, Michael. *Stories of Reading: Subjectivity and Literary Understanding.* Baltimore: Johns Hopkins University Press, 1989.

Storr, Anthony. "Aspects of Adult Development." In *Churchill's Black Dog, Kafka's Mice, and Other Phenomena of the Human Mind.* New York: Grove Press, 1988.

———. *Churchill's Black Dog, Kafka's Mice, and Other Phenomena of the Human Mind.* New York: Grove Press, 1988.

———. *The Dynamics of Creation.* New York: Atheneum, 1972.

———. *Solitude: A Return to the Self.* New York: Ballantine Books, 1988.

Strauss-Noll, Mary. "Love and Marriage in the Novels." In *The Life and Work of Barbara Pym.* Edited by Dale Salwak. Iowa City: University of Iowa Press, 1987.

Strouse, Jean. *Alice James: A Biography.* Boston: Houghton Mifflin, 1980.

Summerfield, Judith, and Geoffrey Summerfield. *Texts and Contexts: A Contribution to the Theory and Practice of Teaching Composition.* New York: Random House, 1986.

"Symposium: Books That Gave Me Pleasure." *New York Times Book Review,* December 5, 1982, 9, 62, 63.

Tannen, Deborah. *You Just Don't Understand: Women and Men in Conversation.* New York: William Morrow, 1990.

Taylor, Elizabeth. *At Mrs Lippincote's.* 1945. Reprint. London: Virago, 1988.

Treglown, Jeremy. "Snob Story." Review of *The Sweet Dove Died. New Statesman* (July 7, 1978): 27.

Vygotsky, Lev. *Thought and Language.* Translated and edited by Alex Kozulin. 1934. Reprint. Cambridge, Mass.: MIT Press, 1986.

Wagner-Martin, Linda. *Sylvia Plath: A Biography* New York: Simon and Schuster, 1987.

Warhol, Robyn R. "Toward a Theory of the Engaging Narrator: Earnest Interventions in Gaskell, Stowe, and Eliot." *PMLA* 101 (October 1986): 811–18.

Waxman, Barbara Frey. *From the Hearth to the Open Road: A Feminist Study of Aging in Contemporary Literature.* New York: Greenwood Press, 1990.

West, Rebecca. "And They All Lived Unhappily Ever After." *Times Literary Supplement,* July 26, 1974, 779.

Wilson, A. N. "St. Barbara-in-the-Precinct." Review of *An Unsuitable Attachment. Spectator* (February 20, 1982): 22–23.

Winnicott, D. W. "The Capacity to Be Alone" (1958). In *The Maturational Processes and the Facilitating Environment: Studies in the Theory of Emotional Development.* Madison, Conn.: International Universities Press, 1965.

————. "Communicating and Not Communicating Leading to a Study of Certain Opposites" (1963). In *The Maturational Processes and the Facilitating Environment: Studies in the Theory of Emotional Development.* Madison, Conn.: International Universities Press, 1965.

Woodward, Kathleen. *Aging and Its Discontents: Freud and Other Fictions.* Bloomington: Indiana University Press, 1991.

————. "May Sarton and Fictions of Old Age." In *Gender and Literary Voice.* Edited by Janet Todd. *Women and Literature.* New York: Holmes and Meier, 1980.

————. "Simone de Beauvoir: Aging and Its Discontents." In *The Private Self: Theory and Practice in Women's Autobiographical Writings.* Edited by Shari Benstock. Chapel Hill: University of North Carolina Press, 1988.

Woodward, Kathleen M. *At Last, the Real Distinguished Thing: The Late Poems of Eliot, Pound, Stevens, and Williams.* Columbus: Ohio State University Press, 1980.

Woolf, Virginia. "Professions for Women." In *Death of the Moth and Other Essays.* 1942. Reprint. New York: Harvest, 1974.

Wyatt, Jean. *Reconstructing Desire: The Role of the Unconscious in Women's Reading and Writing.* Chapel Hill: University of North Carolina, 1990.

Wyatt-Brown, Anne M. "A Buried Life: E. M. Forster's Struggle with Creativity." *Journal of Modern Literature* 10 (March 1983): 109–24.

————. "Creativity in Midlife: The Novels of Anita Brookner." *Journal of Aging Studies* 3 (Summer 1989): 175–81.

————. "Ellipsis, Eccentricity and Evasion in the Diaries of Barbara Pym." In *Independent Women: The Function of Gender in the Novels of Barbara Pym.* Edited by Janice Rossen. Sussex: Harvester; New York: St. Martin's, 1988.

————. "E. M. Forster and the Transformation of Comedy." Ph.D. diss., Case Western Reserve University, 1972.

————. "From Fantasy to Pathology: Images of Aging in the Novels of

Barbara Pym." *Human Values and Aging Newsletter* 6 (January–February 1984): 5–7.

———. "*Howards End:* Celibacy and Stalemate." *Psychohistory Review* 12 (Fall 1983): 26–33.

———. "Late Style in the Novels of Barbara Pym and Penelope Mortimer," *Gerontologist* 28 (December 1988): 835–39.

———. "The Liberation of Mourning in Elizabeth Bowen's *The Little Girls* and *Eva Trout.*" In *Aging and Gender: Studies in Literary Creativity.* Edited by Anne M. Wyatt-Brown and Janice Rossen. Charlottesville: University of Virginia Press, n.d.

———. " 'The Lumber Room': Suffering and Creativity in the Novels of Barbara Pym." Paper presented at the annual meeting of the Modern Language Association, New York, December 9, 1986.

Yonge, Charlotte M. *The Daisy Chain or Aspirations: A Family Chronicle.* 1856. Reprint. London: Virago, 1988.

Index

69; Archdeacon Henry Hoccleve, 24, 43–45, 58, 67, 68, 69, 81; Belinda Bede, x, 3, 43–45, 58, 61, 65–70, 75, 129, 134; Bishop Grote, 45, 65–71, 169n22, 178n31; Edith Liversidge, 17, 71, 122; Harriet Bede, 44, 45, 49, 61, 65–7,1 74
Something to Remember, 52, 56–58, 89, 127
"Something to Remember," 165n39
So Very Secret, 52, 57, 58, 63, 144; Cassandra Swan, 57, 58
Spacks, Patricia Meyer, 96, 154n1
Spurling, Hilary, 3
Storr, Anthony, xi, xiv, 156n10
Strouse, Jean, xii
Summerfield, Geoffrey, 155n7, 158n26, 159n38
Summerfield, Judith, 155n7, 158n26, 159n38
Sunday Times: Jill Neville, 138
Sweet Dove Died, The, 7, 9, 10, 111, 114–20, 137, 138, 141, 178n34, 181n19; James Boyce, 115–18; Leonora Eyre, 118–20, 141, 179n38; Phoebe Sharpe, 111, 117; Rose Culver, 115, 116

Tannen, Deborah, 62, 167n3
Taylor, Elizabeth, 1, 8, 97, 171n42
Thankless Task, The, 175n36
Thirkell, Angela, 90
Thomas, Edward (grandfather) 13, 14
Thomas, Irena Spenser. *See* Pym, Irena Spenser
Thomas, Jane ("Ack") Robson, 17, 50, 53
Thomas, Mary Jane Carr (grandmother), 13, 14
Times Literary Supplement: survey recommending Pym's novels, ix, 136, 137
Tracy, Honor, 5
Treglown, Jeremy, 179n38
"Trivial Rounds and Common Tasks," 42
Trollope, Anthony, 5
Tyler, Anne, 155n13

Unsuitable Attachment, An, 6, 7, 9, 52, 53, 105–14, 121, 126, 139, 143, 148, 177n15; Ianthe Broome, 107–12; John Challow, 108, 109, 112; Mark Ainger, 108–13; Penelope Grandison, 110–13;

Rupert Stonebird, 106, 108, 111–13; Sophia Ainger, 106, 108–12, 121

Vanguard Press (U.S. publisher), 90, 91, 138
Very Private Eye, A, xi, xiii, 7, 13, 31, 48, 102; letters, 48, 102
"Vicar Floating By, The," 16, 18, 19, 42
Vygotsky, Lev, 159n38

Wagner-Martin, Linda, xii
Walton, Hilary Crampton Pym, xi, 4, 7, 9, 11, 13, 14, 17, 19, 22, 29, 37, 38, 47, 61, 65, 66, 70, 76, 77, 85, 94, 98, 103, 115, 125–30, 151, 157n17
Warhol, Robyn R., 24
Watson, Graham (Curtis Brown), 84
Waugh, Evelyn, 90
Waxman, Barbara Frey, 132, 180n9, 181n19, 182n22
"Wedge of Misery Tea Time," 72
Welch, Denton, 97
Welty, Eudora, 155n13
West, Rebecca, 171n47
West-Watson, Alison, 31, 32, 43, 44, 163n20
Wilson, A. N., 155n13
Winnicott, D. W., xiv, 34, 156n10
Woischnick, Hanns, 33, 45
Woodward, Kathleen, 160n45
Woolf, Virginia, 41, 85, 86, 92, 129, 159n35; *A Room of One's Own*, 67; *A Writer's Diary*, 89; *To the Lighthouse*, 85, 89, 90
Wordsworth, William, 122, 131
World War II, 38, 48, 50, 66
Wright, James (Macmillan), 137–39, 142, 184n5
Writers: psychological analysis of, 11, 159n37; relation to audience, 159n38; roles of, 159n38; self-consciousness of, 22, 158n26
WRNS (Women's Royal Naval Service), 60, 62, 63, 71–73; Starky, 64, 95
Wyatt, Honor, 60–63, 82, 104, 161n58
Wyatt, Jean, 156n1, 162n10
Wyndham, Francis, 134

Yeats, William Butler, 2
Yonge, Charlotte M., 6, 15, 18, 41, 73, 158n23, 162n9; *The Daisy Chain*, 39; *The Heir of Redclyffe*, 39; *Young Men in Fancy Dress*, 22, 25, 101; Denis Feverel, 22; Marguerite Duval, 22, 25